BUSINESS DATA PROCESSING

BUSINESS DATA PROCESSING

Gerard Prudhomme

ARCLER
PRESS

www.arclerpress.com

Business Data Processing

Gerard Prudhomme

Arcler Press
2010 Winston Park Drive,
2nd Floor
Oakville, ON L6H 5R7
Canada
www.arclerpress.com
Tel: 001-289-291-7705
001-905-616-2116
Fax: 001-289-291-7601
Email: orders@arclereducation.com

ISBN: 978-1-77361-447-2 (Hardcover)

ABOUT THE AUTHOR

Gerard I. Prudhomme has a graduate degree (M.S.) for Computer Science from University College London (UCL). He has also worked as a software programmer and tech writer for different Fortune 500 companies, and studied at UCL, Harvard, and Oxford.

TABLE OF CONTENTS

LIST OF FIGURES

https://creativecommons.org/licenses/by-sa/3.0/deed.en
Author: Marcel Douwe Dekker

Figure 6.8. UML diagram
Attribution-ShareAlike 3.0 Unported (CC BY-SA 3.0)
https://creativecommons.org/licenses/by-sa/3.0/deed.en
Author: TexasDex

Figure 6.9. A sample deployment diagram
Attribution-ShareAlike 3.0 Unported (CC BY-SA 3.0)
https://creativecommons.org/licenses/by-sa/3.0/deed.en
Author: Kishorekumar 62

Figure 6.10. View example
Creative Commons Attribution-Share Alike 4.0 International
https://creativecommons.org/licenses/by-sa/4.0/deed.en
Authors: Muug1

Figure 10.1. Network
Creative Commons Attribution-Share Alike 4.0 International
https://creativecommons.org/licenses/by-sa/4.0/deed.en
Author: Wvbailey

Figure 10.2. Data model
Creative Commons Attribution-Share Alike 3.0 Unported license.
https://creativecommons.org/licenses/by-sa/3.0/deed.en
Author: AutumnSnow

Figure 10.3. Process of database design
Creative Commons Attribution-Share Alike 4.0 International
https://creativecommons.org/licenses/by-sa/4.0/deed.en
Author: Kitman20022002

Figure 10.4. Flowchart
Creative Commons Attribution 2.0 Generic
https://creativecommons.org/licenses/by/2.0/deed.en
Author: Wvbailey

Figure 10.5. Process of database design
Creative Commons Attribution-Share Alike 4.0 International
https://creativecommons.org/licenses/by-sa/4.0/deed.en
Author: Kitman20022002

Figure 10.6. Cloud computing
Creative Commons Attribution-Share Alike 3.0 Unported
https://creativecommons.org/licenses/by-sa/3.0/deed.en
Author: Sam Johnston

Figure 10.7. Data modeling
Creative Commons Attribution-Share Alike 3.0 Unported
https://creativecommons.org/licenses/by-sa/3.0/deed.en
Author: Paul R. Smith. Redrawn by Marcel Douwe Dekker

Figure 10.8. DB model
Creative Commons Attribution-Share Alike 3.0 Unported
https://creativecommons.org/licenses/by-sa/3.0/deed.en
Author: Wikipedia user X00022027

Figure 10.9. Layers in NoSQL
Creative Commons Attribution-Share Alike 3.0 Unported
https://creativecommons.org/licenses/by-sa/3.0/deed.en
Author: Geetika saini

Figure 10.10. Database systems
Creative Commons Attribution-Share Alike 3.0 Unported
https://creativecommons.org/licenses/by-sa/3.0/deed.en
Author: Чоймаа

Figure 10.11. DDL diagram
Creative Commons Attribution-Share Alike 4.0 International
https://creativecommons.org/licenses/by-sa/4.0/deed.en
Author: Sparx Systems

Figure 14.1. Processes
Creative Commons Attribution-Share Alike 3.0 Unported
https://creativecommons.org/licenses/by-sa/3.0/deed.en
Author: Evan Mason

Figure 14.2. mvc-diagram Creative Commons Attribution-Share Alike 3.0 Unported
https://creativecommons.org/licenses/by-sa/3.0/deed.en
Author: R2G

Figure 14.3. Backbone
Creative Commons Attribution-Share Alike 3.0 Unported
https://creativecommons.org/licenses/by-sa/3.0/deed.en
Author: Electronic Frontier Foundation
Figure 14.4. Survey database
Creative Commons Attribution-Share Alike 3.0 Unported
https://creativecommons.org/licenses/by-sa/3.0/deed.en
Author: Ahessellund

Figure 14.5. ANSI/SPARC three level architecture
Creative Commons Attribution-Share Alike 3.0 Unported
https://creativecommons.org/licenses/by-sa/3.0/deed.en
Author: EPISTLE (the European Process Industries STEP Technical Liaison Executive)

Figure 14.6. Analytics
Creative Commons Attribution-Share Alike 4.0 International
https://creativecommons.org/licenses/by-sa/4.0/deed.en
Author: Fuzzy Logix Staff

Figure 14.7. Database
Creative Commons Attribution-Share Alike 4.0 International
https://creativecommons.org/licenses/by-sa/4.0/deed.en
Author: Tourar

Figure 14.8. N-tier client/server model architecture.
Creative Commons Attribution-Share Alike 4.0 International
https://creativecommons.org/licenses/by-sa/4.0/deed.en
Author: MichelBakni

Figure 14.9. A system
version 3 of the GNU General Public License
https://www.gnu.org/copyleft/gpl-3.0.html
Author: Samuel.mann at English Wikibooks

Figure 14.10. IT service landscape
Creative Commons Attribution-Share Alike 4.0 International
https://creativecommons.org/licenses/by-sa/4.0/deed.en
Author: Newforceltd

Figure 14.11. Diagram of typical barcode system
version 3 of the GNU General Public License
https://www.gnu.org/copyleft/gpl-3.0.html
Author: Jmduncan

Figure 16.1. A. systematic-review
Creative Commons Attribution 2.0 Generic
https://creativecommons.org/licenses/by/2.0/deed.en
Author: Manyando C, Kayentao K, D'Alessandro U, Okafor H, Juma E, Hamed K

Figure 16.2. Map serving steps
Creative Commons Attribution-Share Alike 3.0 Unported
https://creativecommons.org/licenses/by-sa/3.0/deed.en
Author: Carl Sack

Figure 16.3. Local to global
Creative Commons Attribution-Share Alike 3.0 Unported
https://creativecommons.org/licenses/by-sa/3.0/deed.en
Author: Arbeck

Figure 16.4. Materialsdb
Creative Commons Attribution-Share Alike 3.0 Unported
https://creativecommons.org/licenses/by-sa/3.0/deed.en
Author: Fla for

Figure 16.5. Clustering
Creative Commons Attribution-Share Alike 3.0 Unported
https://creativecommons.org/licenses/by-sa/3.0/deed.en
Author: Markkobo

Figure 16.6. Problem-solving solutions
Creative Commons Attribution-Share Alike 4.0 International
https://creativecommons.org/licenses/by-sa/4.0/deed.en
Author: Oxford Creativity

Figure 16.7. Architecture
Creative Commons Attribution-Share Alike 3.0 Unported
https://creativecommons.org/licenses/by-sa/3.0/deed.en
Author: Soumyasch at English Wikipedia

Figure 16.8. PRISMA flow diagram
Creative Commons Attribution-Share Alike 3.0 Unported
https://creativecommons.org/licenses/by-sa/3.0/deed.en
Author: Atizinha

Figure 16.9. Tier diagram
Attribution-ShareAlike 3.0 Unported (CC BY-SA 3.0)
https://creativecommons.org/licenses/by-sa/3.0/deed.en
Authors: Jessica Hall 1230

Figure 16.10. Infodiagram2
Creative Commons Attribution-Share Alike 4.0 International
https://creativecommons.org/licenses/by-sa/4.0/deed.en
Authors: Aadils96

Figure 16.11. Operational threat model
Creative Commons Attribution-Share Alike 4.0 International
https://creativecommons.org/licenses/by-sa/4.0/deed.en
Author: Bbeyst

Figure 16.12. International data encryption algorithm
Creative Commons Attribution-Share Alike 3.0 Unported
https://creativecommons.org/licenses/by-sa/3.0/deed.en
Author: Daniele Pugliesi

Figure 18.1. Classification tree for database system
Creative Commons Attribution-Share Alike 3.0 Unported
https://creativecommons.org/licenses/by-sa/3.0/deed.en
Author: OMPwiki

Figure 18.2. WordPress
Creative Commons Attribution-Share Alike 3.0 Unported
https://creativecommons.org/licenses/by-sa/3.0/deed.en
Author: Samwilson

Figure 18.3. OS 2200 database architecture
Creative Commons Attribution-Share Alike 3.0 Unported
https://creativecommons.org/licenses/by-sa/3.0/deed.en
Author: Gtgray1948

Figure 18.4. Cbir
Creative Commons Attribution-Share Alike 4.0 International
https://creativecommons.org/licenses/by-sa/4.0/deed.en
Author: Jordill2

Figure 18.5. Database parts
Attribution-ShareAlike 3.0 Unported (CC BY-SA 3.0)
https://creativecommons.org/licenses/by-sa/3.0/deed.en
Author: 110808049 nisarg

Figure 18.6. Star schema
Creative Commons Attribution-Share Alike 3.0 Unported
https://creativecommons.org/licenses/by-sa/3.0/deed.en
Author: Dhbw dbi

Figure 21.1. Trigger
Creative Commons Attribution-Share Alike 4.0 International
https://creativecommons.org/licenses/by-sa/4.0/deed.en
Author: Muugl
Figure 21.2. IDA cognitive architecture
Creative Commons Attribution-Share Alike 3.0 Unported
https://creativecommons.org/licenses/by-sa/3.0/deed.en
Author: Graeme E. Smith

Figure 21.3. Interaction between managers and sensors
Creative Commons Attribution-Share Alike 4.0 International
https://creativecommons.org/licenses/by-sa/4.0/deed.en
Author: UNIH

Figure 21.4. Schematic diagram
Creative Commons Attribution-Share Alike 2.5 Generic
https://creativecommons.org/licenses/by-sa/2.5/deed.en
Author: Philipp Fleck

Figure 21.5. Geoservices server
Creative Commons Attribution-Share Alike 4.0 International
https://creativecommons.org/licenses/by-sa/4.0/deed.en
Author: SEWilco.

Figure 23.1. Map reduce job
Creative Commons Attribution-Share Alike 3.0 Unported
https://creativecommons.org/licenses/by-sa/3.0/deed.en
Author: Skamisetty

Figure 23.2. Wikimedia-servers
Creative Commons Attribution-Share Alike 3.0 Unported
https://creativecommons.org/licenses/by-sa/3.0/deed.en
Author: Hk kng

Figure 23.3. Hadoop
Creative Commons Attribution-Share Alike 4.0 International
https://creativecommons.org/licenses/by-sa/4.0/deed.en
Author: Magnai17

Figure 23.4. Database Oriented Usecase Authorization
Attribution-ShareAlike 3.0 Unported (CC BY SA 3.0)
https://creativecommons.org/licenses/by-sa/3.0/deed.en
Author: Sbvb

Figure 23.5. PostgreSQL proces sesCreative Commons Attribution-Share Alike 4.0 International
https://creativecommons.org/licenses/by-sa/4.0/deed.en
Author: Kelti

Figure 23.6. KM Pyramid
Creative Commons Attribution-Share Alike 4.0 International
https://creativecommons.org/licenses/by-sa/4.0/deed.en
Author: Matthew.viel

Figure 23.7. Rights management services
Creative Commons Attribution-Share Alike 3.0 Unported
https://creativecommons.org/licenses/by-sa/3.0/deed.en
Author: SanderVanGysegem

Figure 23.8. Icinga architecture
Creative Commons Attribution-Share Alike 3.0 Unported
https://creativecommons.org/licenses/by-sa/3.0/deed.en
Author: The Icinga Project

Figure 23.9. DbModel category
Creative Commons Attribution-Share Alike 4.0 International
https://creativecommons.org/licenses/by-sa/4.0/deed.en
Author: Alphama
Figure 23.10. Data Modeling Today
Creative Commons Attribution-Share Alike 3.0 Unported
https://creativecommons.org/licenses/by-sa/3.0/deed.en
Author: EPISTLE (the European Process Industries STEP Technical Liaison Executive)

Figure 23.11. WI-FI network
Creative Commons Attribution-Share Alike 3.0 Unported
https://creativecommons.org/licenses/by-sa/3.0/deed.en
Author: Robo56 at English Wikipedia

Figure 23.12. Metadata interoperability chart
Creative Commons Attribution-Share Alike 3.0 Unported
https://creativecommons.org/licenses/by-sa/3.0/deed.en
Author: Primaver

Figure 23.13. Mediawiki math rendering schema
Creative Commons Attribution-Share Alike 3.0 Unported
https://creativecommons.org/licenses/by-sa/3.0/deed.en
Author: Schubi87

Figure 23.14. Dataflow-diagram
Creative Commons Attribution-Share Alike 3.0 Unported
https://creativecommons.org/licenses/by-sa/3.0/deed.en
Author: Edited by User: Autumn Snow with Inkscape, based on Image: DataFlowDiagram Esempio1.png created by User: Ilario

Figure 26.1. Overview of OpenR66 servers and clients
Creative Commons Attribution-Share Alike 3.0 Unported
https://creativecommons.org/licenses/by-sa/3.0/deed.en
Author: Fbg42

Figure 26.2. SQL azure architecture
Creative Commons Attribution-Share Alike 2.0 Taiwan
https://creativecommons.org/licenses/by-sa/2.0/tw/deed.en
Author: 小朱

Figure 26.3. Meronymy db architectureCreative Commons Attribution-Share Alike 3.0 Unported
https://creativecommons.org/licenses/by-sa/3.0/deed.en
Author: Professor Baltasar at Wikipedia

Figure 26.4. DB2 storage hierarchy
Creative Commons Attribution-Share Alike 3.0 Unported
https://creativecommons.org/licenses/by-sa/3.0/deed.en
Author: Scifipete

Figure 26.5. Java EE Enterprise Java Bean
Creative Commons Attribution-Share Alike 3.0 Unported
https://creativecommons.org/licenses/by-sa/3.0/deed.en
Author: 流星依旧

Figure 26.6. Client-Server 2-tier
Creative Commons Attribution-Share Alike 4.0 International
https://creativecommons.org/licenses/by-sa/4.0/deed.en
Author: MichelBakni

Figure 26.7. Lucidworks
Creative Commons Attribution-Share Alike 4.0 International
https://creativecommons.org/licenses/by-sa/4.0/deed.en
Author: Ao4047

Figure 26.8. Architecture diagram for disk resident database systems
Creative Commons Attribution-Share Alike 3.0 Unported
https://creativecommons.org/licenses/by-sa/3.0/deed.en
Author: Praba tuty at English Wikibooks

Figure 26.9. Triple graph grammar
Creative Commons Attribution-Share Alike 3.0 Unported
https://creativecommons.org/licenses/by-sa/3.0/deed.en
Author: Jan Rieke

Figure 26.10. Wikimedia-servers
Creative Commons Attribution-Share Alike 3.0 Unported
https://creativecommons.org/licenses/by-sa/3.0/deed.en
Author: Marco Krohn

Figure 26.11. Property graph model
Creative Commons Attribution-Share Alike 4.0 International
https://creativecommons.org/licenses/by-sa/4.0/deed.en
Author: М.Оюунболор

Figure 26.12. Ignition SQL bridge diagram
Creative Commons Attribution-Share Alike 3.0 Unported
https://creativecommons.org/licenses/by-sa/3.0/deed.en
Author: Not another industrial blog at English Wikipedia

Figure 26.13. Maps-deployment
Creative Commons Attribution-Share Alike 4.0 International
https://creativecommons.org/licenses/by-sa/4.0/deed.en
Author: GLederrey (WMF)

Figure 26.14. Data model
Creative Commons Attribution-Share Alike 3.0 Unported
https://creativecommons.org/licenses/by-sa/3.0/deed.en
Author: AutumnSnow

Figure 30.1. Jet DLLs
Creative Commons Attribution-Share Alike 3.0 Unported
https://creativecommons.org/licenses/by-sa/3.0/deed.en
Author: Rugby471

Figure 30.2. Htsql-web-service
Creative Commons Attribution-Share Alike 4.0 International
https://creativecommons.org/licenses/by-sa/4.0/deed.en
Author: Jcarrascopacheco

PREFACE

Business data processing tools require extremely sophisticated statistical methods. This book aims to understand, in addition to the existing legal framework and the resulting obligations for companies, the security policy of companies in the processing, collection, and storage of personal data. Business data processing should, therefore, provide a complexity which increases the degree of uncertainty and, therefore, precautions for information security in particular. This methodology is suitable for studying an emerging and ill-defined concept: the concept of business data processing.

Business data processing provides the ability to understand the relationships between the elements of a situation and to adapt to it in order to achieve a business' ends. This book is, therefore, intended especially for executives who have projects to achieve, and also for other people who are interested. Computer systems centralize and aggregate a large amount of data and thus constitute a tempting target for those interested in this sometimes insufficiently protected information which, as we have seen, are likely to be used for profit. To illustrate, we may additionally supply the fact that business data processing provides capabilities and constraints at the level of its branch of activity. For example, business can collect information that will be of interest for a business.

On the other hand, to provide an example, we may also use criminal law responses to attacks on companies' computer systems to understand business data processing. Because it is these data and their treatment that will optimize the commercial proposals by making customized, targeted, and differentiated offers. The purpose of a qualitative study is, therefore, not only to explain the reality, but also to improve it, and the primary goal is to formulate the problems that it will be relevant to solve.

These networks and more or less informal links that feed the tools are stronger in a context of high volatility and high uncertainty, like that in which high-tech businesses operate. To illustrate, we may additionally supply the fact that active demonstration of compliance with data protection measures must be integrated into business processes using transparency tools: reviews, policies, and training on data protection.

Indeed, the purpose of a qualitative study is not only to answer questions, but also to rephrase them, and especially to update relevant questions not yet formulated. If these objectives are first, then data processing and analysis will be done in the field, whether in the development of a protocol and a guide those are in their own right, or in the formulation of objectives between the advertiser and the institute with this same model of data processing. One can thus say that it brings together the activity of strategic ideas and the activity of the protection of the information.

Business data processing can take different forms: supervision; specialized watches; environmental alerts (reputation, competitive, regulatory, and so on and so forth); ad hoc studies; monitoring market developments; and so on and so forth. In a business data processing working environment, more than anywhere else, you have the ability to create dedicated spaces, such as discussion forums, where the security team can post the information and keep employees up-to-date on incidents, security threats, and policy changes. The idea is to find an explanation that is justifiable on a theoretical level while being firmly anchored in the observed reality.

To provide an example, new data protection regulations will be effective in 2018 and firms that do not comply will be subject to administrative sanctions. Also, delegates for economic are tasked with developing policy in this area. Business data processing should also provide data protection for employees (current employees, future employees, former employees, and so on and so forth) covering all data concerning personal files, e-mail, physical access control to premises, recruitment, video surveillance, data transfers abroad, time control, biometrics, economic and financial transactions, geolocation, and so on and so forth.

These offers can be triggered according to a specific event, leaving you with the time you need to plan and implement your other marketing actions. You will then be able to send a confirmation email that offers an excellent opportunity to obtain consent to communicate with them afterwards. You will be simplifying technology so that your customers can go even further. To provide an example of any company that has information to protect sensitive information exploitation of open information on the business environment involving staff and partners.

Indeed, depending on your products or services, you will not be interested in the same information. On the other hand, to provide an example, we may also gather the information of users with the use of cookies. The first step is to gather the information of the customers by the appearance of a banner indicating that their data will be used. The products are the knowledge and the information having the decision-making as an objective.

Business data processing should formulate in particular recommendations in terms of management of breaches of data. security, logical and physical access control, archive protection, the reduction of the causes of vulnerability of networks and computer systems, data integrity control, traceability of the activity on the computer system, the fight against malicious codes, data backup, and so on and so forth. The process concretizes by behaviors and acts of management practically daily. The choice to reduce the costs and delays at the start and during the project only moves a problem at a later date. Learning is essential for the adoption of a business data processing strategy.

It is understood as an approach of anticipation and projection in the future, based on the links that unite the networks of companies and those of economic operators. Finally, be aware that sometimes the best protection of an idea is its disclosure. Secondly, a synergy between the public and private sector must be created, this allows and reflects the desire for competitiveness between them. It is also quite possible to collect data retrospectively, that is after the completion of a sale or service.

1
CHAPTER

FUNCTIONAL APPROACHES

A functional approach of the business data processing, with for each function an operational variation within the company, is today largely studied and diffused. This gives you time to prepare it. The process represents all the stages of the information system which were studied and on which we will come back. The process will only be effective if we go beyond the stage of concepts and concepts to a genuine involvement of individual and collective will.

At the research level, several concepts are used to define the concept of performance. This is a little explored area. It is about influencing the interventions or decisions of the public authorities or organizations. Safety issues are rarely the primary concern of an employee who already has his own daily tasks and concerns. Technology, however, brings new tools. With business data processing strategic specialists, however, we note that security is key.

It is, therefore, essential and vital to warn of the misdeeds of security in an inadequate spatial and human context, and to make specialists aware energetically against this type of leakage or failures of a human nature. Information reveals data as the most valuable asset of an organization. Feel free to reorient your searches according to your specific needs. On the other hand, to provide an example, we may also use coordinators, monitoring officers, producers of information, and so on and so forth, for business data processing.

We confuse security with the very different expressions of economics, intelligence, and strategic intelligence. This activity must also ensure monitoring of the regional and global environment. Its purpose is the competitiveness of the economy and the security of the business data processing of the state and companies. To provide an example, business data processing is aimed at ensuring a sufficient level of protection for data transferred to a third country. On the other hand, to provide an example, we may also have stakeholders with too many problems inherited from the past.

Consumers are inevitably exposed to risks, so they expect e-commerce sites to manage their data according to applicable legislation and to protect against internal and external threats. Thus, we speak of technological performance, commercial performance, economic performance, and so on and so forth. It is a question of finding a balance between the protection of the interests of the company and the protection of the private life of the employees.

So impunity remains de facto. On the other hand, to provide an example, we may also use competitive governance of academic and research institutions and business data processing. Remember, however, business data processing is real only if grasped with both hands.

As a result, high technology business data processing has a culture of innovation. On the other hand, to provide an example, we may also use corporate culture in a new power of knowledge imply questioning assumptions that we had made. To provide an example, a coordinator is installed, he works with the project manager, his mission is to coordinate all the functions of a business data processing structure. To illustrate, we may additionally supply the fact that an orientation of behaviors should, therefore, service these actors to the point where business data processing will become a habit where each element will be involved.

Their missions are then reinforced and focused on spreading the culture of to companies and players in the economy in a region. This approach can be summarized as follows: the business data processing is essentially social; the adoption of the strategy is necessary in the implementation and is guided by values: personal and organizational; business data processing is not enough; business data processing is always guided by identity; business data processing is a complex and cultural process; business data processing is a central issue in the implementation of the strategy; and so on and so forth. Locking out access with passwords, raising employee awareness, or setting up confidentiality clauses with employees and partners are strong guarantees to help with business data processing.

Although business data processing appears to have an impact on the company's performance, few research projects have explicitly addressed this relationship. With economic actors, and so on and so forth. A desire to innovate, to do things differently and to be a market leader serves as a catalyst for business data processing as it amplifies the need for vigilance towards the environment. On the other hand, to provide an example, we may also use business data processing for protecting your company network. Business data processing imposes on economic operators more transparency towards their customers, employees, and partners, in the processing and collection of personal data.

The concept of business data processing is less sexy, as long as it is not supported in the minds of the public. The imperative of security must, therefore, accord with fundamental rights. The next step is the proper allocation of resources and the definition of responsibilities by activating a network contributing to the system and relying on external and internal sources

The added value of information content, a high level of analysis of value is a main objective. Similarly, in partnership, companies are developing corporate rules, internal codes of conduct that define a group's policy on data transfer. On the other hand, to provide an example, we may also determine the essential themes to be monitored in the exercise of the activity and essential also in relation to the objectives that is fixed the company. Business data processing is considered as an activity of processing, collection, analysis, and dissemination of relevant and useful information that contributes to the production of knowledge essential for the decision-making and management of companies.

Business data processing suffers when there is little or not enough ambition to follow the technological evolution, with all the expected consequences. On the other hand, to provide an example, we may also ban endless forms, use and implement progressive profiling, and prefer several questionnaires of a few fields different according to information that you already have and organized in a sequence. On the other hand, to provide an example, we may also use a support on the essential of the control of the information.

On the other hand, to provide an example, we may also use pseudonymization or data encryption as well as the use of sophisticated tools for leak detection and reporting. On the other hand, unfortunately, we are confined far too often in ceremonial speeches and good intentions. There is often little or no concrete action behind, in the "back office." As a result, business data processing constitutes tools, products and a process, and products. How can business data processing help to ask the right questions in the context marked by a strong desire to evolve and change administrative and economic structures?.

Legislation also assigns obligations to subcontractors, such as hosting providers or SaaS service providers. Obviously, the company has to define a general policy of internal security vis-à-vis its employees and visitors: work rules, physical access rights and logic and so on and so forth. To be effective in a global competition, and as part of strategic business data processing, we include the following: communication in forms; the acquisition and optimized processing of information, as without information nothing can be done; the protection of this information, since the adversary, the competitor, or the enemy will do the same thing as us; and so on and so forth.

To illustrate, we may additionally supply the fact that for a booking confirmation method: you may, at the end of the booking by phone, ask your customer's email address to send him a confirmation by email immediately. Whether a natural person (first name, last name, phone, address, age, greeting, and so on and so forth) or a company (job, business name, sector of activity, workforce, position in the industry, and so on and so forth), these interactions are an opportunity to acquire information.

On the other hand, to provide an example, we may also use an online order service with withdrawal in store and sends you information to warn you that your order is available and when it is best to pick it up for off-peak hours. In the hotel groups, you are asked for your e-mail address when requesting access to free Wi-Fi. Remember, obligations go hand in hand with the rights of the customers as well as their right of rectification. Research firms have underlined it, explaining that the added value of studies must be redefined. In addition, if you add a subscription option for a recipient, you increase your chances of getting a new adept of your publications.

To illustrate, we may additionally supply the fact that we may use a post-stay method, where we send an e-mail to measure the satisfaction of your host, just after his stay. Therefore, what information should a company use for its customer database? Integrated in the information system, these platforms are used in all functional areas of the company when it comes to collecting and analyzing information through questionnaires: research studies satisfaction, evaluations and R&D experiments, internal control, marketing studies, internal surveys, and so on and so forth.

Remember, only a behavioral tracer requires the express permission of the visitor. While for the customers, the sources are essentially internal, for the prospects, the external files will come to enrich the information that the company already has. Often we collect this information through a contact form placed on its website. On the other hand, to provide an example, we may also use and develop awareness of business data processing among students to ensure the use of business data processing in any company.

Long and tedious, these steps are, however, essential. A majority of company customers surveyed believes they have increased their collection of valid email addresses by opting for these steps. This is why company customers have the right to access their data. Once your customer database is enriched, it will be necessary to ensure that customers are identifiable on all channels. The fields of application are numerous.

2
CHAPTER

KEY DATA

In the same way that driving a business requires identifying key performance indicators, driving a business relationship requires identifying the key data of a target audience. To illustrate, we may additionally supply a sample question to ask yourself when developing your strategy: "What essential information do you want to know about your prospects?" On the other hand, to provide an example, we may also use a standard plan of a competitor's net strategic business data processing position.

On the other hand, to provide an example, we may also use the following scenario: a potential customer enters your store, therefore, knowing and optimizing the level of satisfaction of your customers is essential in determining the friction points of your customer experience. To illustrate, we may additionally supply the fact that action data involves recording the actions taken with a client over as wide a period as possible.

And yet, surveys of leading brand marketers around the world reveals that a large number of them admit to not collecting the email addresses of their customers at the point of sale. This is only a first step, certainly essential, but must be followed by other attentions to retain online shoppers. On the other hand, to provide an example, a company may also use a contest and organize a raffle every night among the customers at a store and among those who left a company their e-mail address.

In fact, you do not have to be a multinational to use customer data for business purposes. Customer knowledge is a major issue for all companies. Intelligent questionnaires allow you to ask the right question to the right customer and at the right moment on the customer journey. Remember, as we saw earlier, a company has an obligation to provide customers with all the data they have about them and to indicate what it has been used for.

To finally reassure consumers, implement a clear data policy. The question is how to reassure them to agree to share some information about them, essential for marketers to customize their approach. Remember, customer knowledge solutions and CRM make it possible to build and enrich your databases.

The user must show his will, whereas for technical plotters the e-merchant does not need his consent to collect his data. It is, therefore, vital to ensure the quality of the information collected. All these practices have forced us to learn new languages such as the mixture of alphabetic and alphanumeric codes, phonetics, the use of codes, and so on and so forth. The customer database serves as a support for all marketing actions.

Remember, consumers appreciate being able to contact customer service agents when they have questions or complaints. Thanks to the omnichannel dimension of these solutions, you choose for yourself the best way to interrogate your customers, among all available channels (email, website, sms, and so on and so forth). These steps help to restore consumer confidence in the processing of their data. This calls into question the hypothesis which consists of eliminating the intervals of non-surveillance by the omnipresence of technology.

This is a step that should not be taken lightly. The goal is to take advantage of this mass of information instead of letting it wither in some Excel files. Treatment is an important part of a study, the foundation of our profession; it allows us to draw good conclusions. Then you have to store your data in an Excel file or in a Customer Relationship Management (CRM) software if you have. After that, it goes without saying that the nature of the data to collect on your customers depends on your objectives and your activity.

The interest can also be a saving of time: by connecting via his Facebook account, the customer will not need to complete the registration questionnaire and all his data (address, first name, surname, telephone number, and so on and so forth) will be automatically transferred to his customer account.

A physical store, for example, will collect data at the cash desk, when the customer is in a state of mind that will invite him to provide his personal data, especially if there is a promise of offers. At a time when we are talking about "big data," it is important to return to one of the fundamentals of the commercial relationship: data. Customer data is growing more and more. Indeed, if conventional treatments, based on the contributions of psycholinguistics (socio-semantics, thematic analysis, and so on and so forth) remain useful, they become less effective when it comes to analyzing new facts, languages, and figures.

The road to the control of our data is still long, but the laws of several countries are working more and more for a better management of these data and a protection of the privacy of Internet users. In addition, for employees to use the data, it must be clear and easily accessible. How and where to store them? On the other hand, to provide an example, we may also use a map consisting in delimiting the features with which the company requests the information belonging to the external environment.

What kind of communication do you want to put in place? Without commitment on your part in the long term, you will not get any results. If you do not have this information, data experts can help you to enrich your repositories with this strategic information. On the other hand, to provide an example, we may also use for an evaluation of the competitor's strategy in terms of key factors of success or non-success.

Note that this is the data to be collected in all circumstances, regardless of the company and its business. In the short or long term, communication about products or services, and so on and so forth. Today plays a key role in the valuation of data studies and treatment.

Finally, it is also key to define the level of information that we will ask the customer. The regulations provide that websites must collect the consent of the user before the deposit of these cookies, tell us what they serve and how we can oppose them.

Data processing and storage remains a real problem. On the other hand, when buying a client file, you do not know when it was done. Normally, it has an e-mail sending function automatically taking the fields of the reservation.

What level of qualification of customer data? How to get around this difficulty without harming the Customer Experience? Does your company organize activities offered to the public or participate in trade shows? However, we cannot engage in business data processing if we have not previously asked the question of strategy, itself consubstantial with the awareness of an identity.

It is necessary to highlight the significativity, the margins of error, the possible biases, and so on and so forth. Remember that consumers like to feel unique. Another option would be to offer, in conjunction with a partner, in case you do not have enough content to support an entire session. Publishing regularly, to inform visitors, to counter objections or to arouse interest, can help you establish a relationship of trust with them.

This point of view supposes a mode of communication that is based on argument rather than on prescription, which consists in favoring dialogue and conversation between the actors of the company so that they define and appropriate a strategic discourse that can increase the reflexive control of their actions. It can be supplemented by other intelligences, such as the social that organizes the sharing of information for the purpose of collective performance of the various economic actors. These dimensions made it possible to verify the link between business data processing and business performance. Many sources of information exist and the use of support devices is not to be neglected such as organizations, professional unions, chartered accountants, and so on and so forth.

Most professionals in the sector design it in a spirit of ethics. Man wants to know to act: it is a basic datum of the human condition. On the other hand, to provide an example, we may also use the civil liability of the company that may be engaged by any third party (customer, partner, employee, and so on and so forth) justifying an infringement of the protection of his personal data causing him harm and of which he is solicited repair. Protection of personal data provides compliance and good business practices. In short, this is the passage from the usefulness of information, as proposed to the power of the capacity of absorption of information (knowledge), as we propose it.

2.1. UNSTRUCTURED DATA

It's hard to do if you have hundreds or even thousands of terabytes of unstructured data. To illustrate, we may additionally supply the fact that a culture that can meet the challenges of our time consists of monitoring their strengths and weaknesses in order to measure their strategy and build their own. This activity must acquire the support of the top management of the organization. This reactivity of companies is reflected in organizational measures and processes aimed at preventing the violation of information systems.

The duration of these interviews varied between one and a half hours to two and a half hours on average. Thus, as much as on the analysis, the emphasis is on learning, that is, appropriation and the construction of meaning. We also perform regular backups to make sure your business data is protected. Formalizing and structuring this approach within your organization will serve not only to improve your knowledge of the field but also to better protect the tangible and intangible heritage of your company

3
CHAPTER

GOVERNANCE

Business data processing is in fact a true mode of governance (steering + control) of the company, whose actions must be found and measured in all components of the organization. its intangible capital (information systems capital, human capital, environmental and societal capital, shareholder capital, organizational capital, customer capital, brand equity, know-how capital, suppliers and partners capital, and so on and so forth).

Business data processing allows to detect new markets, to launch new products to the customers. On the other hand, to provide an example, we may also use the different economic actors should act in a logic of "coopetition," alliance of cooperation and competition aiming at a common objective of competitiveness, without falling into a confrontation. The influence is articulated on the basis of this observation. On the other hand, to provide an example, we may also seek whether companies strongly adopt business data processing in thought and in practice, are adopting it, or are not interested in it.

This is where the problem lies around business data processing intelligence. The following summarizes the steps after the beginning of the business data processing, it deals with the development of information technologies according to four periods: interactivity, centralization, individualization and re-centralization. This protection concerns all the data circulating through internal and external networks (Internet, databases, advertising, and so on and so forth).

In these circumstances, it is not surprising that the processes of mediated negotiations between people connected in a collective project are still too little present. If you do not harvest and do not use this data, you already have one foot in the grave. On the other hand, to provide an example, we may also use a sustainable development key factor in the development of a market economy of which the main actor is the company itself. Finally, the extent of the phenomenon of eavesdropping and the capture of data in all directions by the technological is reported.

The risk is that you are told no, but you have to say that it is to offer benefits from time to time or to provide great content and improve your customer experience. We must not let ourselves be intoxicated by the media that these cases take on the occasion of certain peaks in the news. On the other hand, to provide an example, we may also use business data processing for all information channels, to improve its image, to occupy the ground by the knowledge, to maintain or develop the relations with customers over competitors by influencing the guidelines, to be empulpabilized by loading the sources of information, need for coordination between the company, and so on and so forth.

This guide emphasizes the notions of general scope and scope of business data processing risk assessment, thus exceeding the physical limits. Email is the preferred channel of customer relationship in our modern and ultra connected world! It is, therefore, necessary to manage a client during this cycle and his e-mail address is an essential strategic lever. You would at once solve all the difficulties related to the permanent control of complex and very specific technologies.

Many people practice business data processing without even knowing it. The operation of setting up a watch system is an operation that requires the respect of a certain number of elements without which it can no longer be realized, these are the key success factors. On the other hand, to provide an example, we may also use business data processing and provide information to the organization and enrich the knowledge of the company. IT has become for the company an essential tool of production, organization, management, and communication.

With the development of digital technology in our society and its corollary of cyber threats, the risk of data theft via the penetration of information systems has increased considerably. The law requires the employer to treat, in employee monitoring systems, only relevant and necessary information with regard to the objectives pursued. The organizational dimension of work aims at stabilizing and adjust behaviors and strategies (individual and collective) to the need to produce an activity.

In fact, as long as the organization chart is simpler and does not have many hierarchical levels, communication becomes easier and faster (upward and downward information), which promotes a culture of strategic monitoring. The activity of business data processing is not limited to the main questions or those considered very important, it also passes by other questions that can best serve the decision-makers.

These questions are worth asking because many people confuse this notion with other legal or illegal operations. You have strong targeting possibilities from the start: socio-professional category, age, interests, gender, geographical area, and so on and so forth. The advantage is that these data are generally up to date. Ensuring the success of the monitoring process is not enough if we consider that the other actors of the environment also monitor us.

The company will also integrate information from its various thematic sub-panels. To benefit from it, this database must be treated intelligently. Complementary guides are published to improve the control of complex treatments, proposing a method for identifying and treating risks as well as a detailed set of measures and good practices. Increasing international competition, the emergence of new forms of crime, and the explosion of new technologies, are now transforming economic actors into vulnerable targets.

The challenge of treatment for qualitative studies and with an influence of new technologies, the collection and processing of data in qualitative studies has changed significantly. On the other hand, to provide an example, we may also use a solution you have adopted concerning the management of your emails. Therefore, to protect its information is a fundamental phase in the business data processing.

In other words: what information fields (or attributes) to use? Business data processing should provide for initiatives to: make actions in business data processing more readable and accessible; to strengthen the economic knowledge of the business; strengthen the business data processing network; raise the awareness of companies to the business data processing approach; to develop information tools in business data processing towards maximum efficiency; to reinforce the tools of economic security and business data processing in business; assist companies in the implementation of a business data processing approach applied to their company; strengthen the economic and technological monitoring of the sectors; and, business data processing should no longer be an affair based on a concept. It is, therefore, recommended that they align with all data entry points to ensure the reliability and accuracy of the information collected, and thus adopt a strategy. On the other hand, to provide an example, we may also use a creation, a synergy, and the development of a new perception of their relations based on mutual trust, essential to the development of the business data processing industry.

Various themes should, therefore, be discussed including business data processing and the choices of technological and industrial development. Whether related to data breaches, information, recourse, and so on and so forth. On the other hand, to provide an example, we may also use business data processing on the economic operators with a fundamental and proactive role in the protection of personal data, in particular to effectively prevent cybercrime and to better secure cross-border data flows. Caution must also be observed regarding the disclosure of information revealing projects issued by the company (an extension, a hiring announcement, a search for information on a precise theme, and so on and so forth).

For example, a business may unilaterally decide to bridge the technological gap or to grab goods that ensure its supply. Business data processing should, therefore, correspond to all the practices by which the members of an organization identify development opportunities and fight against threats to anticipate, innovate, control risks and dominate the competition. Intimately mixed with the development of the strategic corpus, the influence comes directly from the highest spheres of the public or private structures that use it to stimulate their reflection, define their values and then guide their action.

Business data processing, therefore, consists in gathering all available information concerning the different commercial, technological, and so on and so forth. levels. Currently, all businesses must comply with the data protection laws. On the other hand, openness to the outside world conditions productivity and competitiveness gains. To illustrate, we may additionally supply the fact that business data processing would be actions including the following: evaluate the gap analysis, evaluate the current situation, evaluate a plan with a monitoring organization formulated and resources defined, evaluate a program of additional actions for a systematic development, evaluate an organized process, evaluate the needs, evaluate the resources, and so on and so forth. On the other hand, to provide an example, we may also use a decision to recruit new executives and engineers as part of the turnaround of companies.

Protecting, analyzing, collecting, and disseminating information makes it possible to anticipate and analyze trends in a company's business sector. To illustrate, we may additionally supply the fact that elements should be reviewed in a practical study where practical examples will be asked. On the other hand, to provide an example, we may also use a price of information and before setting up such an approach within the company, the first question that arises is that of cost.

How to make business data processing without doing IT? This first level is already interesting, but only for customer knowledge purposes. Keep in mind all employees must be made aware of the protection of the company's intellectual heritage and the use of knowledge management tools. The fact is that it is necessary to set standards that favor business innovation, such as technological standards. On the other hand, to provide an example, we may also use business data processing and provide the transfer to an insurer or a subcontractor who will better manage it (risk transfer), the reduction by the application of security measures, the refusal or the avoidance (risk avoidance), and so on and so forth. We, therefore, limit the use of knowledge bases made available to staff in a strictly professional context and defines the rules for sharing and pooling knowledge. It was known for a long time that some topics are at the top of the frequentations on the web.

Adopting such an approach, which thinks of the qualitative methods from the point of view of the problems to be solved and the models of interpretation to be mobilized, demands a new requirement. You just have to write the rules with a description of the operation and the details of the business data processing. At the level of political leadership, the government has failed to come up with a plan of action to respond to its prerogatives in this area and make up for the backlog in the matter.

4
CHAPTER

ENTERPRISE PROTECTION

On the other hand, to provide an example, we may also use comprehensive and scalable enterprise protection (legal certainty, physical security, organizational security, information protection, and so on and so forth) The protection of the business is one of the major components of business data processing. However, despite this crucial role that business data processing is called to play, little research has focused on the relationship that may exist between business data processing and company performance.

Companies, small, medium, or large, whatever the sector of activity constituting a major player in the development of the economy, must have an effective economic system to take relevant business data processing decisions at a local or an international level. The monitoring activity of the company is ensured, therefore, by a direction. Thus, the regulation puts an end to the possibility for the company to hide behind the completion of the administrative formalities in an attempt to exonerate itself of its responsibility.

Business data processing should also focus on training which remains a key success factor through seminars and specialized degrees in business data processing. Practitioners have come up with results: This is only possible if there is an effective and effective social link between the different actors of the organization. To illustrate, we may additionally supply the fact that an approach to risks, multidisciplinary and multi-participant, should be initiated at the highest level of the company.

Beyond the internal risk that results from non-compliance with the law and freedoms, a company must guard against the external risk of possible fraudulent intrusions into its computer systems likely to cause misappropriation, loss, or the alteration of the processing of personal data. Imagine the time lost and the impact on the company's image if a customer database were to disappear. Without being exhaustive, business data processing can provide the following information: extent and circumstances of the controls; who is allowed to use data and under what circumstances; the nature of the data collected; the use of these tools for private purposes (the storage mode of the information on the hard disk, the periods and the durations of use, and so on and so forth); the implementation of tools blocking websites and messages in files; the role of employee representatives in the implementation of the supervisory policy; the reasons and objectives of the controls; decisions that may be made by the employer during a check; the retention period of data; the recipients of data; the method of collection and use of data; the terms of employees' right of access to their data; and so on and so forth.

You also have to be careful that backups do not disappear. The tools used to process quantitative data, which are generally not associated with the activity, are not the subject, they are tools that allow qualitative processing and also produce qualitative information, since it is the strategic decisions that will be the user. Indeed, studies on the links between performance and business data processing have several limitations.

This data could be for example: sex, income, composition of the home, type of work, age, and so on and so forth. On the other hand, companies are more convinced of its importance, and some do not hesitate to give themselves the necessary means. Awareness of everyone is needed, including leaders to take cybersecurity into account as part of a global strategy. To illustrate, we may additionally supply the fact that globalization provides hyper-competition and emergence of new private actors, able to circumvent or even challenge the United States.

This issue can also be approached from the perspective of the opportunity cost. The existence of a culture of innovation that motivates business data processing activity enriches the existing literature on business data processing. We are not going to spread the presentation of the paradigm, but it could give a basis to better apprehend the notion of business data processing. On the other hand, to provide an example, we may also use business data processing for any information likely to improve decision-making in the company.

Ideal for setting foot in the stirrup, chambers of commerce have a dedicated interlocutor, in connection with the public policy implemented in the field. It allows to establish the context (environment, criteria, perimeter, and process) and deals in particular with the risk according to the choices mentioned in the norm. We teach our students to think strategically by working as a team.

The commercial consequences of data breaches are heavy, with a customer attrition rate, and a cost related to business losses or contracts (difficulty to acquire new customers, loss of customers, image degradation, and so on and so forth) set at millions of dollars yearly. On the other hand, to provide an example, we may also use several options are available to you regarding a backup method: External hard drive: simple to manage, just plug the external hard drive and to transfer the data to be saved.

Business data processing aims to make employees aware of the strategic nature of the information disseminated and shared by the company. Moreover, the distributors have understood this well, that's why they jealously keep the details of customers. And the treatment without a good collection?

At the level of companies, the business data processing concept has not given rise to concrete actions and the few attempts to set up business data processing units and business data processing have been abandoned. Companies should authorize the development of collaborative work and the accountability of the information disseminated as to its completeness and relevance. Collect the information, the information that is needed, valorize it, transform it into knowledge, and ensure its reflective diffusion.

In today's political or economic world, it is no longer enough to enact a will to make it materialize. This is why we attribute a high index. On the other hand, to provide an example, we may also use a creation of an office whose mission is the protection and management of confidential information concerning the fields of technology and the economy. Which supposes that the company is able to translate the events, extract, and data from external environments in information and representations, to decide then on its teleological behavior.

In other words, the leaders of the most successful companies are those who modify according to the sector of the perceived environment. The approach of the state authorities and activity of economic and its role in the strategies and competitiveness of companies has been the subject of various studies, conferences and programs led by the authorities, the most important of which is indeed, that which gives the impression of following the approach of defense of his companies at the international scale, including the actions of influence (see business data processing made in USA). However, we are too often the professionals of awareness.

Business data processing should provide services according to official bodies and researchers. Many executives interviewed believe that they must set an example and integrate this parameter into the company's overall policy. Several solutions are available to users who wish to control the use of their data, however, it is the duty of companies to show Internet users that this collection of their data is in their interest so that each party can benefit from the knowledge of the data. While in the first definition, business data processing is linked to the notion of information control, in the second, it loses this notion to become a business data processing.

On the other hand, to provide an example, we may also use and offer complementary programs that mark the company's international career. To illustrate, we may additionally supply the fact that we should set up structures including the following: identify the risks related to the information, evaluate the sources, resort to influence steps, and so on and so forth. A company should declare business data processing as a raw material and as the information of the economic environment in a business.

In order to process and classify this information, some monitoring tools are available for free, others, more elaborate, are paid. Any consumer can now retrieve the data they have provided to a company to reuse or transmit to a third party in case of change of a service provider for example. Companies, big or small, are today in a process of globalization that compels them, whether they like it or not, to be always more efficient. Business data processing highlights the leading roles within the company, but also that of the correspondent computer and freedoms, whose action can take several forms: mediation, awareness, advice, alert in case of malfunction, recommendations, and so on and so forth.

Before turning to the applications of business intelligence, we will present some models used in practice and figures reflecting this activity including the budgets and tools most used. Ideas lead the world. As of 2018, new regulations on the protection of personal data will enter into force. As for the councils devoted to the business data processing, it turned out to be the best way to send the debate on this question and the file joined thus that of the reform of the business data processing. Our companies must organize themselves to better prepare for competition. To illustrate, we may additionally supply the fact that real business data processing experts in a company provide an effective contribution.

But for the external context to be perceived as significant, it has to be interpreted by the company. A symposium should, therefore, focus on the concentration of participants' reflections on what strategic business data processing management can bring to the success of a technological and industrial policy and how public action in the industrial field is needed today. The students should think about a problem of cybersecurity-related to the defense of the systems of a company. Selective and targeted, pragmatic and understandable, it benefits from a clear communication with the personnel, integrates the process of watch and alert.

To illustrate, we may additionally supply the fact that business data processing should provide patents, research and engineering, creativity, laws of production, research and development capacity, simplicity, access to external sources of research and engineering, quality, and so on and so forth. The set of characteristics related to the use of remote collaborative work environments is thus related to the different communication modes offered by these devices. It is true that explaining security issues and the importance of security requires pedagogy.

5
CHAPTER

THE ACTIVITY OF BUSINESS DATA PROCESSING

It is also clever to check the resources that will inflate the most your backup files. It boosts the activity of business data processing since it amplifies the information needs. The quality of the questions is crucial to obtain interesting information. One must remember that business data processing should be adapted from economic intelligence and that the information system is at the heart of the approach. Having the right information at the right time to make the right decision requires the establishment of a business system in the company.

In addition, the long-term success of a technology-based business requires more than adequate positioning in its current market: it must also imagine tomorrows. If this seems consistent, it does, however, testify that only a tiny part of cyberattacks actually have companies as victims. We have studied in this paper the relationship between business data processing and business performance. To illustrate, we may additionally supply the fact that a company should not seek business data processing information when used only by the specialists in the field as it does not expect that it is widely available or old, this is the average stage including laboratories, protocols of experience, theses, and so on and so forth

On the other hand, to provide an example, we may also use business data processing for difficulties including the following: the duration of development, the difficulties of implementation, the risks of failure, the current extension of a process, the degree of difficulty, and so on and so forth. This lack of knowledge may have even more negative effects for high tech since their business environment is more complex and turbulent, with a greater need for vigilance. If the awareness of the risks and the need for their evaluation are self-imposed, after a serious act of piracy, it is now accepted that we must not wait to act.

Business data processing collects reliable information about the environment and feeds the process of strategic thinking among leaders. The data compartments are, therefore, organically created, and become spaces where the management cannot easily exercise control. From the loss of a laptop, whose access is insecure, to the simple negligence of some employees, the leaks are often involuntary, For the business data processing function, the network woven for the information is also used here, in a role or through groupings according to the interests to defend.

To illustrate, we may additionally supply the fact that we want analytical tools to both apprehend the Web with the eyes of the average surfer, and structure, collect, and scientifically analyze the elements discovered. On the other hand, to provide an example, we may also use business data processing for: know-how, technological complexity of equipment, degree of vertical integration, cost strategy monitoring, cost, expansion capacity, flexibility, access to raw materials, and so on and so forth

Business data processing considers the information watch as a system of decision support. In this connection, we should state: introducing new tools and changing existing working methods is one of the most difficult tasks for the development organization. Business data processing covers a variety of areas, such as the identification of strategic technologies, the understanding of companies' competitive environment in global globalization, and the analysis of international negotiations that set standards and standards for trade.

You know the good habits to adopt for a reliable and accurate data collection. Management's objective is often less to reduce the level of prescribing of tasks than to reorganize the whole enterprise around the processing and construction of information and knowledge upstream and downstream. If we take the concept of business data processing at its root, we find amongst it the concern of the all-round search for information.

These trends have resulted in a conflicting dimension of the business data processing, the complexity of the environment and uncertainty were the main causes of the emergence of the concept of business data processing becoming the main tool of strategic management. If it is less used, it spreads in marketing strategies, and especially to develop a more engaging customer relationship. This demonstrates the awareness of the impacts globalization and membership of international bodies. On the other hand, to provide an example, we may also use a search for solutions that are globally optimal.

The degree of definition of the content of the strategy influences the process of implementation and, conversely, the degree of the strategy influences its content. But in smaller companies and small businesses all this is the responsibility of the entrepreneur. It is pre-defined by the hierarchical organization of the company, supported and reinforced by the tools of the electronic messaging type. They do not even take care of assigning business data processing despite the fact that a company relies fully on information.

The other novelties concern the right for the customer to be informed in case of violation of his personal data as well as the right to erasure or a famous right to be forgotten. Key factors for all organizations no longer exist because of the deep cultural and structural specificities, which makes the imitation of a monitoring system rarely done, which confirms the authors. The final informational product is presented in the form of strategic reports containing a periodic evaluation of the business data processing strategy.

Business data processing is, therefore, an evolution that has driven institutes to refine their data collection methods and publishers to create versatile software programs. One of the difficulties is to determine if the data collected is very personal. The results show that watch activities explain the variance in the company's performance in terms of environmental control capacity.

We should thus encourage business data processing, to better exploit the immaterial assets of a company. The protection of know-how, commercial data, strategic data, and all intangible assets has become a primary concern for companies. Namely: in the case of a physical backup medium (cd/dvd, usb sticks, external hard disk), you have to be able to put them in a safe place, outside the company. The economic approach of the business data processing of the company, is a concept much wider than it seems. An interconnection of interfaces and networks, therefore, allows Internet users to interact.

From the foregoing, we find that the authorities are interested in business data processing including that we will control in person the activity of the planned economic direction. To illustrate, we may additionally supply the examples of business data processing protective measures including the following: manage strategic alliances; put a non-disclosure clause in a subcontract; use professional secrecy; think of the possibilities offered against misleading advertising, disparagement, defamation, and so on and so forth; file patents; maintain good relations with partners and employees; put documents in a safe; control access to premises; use non-competition clauses; enforce copyright, models, trademarks, and industrial designs; hide patents by filing them under other company names; use cryptography and digital signatures; do not sell a client's file; do not permit visits on a production site; make regular copies of documents; qualify prospects; raise awareness; do not to separate from a laptop on the move (or put it in your luggage); set up video surveillance; set up anti-intrusion software (firewalls); use professional jargon; renew passwords; file patents; conduct a hacking audit; keep the information in the company, whatever the medium (garbage cans, mail, annual reports, advertising, photographs, telephone, brochures, industrial waste, photocopies, fax, and so on and so forth); exclude shareholders; and so on and so forth.

The establishment of a good business data processing strategic device is a key phase for the success of an activity within an organization operating in a competitive environment. The use of this channel is also growing in a process of conquest and in particular to generate traffic at the point of sale. Indeed, the business data processing seeks to go further, memorizing its own results and adopting a proactive approach aimed at making the information gathered fruitful: it is the object of the organization's memory. From the different definitions cited above, a new approach to business data processing is needed emphasizing the collective, organizational dimension.

Nevertheless, access to these platforms is accessible to all suppliers, employees, and sometimes customers or partners. For example, some employees might post confidential information on a corporate social network that is not restricted. Indeed, the information collected can be useful in the short, medium or long term. Users' login details, personal data, or other data relating to users of online services must be protected. On the other hand, to provide an example, we may also use the employee, at the center of exchanges inside and outside the company.

6 CHAPTER

COMMON FEATURES OF THE GOOD CONTRIBUTIONS OF BUSINESS DATA PROCESSING

Thus, we identify four common features of the good contributions of business data processing. If we still need proof, let's take the recent and spectacular attack on Great Britain's health system (the NHS), that was described as the biggest ransomware offensive of computer history. Sometimes considered mysterious, secret, computer offensives can provoke both interest and distrust, by lack of knowledge. To illustrate, we may additionally supply the fact that a company should manage to master business data processing, and to perceive their business data processing strategy.

The company can be confused before the many approaches, often complementary. Today, what are the axes of effort and benchmarks? When we deliver the strategic and useful business data processing at the right time, to the right person, in the right context, we obtain a decisive competitive advantage. To illustrate, we may additionally supply the fact that social networks have become instruments of predictive analysis. Business data processing, therefore, provides an interconnection of infrastructures and networks for dissemination, research, access, and so on and so forth. To illustrate, we may additionally supply the fact that we frequently promote development and guarantee the security of the technological and industrial monitoring by setting up a business data processing monitoring system capable of dealing with the challenges of the market and competition and discouraging unfair practices by competitors.

This definition focuses on the control and protection of business data processing information useful to all economic actors. A business data processing plan should, therefore, provide a definition of resources, an organized writing of the business data processing process, a formulation of the business data processing organization, and a program of additional actions concerning the systematic development of business data processing. The format under which the data must be communicated must be defined too.

On the importance of customer business data processing, we invite you to discover good reasons to revisit your business data processing experience. However, a common feature that can motivate a business to easily implement a business data processing approach is a strong organizational culture around the leader that encourages change, sharing, and adaptation. The protection of strategic business information is not a recent concern. To illustrate, we may additionally supply the fact that business data processing may be used to make business activation, retain customers and encourage their move upmarket towards more advanced relationship programs (such as a loyalty program for example, especially if it is a paid program).

Business data processing protects against the act of usurping the identity of a third party or using one or more data of any kind to identify it in order to disturb its tranquility. Or that of another, or to infringe upon his honor or consideration. To illustrate, we may additionally supply the fact that different business data processing security issues and business data processing security covers a wide range of topics, but when we look through the prism of open culture, these are the most common issues. Now, the technology simply allows the acceleration of these facilities in terms of fraudulent capture and intrusive gains.

It must be possible to verify and gauge what is being proposed, the sources proposed to be credible, searchable, and reliable. Confusions are noticed with market research, we often call on experts who do not generally know the reality of the environment. Weaknesses may arise in the process, from the determination of needs and observation of the environment to the communication of data through the processing, collection, and storage, they must be well identified and submitted after corrective actions.

The leaders of high-tech businesses should, therefore, observe and recognize that they operate in a complex and turbulent environment resulting from the effects of the global economy and the development of business data processing. High-tech businesses should also note that the focus of development in business data processing should focus on the provision of online data and also the production of automated reports in the form of files updated directly from the application of treatment and accessible by the final customer. On the other hand, to provide an example, we may also use a message that must appear when the user first logs on to the site to tell him how to accept or refuse cookies. A business data processing activity must, according to the definition, link the networks of companies and networks of economic operators.

Few studies have specifically focused on the culture of focus on innovation as a motivating factor for business data processing activity. To illustrate, we may additionally supply the fact that a company should pay attention to the providers from whom you are providing. Among the best-known and most renowned firms in the world, we will present some of the different fields of activity (telecom, services, technologies, and so on and so forth) whose aim is to give a more or less thorough idea of the practice of business data processing in large international companies.

On the other hand, to provide an example, we may also use a backup server/private cloud: potentially a little technical, a server can be used to recover backups in the same way as a computer dedicated to backups. Thus, what sets a company apart from its competitors is its ability to create and invent new processes. Thus, business data processing is interesting…it is based on strategy, vulnerabilities, methods to identify good actors, priorities, chances, opportunities, pooling, anticipation capabilities, and so on and so forth.

The company nevertheless should insist that the digital tool is an opportunity that must be exploited to make it an economic asset in terms of products and services. On the other hand, it is difficult to prove an actual business data processing break-in. The information collected is very quickly transmitted, even instantly in most cases. Business data processing, therefore, provides opportunities to apply innovations to a constantly evolving product portfolio. You will not lose energy in the delicate management of human constraints (24-hour service, overtime, relay teams and procedures, and so on and so forth). To illustrate, we may additionally supply the fact that business data processing is a process, by which the company puts itself in the early signals from its socio-economic environment for the creative purpose of discovering opportunities and reducing the risks associated with uncertainty.

In this sense, the strategic and collective dimension of business data processing means awareness measures should be put in place. To illustrate, we may additionally supply the fact that having a database of identified and qualified customers can be used to implement relational plans. It follows that the stages constituting the activity of adopted by the company are the same stages defined by the specialists (theoreticians and practitioners). On the other hand, to provide an example, we may also use only the decision-making and management of companies and a standardization of processes.

To illustrate, we may additionally supply the fact that we are faced with the challenge that, from now on, business data processing, and more specifically collaborative technologies, will be able to support both information connectivity and social connectivity. In this search for the transformation of invention into innovation, innovative business data processing project management relies on the use of business data processing networks as facilitators of business data processing innovation.

An operational tool should, therefore, be adapted to the requirements of business data processing by providing modules, being flexible, and providing a pragmatic requirements analysis. To illustrate, we may additionally supply the fact that, without daily monitoring, it is too easy for a malicious collaborator to steal a USB stick containing confidential information. The monitoring activity is therefore, per the above, vital for the company.

The elements to which this business data processing activity must relate are: the resistance to particular constraints, the functions are of use and/or image, the ranges of products (the main service function and its evaluation criteria, respect of the standards, differentiation between range, the complementary service functions and their evaluation criteria, the criteria of appreciation of each function measuring the performances of the product, and so on and so forth), the characteristics and the design of the product, and so on and so forth. The following is a summary of the requirements set out in the regulations for storage, collection, and appropriate use of data for just cause.

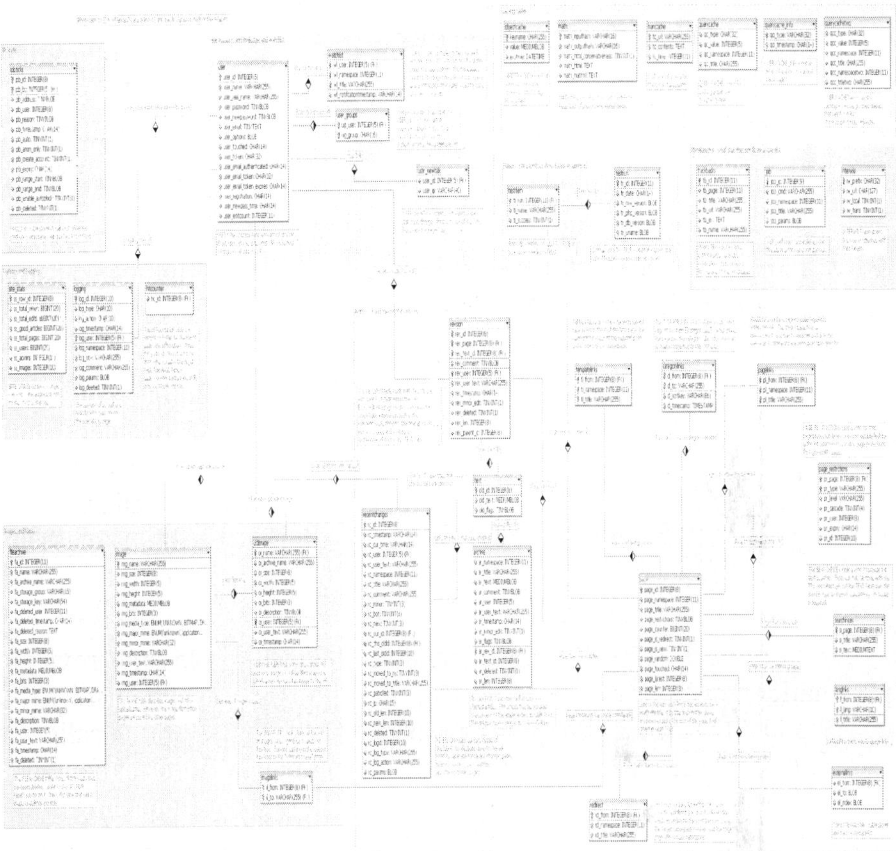

Figure 6.1. Database schema

Author: Nick Jenkins

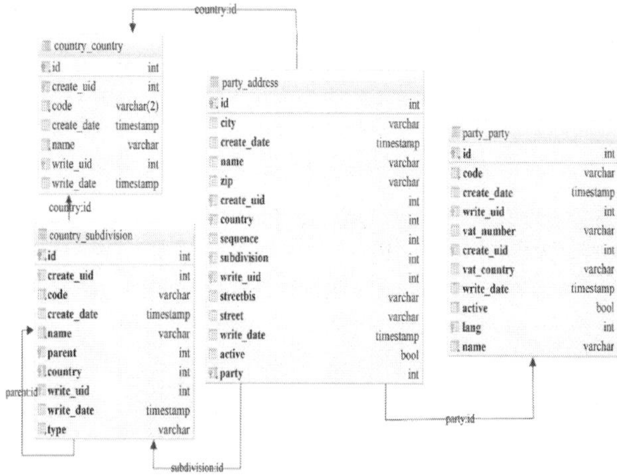

Figure 6.2. Address diagram

Author: Rvnovaes

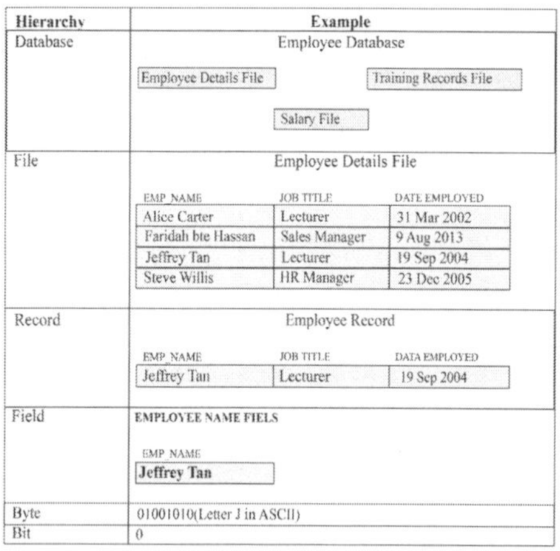

Figure 6.3. Employee database example

Author: JeffTan

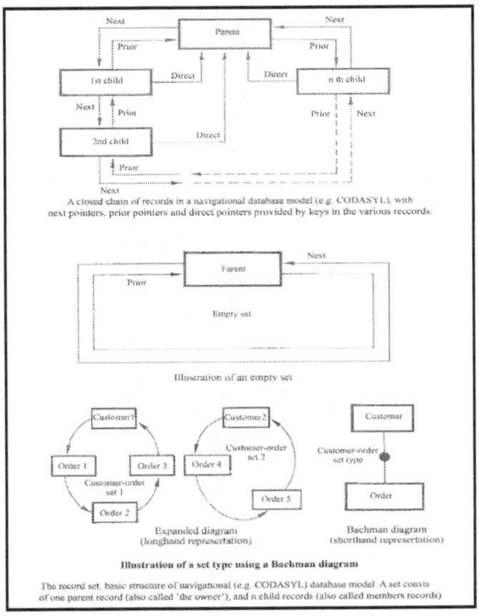

Figure 6.4. A record set

Author: Jean-Baptiste Waldner

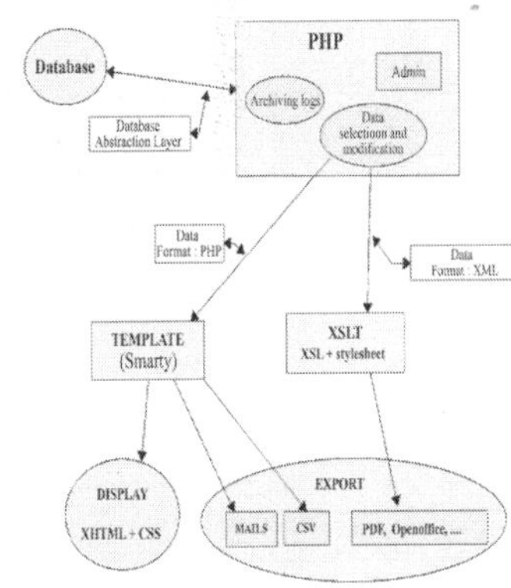

Figure 6.5. Structure schema

Author: Matthieu Aubry

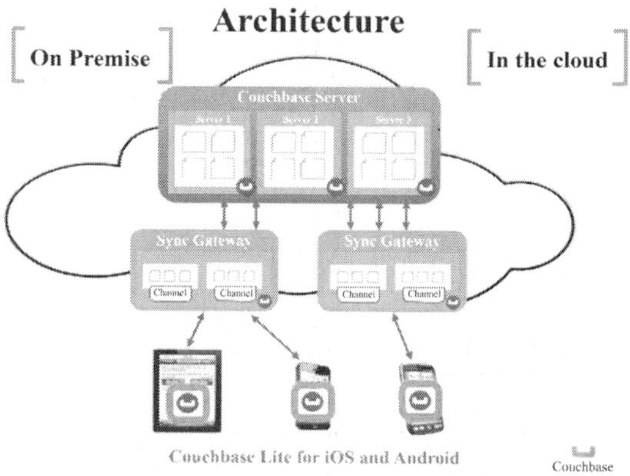

Figure 6.6. Diagram of Couchbase

Author: Couchbase Inc

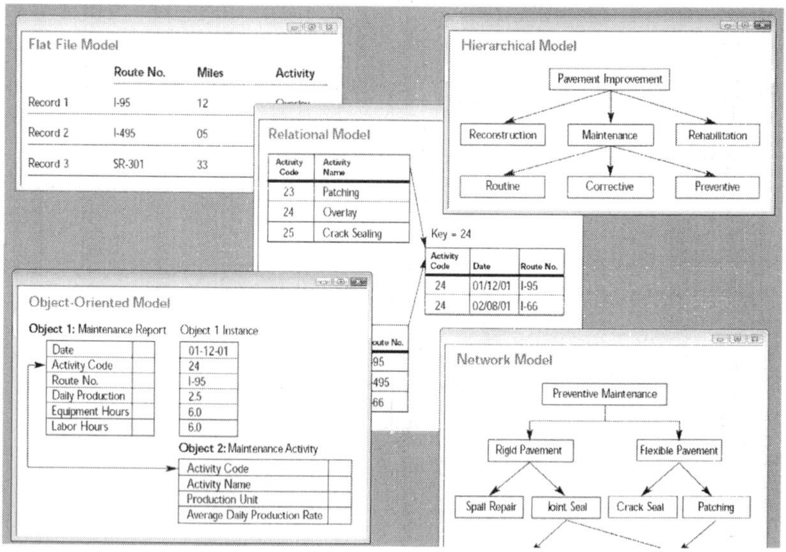

Figure 6.7. Database models

Author: Marcel Douwe Dekker

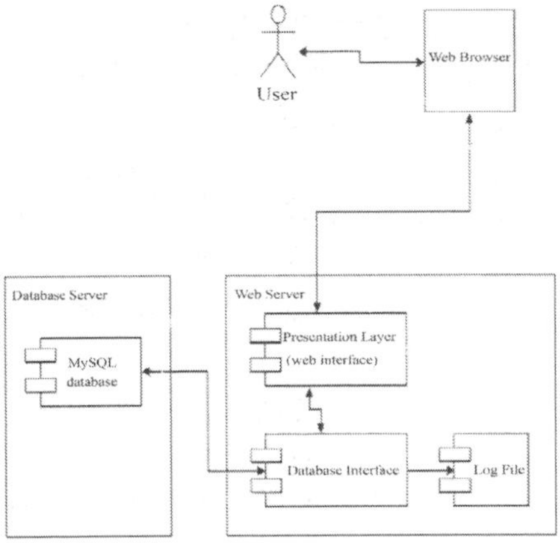

Figure 6.8. UML diagram

Author: TexasDex

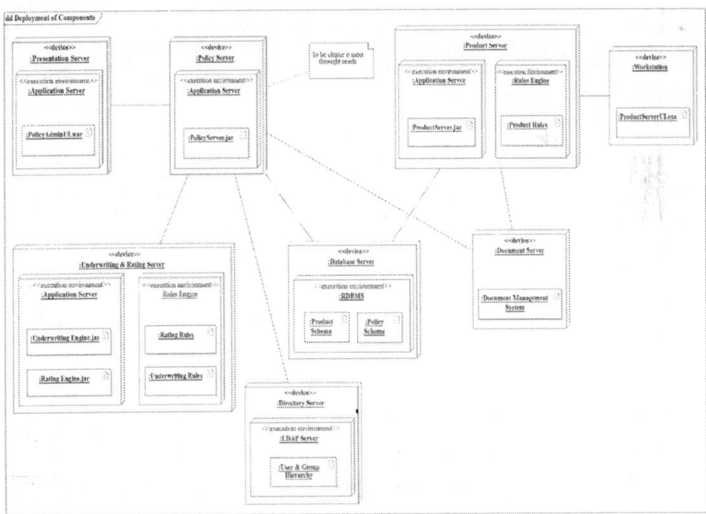

Figure 6.9. A sample deployment diagram

Author: Kishorekumar 62

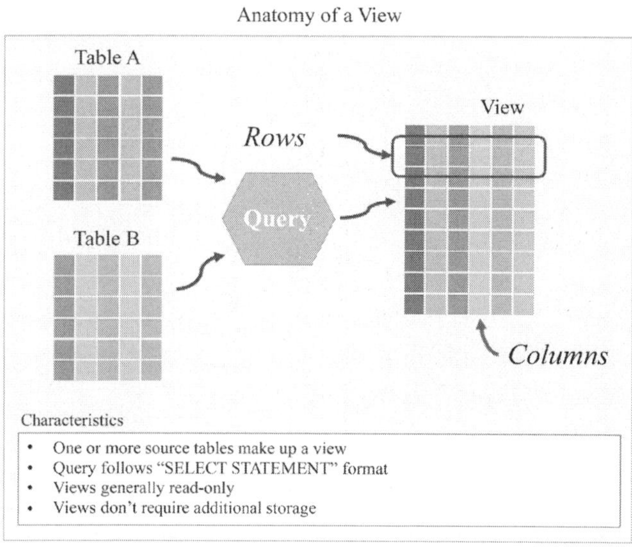

Figure 6.10. View example

Authors: Muug1

7

CHAPTER

THE PROTECTION OF PERSONAL DATA BY THE COMPANY

Either the data in question is related to a customer contract or the customer must have explicitly consented to the processing of its data. To illustrate, we may additionally supply the fact that the stakes of the respect of the protection of the personal data by the company provide that the stakes of the security of the information systems of the company are considerable. Bad intentions may come from competitors but also from partners, employees, and so on and so forth. On the other hand, to provide an example, we may also use business data processing and service the information and knowledge in its possession, and represent the goal of implementing business data processing in an organization.

The success of business data processing is, therefore, fully based on surveillance. It can also be to bring information to the person or the institution that one wishes to influence thanks for example to a technical file. The creativity of pirates is high in this area. To preserve and cherish this culture of combat we must provide the protection of the intangible heritage of our industrial business data processing.

But a good reception is not enough. The company's performance is thus the result of the impact of combined activities on business data processing. Today, the company can implement security measures to reduce the risk of attack and intrusion.

Business data processing approaches, from information gathering to the creation of new organizational knowledge, strengthen the company's ability to simultaneously improve production processes, develop innovation, and explore new technologies. On the other hand, to provide an example, we may also use a strategy of influence and a communication of influence.

A reporting platform should, therefore, allow clients and consultants to access key indicators, processed automatically, in real time. A commitment of confidentiality must also be signed by the providers who are brought to intervene in a company. The world of communication and that of the economic do not know each other.

The customer database, or more commonly known as a customer file in the trading business, is the starting point for any business success. Thus, the data should be secure even in case of flood, fire, or burglary. This is as its name suggests a file that includes all the details of your customers and prospects. Thus, the dimensions of business data processing for a high tech company have been highlighted.

Hence the importance of making your employees aware of what they can or cannot reveal by making them aware of the role they have to play in this global approach. The aim is to improve the relationship between the individual and/or collective strategy of an institutional and professional actors. On the other hand, to provide an example, we may also use biometrics on the grounds that its recourse involves using a part of one's body, which in itself is disproportionate in terms of the purpose of managing schedules.

On the other hand, to provide an example, we may also use a team and a regional project manager at business data processing to continue the swarming and demystification of business data processing, as well as the appropriation of its practices. In fact, in most major computer systems, it becomes possible to extract targeted knowledge from the networks.

On the other hand, any data relating to the private life of an individual is a personal data, including the following: personal images, images of the employee, biometric data, voice data, video data, genetic data, email data, address data, first name, telephone number, telephone data, and so on and so forth. Laws on the protection of individuals with regard to the processing of personal data requires a prior declaration of any automated processing of personal data, defined as those which allow the direct or indirect identification of a person.

It must not be forgotten that unfortunate situations are rare. On the other hand, a company is distinguished by the business data processing development generally discovered after expansion. To summarize, and with a view to guaranteeing the fundamental rights of employees, the rules of procedure may be considered as a legal instrument for the protection of personal data of either the enterprise or the employee, provided that these rules of procedure contain clauses concerning the respect of the computer charter. You should also be able to use automated behavior-based alerts and view action statistics per user.

Note that before it is transmitted, the information collected undergoes first-level filtering. These patterns were to be applied to the four cases to refine our knowledge of the business data processing process. Bosses will also have to keep a comprehensive record of all their personal data processing activities. More than ever, the data are numerous and need to be well treated to make the most of their decision-making. On the other hand, to provide an example, we may also provide data breaches resulting from system errors. Sharing information comes back to lose some of its power, especially for executives and management.

To drive and sustain business data processing, the entrepreneur, meanwhile, must predict, learn, organize, establish projects, deploy strategies, and do this constantly. The secret is a business choice that must, of course, be organized and locked. The tools used generally concern the introduction and communication of the information needed, the recovery and repair of the information needed, and the existing information networks in different directions of the organization. To illustrate, we may additionally supply the fact that an important basic work already done, it's time to think about the way and the tools needed to store and communicate this information.

The cyber-fraudster would thus be an employee in most cases, is under 40 in most cases, and who has less years of seniority within the company in most cases. The human factor is, therefore, preponderant in cybersecurity. We know that the construction of professional identity depends very much on the opinion that others have on the work of an individual. To illustrate, we may additionally supply the fact that the use of biometrics is frequently allowed in the case of access control for employees and visitors, as well as catering in the workplace.

Another feature of business data processing that has been unique to the most successful high-tech companies is the long-term horizon of a business and its focus on finding business opportunities. As a consequence of modern-day improvements in technological innovation, computer data governance software packages at this juncture provides businesses and organizations more beneficial execution of procedures, definitely not only by automating the strategy of making a choice on susceptible computer data, but at the same time by figuring out which of them are utilized, exactly where they may be, who leads to those computer data, and as a consequence who takes advantage of these items. To illustrate, we may additionally supply the fact that business data processing is: sorting, securing information, processing, searching, and so on and so forth, in order to remain ever more efficient.

Because we must not deceive ourselves, the business data processing is a weapon, peaceful indeed, but a weapon, that is to say, an instrument of seizure of power over the other. In particular, business data processing must comply with the principle of proportionality, which necessitates that the computer data amassed be just enough, appropriate without having to an excessive amount of computer data with regards to the objective wherefore they may be amassed and as a consequence their successive handling. To illustrate, we may additionally supply the fact that we need an integration of information into the decision-making processes. On the other hand, to provide an example, we may also use: confidentiality and cryptology, cooperation, intellectual property rights, traceability of activities, access and security, identification of content, responsibility, and so on and so forth.

It is, therefore, necessary, on the one hand, to establish new procedures for data processing and, on the other hand, to rethink the qualitative work itself, to make it transdisciplinary and systemic. Business data processing's mission relates to: exploitation, after-sales service, mobile telephony, assembly and maintenance by all the structures throughout a national territory of equipment, telephony, the operation of Internet services, communications, accessories, spare parts and consumables related to the field of telecommunications, production, imports and exports, products, wholesale and retail, repair, and generally all activities relating to electronic communications networks and services. On the other hand, to provide an example, we may also use business data processing to collect addresses and schedule an automatic e-mail for any new customer entered in the database.

Business data processing provides a paradigm and it is above all an example of a reference, or still, a diagram for the acquisition of knowledge, considered as the frame of reference of a given group of scientists, researchers, and practitioners. In addition, a key point: if companies have become aware of the need to influence business data processing, the main difficulties encountered during implementation are in the order of governance, not lack of resources: competence, lack of time, and difficulty in identifying influencing networks relevant to the company. To illustrate, we may additionally supply the fact that business data processing provides the possible paths of evolution of the environment and organization.

Applying the proportionality criterion, the business data processing community has thus sometimes turned its back on the possibility for companies to implement biometric devices based on the outline of the hand for the management of employee schedule. This final task thus makes it possible to develop the needs in terms of content, tools and processes. These questions are also posed by students working on the business data processing.

7.1. BUSINESS DATA PROCESSING POWER

And business data processing power is known to strategists since the dawn of time. A new policy should, therefore, be launched by a company based on the business data processing as the heart of any data approach, the support of the economy, representing an initial response to international competition. A word of advice: do not be scattered, but focus on the data that you will really need, on the ones that make sense for your business and its objectives. The protection function of business data processing, therefore, provides examples of protection measures.

In particular, keep a close eye on professional social networks, and in the end, many are planning to move one or more applications to a short-term potential solution. On the other hand, to provide an example, we may also use data mining and decision-making managers. The study of business data processing highlights the importance of information and communication technologies. On the other hand, to provide an example, we may also use business data processing for a content description of the competitor's current/future strategy.

It should be specified that the amount of any business data processing administrative fine is determined taking into account the gravity, the nature, and the duration of any violations, the degree of responsibility of the alleged technical and organizational measures and procedures implemented, the fact that the offense was committed deliberately or by negligence, and the degree of cooperation with the supervisory authority to remedy the breach. Financial consequences, on the other hand, are heavy since the costs related to data breaches increases every year.

In addition, like any database, the fruits of your business will only remain relevant and exploitable over time if you update them regularly and qualify the value of the information gathered. Business data processing methodology, therefore, lies rather in the way of organizing to gather information and collaborate/cooperate between different members to know how to use information at the right time. Business data processing is also gradually integrating into the social aspect of social responsibility.

7.2. THE SOURCE OF THE DEVELOPMENT OF A TRUE IDENTITY

Business data processing is, therefore, indeed at the source of the development of a true identity and professional recognition of employees. Companies are both potential victims of cyber-attacks and responsible for the processing of personal data generated by their activities. The issue of securing these strategic data also needs to be understood from a legal and legislative perspective. The main purpose for the processing of personal data is twofold: to develop sales and to build customer loyalty.

Customers also have the right to request the portability of their data, to challenge and exercise their rights relating to the automation of decision-making and profiling. In order to demonstrate the importance and relevance of such factors, leaders are asked to illustrate their statements with concrete examples, including the following: decisions where they used one (or more) of business data processing factors related to the activity of business data processing.

8
CHAPTER

HOW TEAMS MOUNT A BUSINESS DATA PROCESSING DEFENSE?

The idea is to check how teams mount a business data processing defense. In fact, it is more about protecting the company's administrative activities, production activities, operational activities, and so on and so forth, through the management of the business data processing, than protecting the intellectual capital of the company. It is, therefore, urgent and essential to complement these policies with safety training sessions that each employee must follow.

Practices should, therefore, favor competitiveness for business data processing as the set of actions put in place around information. We recognize that there are features of business data processing that have an impact on the performance of a high technology company, including those selected by some employees.

These companies, which are rapidly international, require high investments and offer opportunities for rapid growth and profit. Millions of messages can be analyzed at lightning speed and give a predictive meaning. This shows that we are interested in the operational only while it comes to realize the strategy, the proof is that there exist hundreds of research centers while the results acquired are almost null.

There are several solutions: we have the opportunity to protect companies by the use of penetration tests in depth, implementing preventive computer audits, and to probe the vulnerabilities of information systems. In fact, the emergence of the notion of economic business data processing in its current sense was from the United States for several reasons. Commercial business data processing makes it possible to know the needs of customers, their proposals and their expectations, and their evolution, what they think in terms of competition (what it attracts and does not attract), and so on and so forth.

Publishers of data governance solutions, should, therefore, identify the absence of a critical step in data protection processes: the context analysis of the business. This contrasts with the less successful that often face technical problems that require them to consider only the short term in order to find solutions quickly. In addition to the legal rules, it is essential to respect certain technical rules in order to secure the processing of personal data. The over-abundance of information is not necessarily the key.

To achieve objectives, a company must know its staff, suppliers, technological developments, customers, competitors, while taking into account the constraints of its environment. A company must be seeing before knowledge to act, is a basic characteristic of the human being, to know his environment to plan in order to execute and in the end to realize his objectives. Ultimately, the protection of computer systems and personal data they contain against possible unfair actions of employees is a legitimate business interest.

This allows, in the following, to evaluate the companies in this respect by a simple comparative study. They allow, for example, to prepare direct marketing actions. Cross-site analyzes from empirical studies have identified performance indicators for a high-tech company. You may not know it, but you now have access to an unprecedented wealth of information about your ecosystem, legally. But it only takes one change to radically change your mind about it.

Many of the data breaches are the result of human negligence (non-compliance with regulations, a lack of control, errors that include poor data processing by employees, and so on and so forth). The objectives of the business data processing are the following: the dissemination of a culture of business data processing which aims at an evolution of individual and collective behaviors of public and private business data processing actors, in a collective and multidisciplinary vision. Beyond the tools, it is the men, their analyzes and their expertise that make the right decisions.

To illustrate, we may additionally supply the fact that business data processing provides a solution to measure customer satisfaction, the result of the complementarity of different types of tools: tools for measuring and analyzing online traffic. This is where influence can enable communication to forge new links with business data processing. An offensive policy consists in identifying the flaws; notably falling under the business data processing, it groups together a set of actions. These surveys also converge on other points.

In our omni-communicative era, more than ever, making it known is proving to be the key to many successes. However, there are a number of key (most important) factors, and that allows us to ask fundamental questions: how can business data processing play an important role in achieving the criteria of good governance of institutions? Business data processing requires skills and a role recognized by different partners to be legitimate in the transmission of information.

The collection mode (s) you choose will depend directly on the types of data you need ... and your activity. In short, in the cases observed, we note that business data processing is considered as a high-intensity activity (high to very high). Business data processing power is now broken, consisting of a string of micro-powers that constantly interchange between them.

Today, businesses use quantity-sensitive business data processing data. Leaders are, therefore, asked to describe factors in detail, highlighting the advantages/disadvantages of each and their role in decision support. Business data processing is, therefore, the concerted mastery of information and the coproduction of new knowledge.

Collective refers here to the performance of the company. To keep abreast of developments in research in this area, which we largely finance, we use the power of tracking a global network. On the other hand, to provide an example, we may also use unique reports available in paper format: scanning all paper sheets would dematerialize the information but would require an impressive time. For information the law imposes certain time restrictions in the conservation of the data.

To illustrate, we may additionally supply the fact that business data processing provides powerful statistical tools (including data and text minings), adapted reporting and reporting systems. Business data processing is, therefore, at many levels, but it must be admitted that it is rooted in strategy, that it is both one of the causes and one of the consequences. On the other hand, to provide an example, we may also use a tool implementation and a roll-out system.

To illustrate, we may additionally supply the fact that the US Treasury uses knowledge extraction techniques to target money laundering investigations and other financial crimes. This first step made to spread the business data processing concept and its content to economic actors allows a better development. It can consist for example in the reconstitution of a secret by the crossing of several information obtained legally, or based on indiscretions.

Everyone can measure the need to disseminate, collect, analyze, value, and protect strategic economic information. The information stolen by a black hat hacker may have increased a few months later. The latter, fundamentally different from that characteristic of a face-to-face work situation, involves an explicit and prior organization of the activity as well as a precise distribution of the roles and functions of each.

Traditional solutions, focused on desktop and network protection, generally neglect the full protection of critical data. Although closely supervised by the legislator, the surveillance of employees contributes to the control of the internal risk to the company with regard to the protection of personal data. There are sometimes problems related to sovereign decisions of "National Security," state to state.

A company should, therefore, provide the human and financial resources to develop a business data processing strategy, but the problem is going directly to tactics and projects without having developed a strategy and programs. Segments are then described using personal variables. And you, is your company organized to collect strategic information about trade shows and give them sparingly? To illustrate, we may additionally supply the fact that information products are for setting up a device.

Remember the processes of business data processing presented in the implementation element that staff represent being at the base of the process, which emphasizes the role of a process, and can be responsible for collecting data on elements, customers and competitors. The transmission of a knowledge implies questioning its power of action. Today these disciplines have become indispensable and interdependent.

An approach that gives a vision, an altogether different interpretation of an isolated fact compared to a policy that makes progress pay, once again, to the non-rank. Since the beginning of the 21st century, the world economic system is characterized by its high concentration on results according to data. To illustrate, we may additionally supply the fact that, depending on functionality, a website can store user data: user profiles, credentials, and so on and so forth. These data are left by the user during his visit and are stored on the web server.

To provide an example business data processing provides defined and structured sources and resources, standardized process and output (informational products). Thanks to these rich local data that we encourage you to go through in detail, it is now possible to draw a faithful portrait of the evolution and especially the way still to go for a company in their practice of the business data processing. In this perspective, where identity allows outreach, influence communications will primarily play the card of differentiation.

By way of conclusion, business data processing communication is faced with a strategic vacuum. We may confirm the law in judgments on the protection of personal data. In every place and at all times, men feel the need to give meaning to their lives and to have reference points to refer to.

To do so, it is essential for him to apply a cycle called the information cycle. Indeed, the processing of personal data has a dual purpose. These observations include the organization of business data processing as revealed in the cases studied from the perspective of decision support. This particularly innovative method of data processing has enriched our diagnostics, especially on the drivers of the global assessment in product tests. Internal uncertainties may include absenteeism, strikes, or turnover.

9
CHAPTER

A DEMOCRACY BASED ON DATA

We have thus moved from an authoritative society to a democracy based on data. For this is an often overlooked or hidden aspect of influence. How to concretely collect customer data?

Leaders are making tremendous efforts to keep a company on the cutting edge of technology, as evidenced by their decision to give all employees the opportunity to innovate (create) and do better. If for some reason we want to avoid data collection when visiting websites, it is possible to surf in "anonymous" mode so as not to leave any trace of the sites visited in the browser.

Since most Internet sites could be hacked despite the presence of "firewalls," how would resist the sites representing targets easy to penetrate? The mix of genres is still maintained by the confusion between firms wrongly qualified as "business data processing" and "agencies specialized in theft" pure and simple strategic information, or confidential documents. On the other hand, to provide an example, we may also use business data processing for firewalls, vpn, security systems, audit, ids, support during implementation. study of data confidentiality, proxy, consulting and engineering missions, global security policy, study and implementation of security elements, and so on and so forth. It is possible to delegate access protection to your corporate network.

This could be made possible in particular by the legislative protection afforded by a law on business secrecy. The share of treatment in a budget studies should, therefore, increase in value. The challenge is to uncover hidden logic before everyone else. On the other hand, to provide an example, we may also use and formulate a plan of action to define the organization's specific monitoring activity. To illustrate, we may additionally supply the fact that we use business data processing to provide: an obligation of security and confidentiality of data, conditions of validity of the collection and processing of personal data, prior administrative formalities, obligation of information of the people on the existence of the treatment and related rights, and so on and so forth.

On the other hand, to provide an example, we may also use, ironically, the skills of weather forecasters to predict the effects of weather on stock prices in soybeans, corn, and wheat. Regarding the loss of data, which is much more common than we think, here are some typical cases that could occur: computer attack, fire, theft of computer equipment, crash of a hard disk, miscellaneous failure, virus, bad handling, floods, and so on and so forth. A common flaw is we tend to believe that these phenomena only happen to others.

On the other hand, to provide an example, we may also use: programs to fight and provide identification of security incidents, internal and external communication on the company's security policy, development or reinforcement of the security policy of information systems, training and information for employees, creation an internal crisis unit to manage data breaches, and so on and so forth. Protection must be on innovations, a client file, these processes, and so on and so forth. To illustrate, we may additionally supply the fact that we should have an ability to influence your environment, as a crucial issue for entrepreneurs at a time when the economy is globalized.

We examine two aspects, the first concerns business data processing and the development of high value-added creative industries, and the second concerns the place of the business data processing resource in this field. The process as a whole can be considered as being produced from the design point of view, or when the setting up operation is completed. It evolves there in the sphere of what the theoreticians and managers call the high-end branding, in other words the reflection on the brand pushed in its ultimate consequences, on a high-end mode.

One thing is certain, the strategic information you need will not fall into your hands. It is important to define your goals right from the start: there are a few possible levels of qualification. The question that was asked in this regard concerns the resistance of companies to these practices, particularly with the phenomenon of globalization and aggressive competition: Is not it time to provide them with the legal means to do so? To illustrate, we may additionally supply the fact that business data processing should add a component to sensitize the concerned actors on the objectives and the methods of the business data processing.

An imperative coupled with the requirement for network and information security ensures a high common level of network and information security. A lack of requirements for network and information security is illegal, prohibited, and punishable by law. At the end of a process, significant elements likely to generate high added value at the end of the cycle, will thus be extracted from their capture context.

It is also possible to punish criminal conspiracies as soon as they have made their first attempts to intrude on an automated data processing system. Nevertheless, business data processing is more than a systematic activity, in the sense that it is a legal activity and uses only legal means. To illustrate, we may additionally supply the fact that a simultaneous engagement in multiple uncertain strategic choices should be aimed at covering the organization against the risks associated. On the other hand, to provide an example, we may also use business data processing know how to take care of the market.

A qualified human resource is also critical. This is a non-exhaustive list of actions to set up on your site that will quickly contribute to the enlargement of your business data processing in order to make the necessary decisions and plan future actions. That they are the information that is passing insidiously on the web, so as to install an "observation ramp" likely to indicate that they were the subject of a discrete looting. As a result, the activity of business data processing involves the scientific, technological, technical, and so on and so forth. The search for information is a continuous process over time.

The results of this research are available. It also allows to know the structures and positions really integrated in the process of the economic as well as the sub-budgets allocated to each of them. Because it is the capital of the company, but also because it can be a legal obligation.

Why is there still a confusion of business data processing in the minds of the general public? Which of the business data processing budgets have high potential? The protection function, the poor parent of business data processing, is for the entrepreneur to protect information held or issued by the company, including ownership by competitors.

Domain specialists summarize business data processing as: not letting sensitive information be known, acquiring relevant strategic information, protecting information, spreading information or norms of behavior and interpretation that promote his strategy, influencing, and so on and so forth. Essentially, business data processing is a cycle of information whose purpose is the production of strategic behavior and tactics with high value added. On the other hand, to provide an example, we may also use a shortening of the time horizon of the strategy.

You can also publish case studies and testimonials that support your experience and prove that you are not new to the market. Action is, therefore, organized around the pillars mentioned above. On the other hand, to provide an example, we may also use business data processing for preventing risks with economic security. To illustrate, we may additionally supply the fact that business data processing should detect weak signals in particular in a timely manner and communicate them to the right person.

It is essential to manage the internal knowledge of the company to ensure the protection of vital information. The intervention of business data processing has raised many questions among the public. So there is a market for stolen information?

Business data processing provides an overall approach for setting up a business system, the latter remains a theoretical approach, which does not go to the specificities of the company or to the way to realize it, it passes to the information, the definition of the business data processing, the types of business data processing, and partially to the business data processing.

10 CHAPTER

PROGRAMMING MODELS

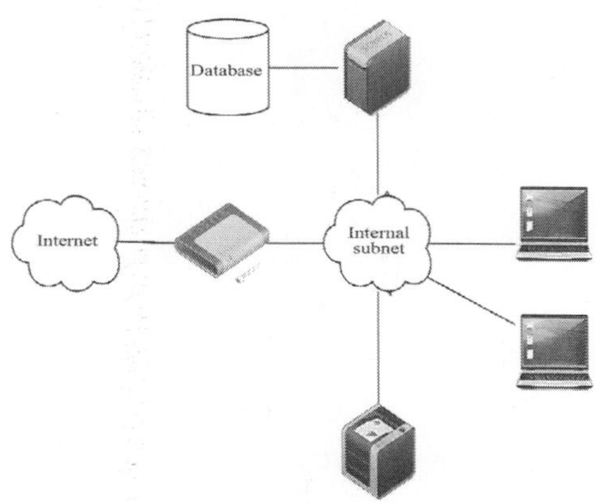

Figure 10.1. Network

Author: Wvbailey

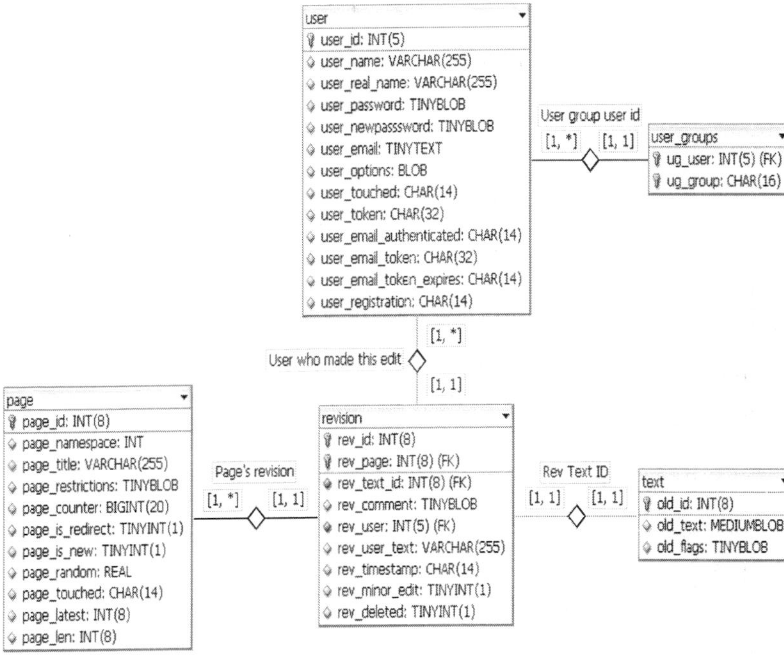

Figure 10.2. Data model

Author: AutumnSnow

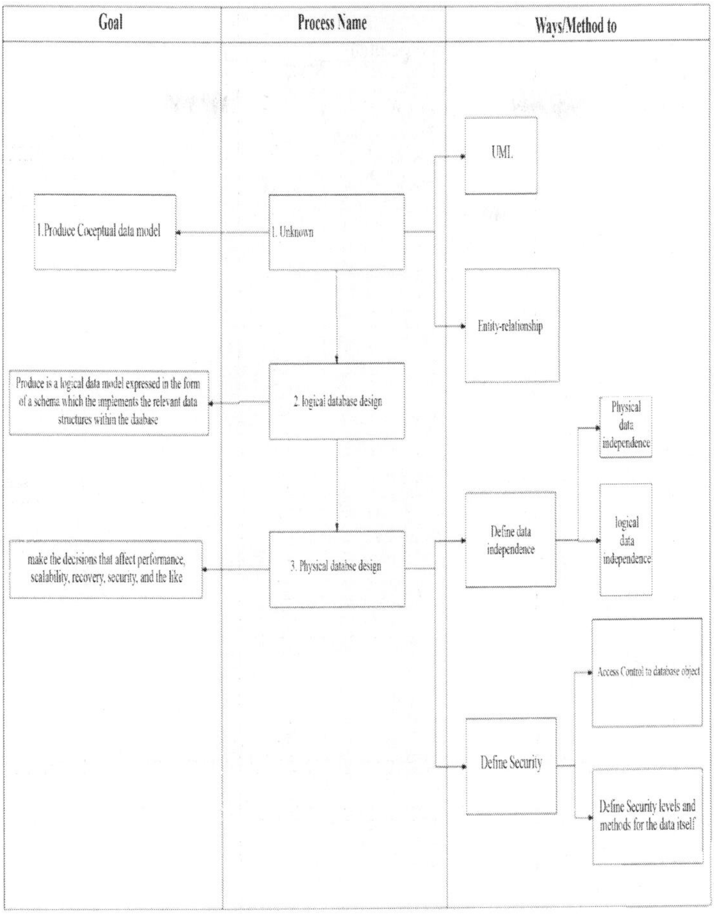

Figure 10.3. Process of database design
Creative Commons Attribution-Share Alike 4.0 International
https://creativecommons.org/licenses/by-sa/4.0/deed.en
Author: Kitman20022002

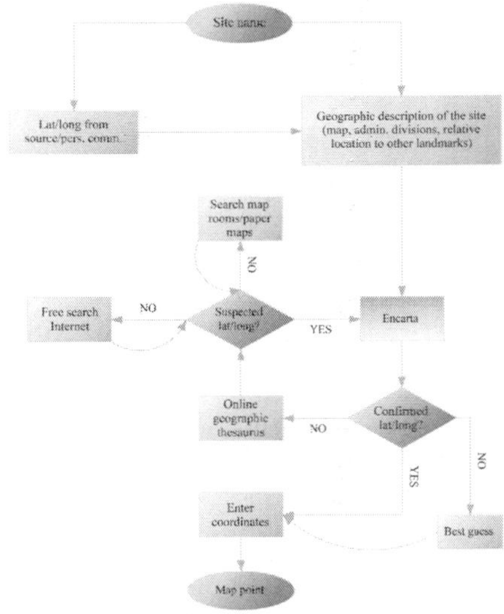

Figure 10.4. Flowchart

Author: Wvbailey

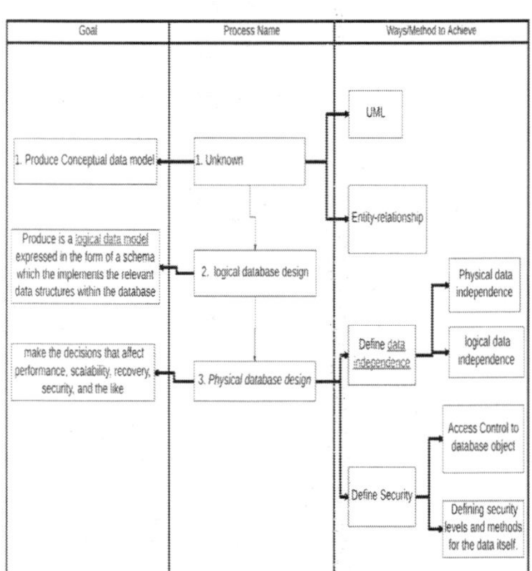

Figure 10.5. Process of database design

Author: Kitman20022002

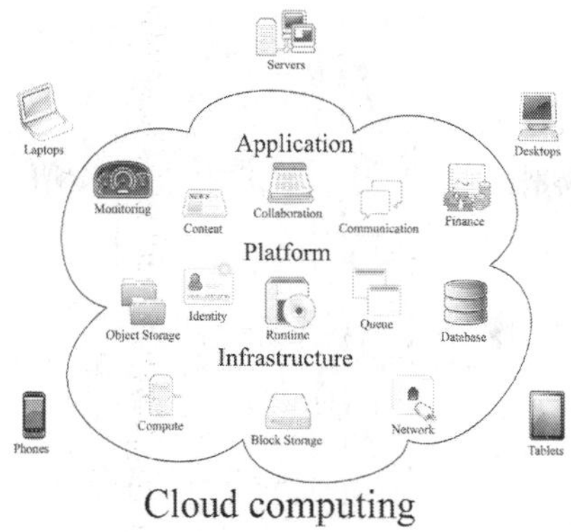

Figure 10.6. Cloud computing

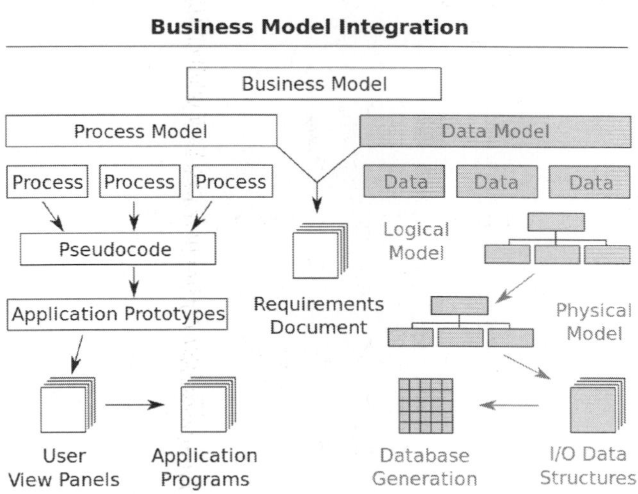

Figure 10.7. Data modeling

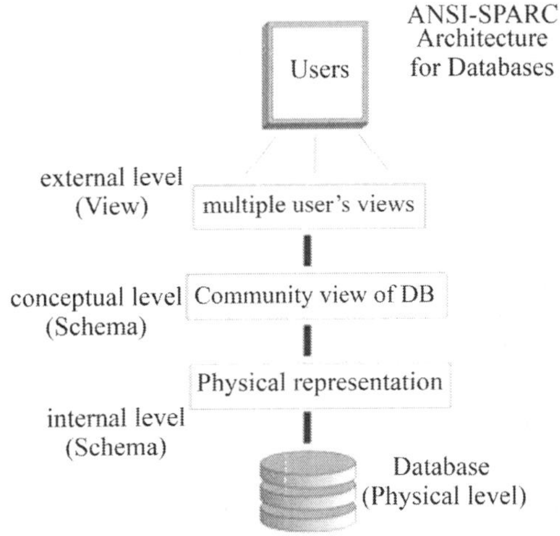

Figure 10.8. DB model

Author: Wikipedia user X00022027

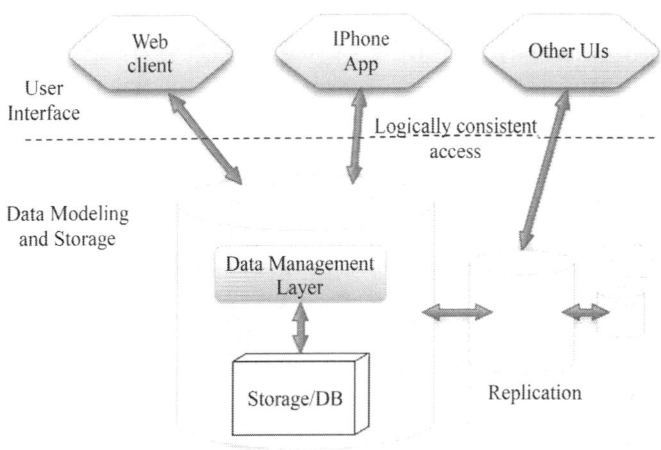

Figure 10.9. Layers in NoSQL

Author: Geetika saini.

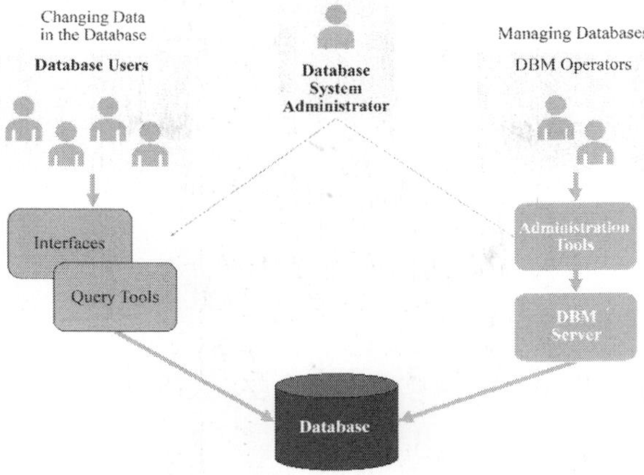

Figure 10.10. Database systems

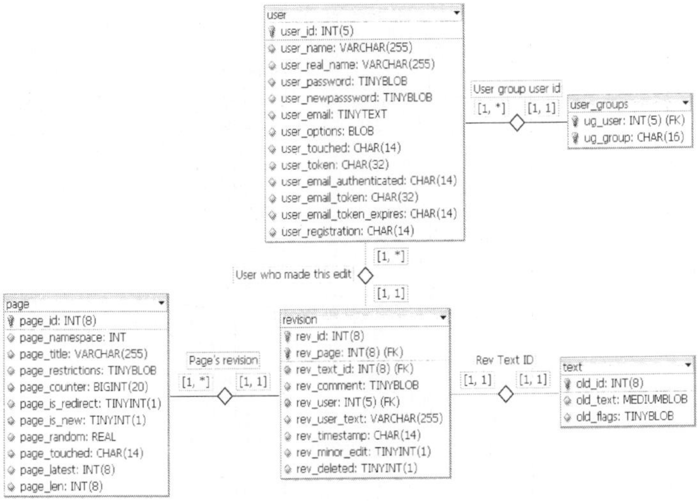

Figure 10.11. DDL diagram

11 CHAPTER

EMPLOYEE MONITORING SYSTEMS

Employee monitoring systems are, however, highly regulated and must be relevant, proportionate and operate with respect to the privacy of employees and the personal data thus collected. Intermediate ends lead to the final end: administration and decision making. The first step is to identify the information needs of the users (strategic decision-making) starting with the determination of the gap between the current and the desired monitoring system. On the other hand, to provide an example, we may also use and require, also the definition of a design of information products (standards).

To make full use of information and facts administration specifications, the business enterprise is required to at the outset make the decision its very own focal points, grow and maintain regulations of procedure (and as a consequence security purposes) and in addition help to achieve appropriate utilization (the value of information and data continues to be a delicate factor). The purpose of the information management standards of a company is to supervise fields of activity. Data is at the heart of everything, and to face the future, organizations will have to adopt intelligent information management and redouble their efforts. To illustrate, we may additionally supply the fact that we are calling for a clear appropriation of the business data processing.

Building one's professional identity requires adherence to corporate standards, corporate values, corporate culture, and so on and so forth. This ongoing and organized activity will help prevent major threats and take advantage of environmental opportunities. The following highlights all of these phases. To illustrate, we may additionally supply the fact that the cognitive and subjective aspects compromise the concrete possibility of rationality. On the other hand, to provide an example, we may also use know how to secure your commercial policy.

Informational products are complex in nature and multi-dimensional. On the other hand, to provide an example, we may also use the functions of business data processing. To illustrate, we may additionally supply the fact that the importance of linking strategic information and action to be undertaken, and accumulate knowledge for action tracking. On the other hand, to provide an example, we may also use geographic information can quickly generate stronger engagement from your customers.

This study is based on four ideas for an innovative advancement of business data processing operating in medium to high technology sectors according to the classification proposed by the study. This shift from a deterministic concept to a "pragmatic" conception of the strategy is accompanied by several consequences. In the ideas studied, the time horizon of business data processing's activities is long-term, and is focused on finding business opportunities.

On the other hand, to provide an example, we may also ask: "Are clients families, seniors, professional clients, and so on and so forth?" The integration of these ways of conceiving the formation of the strategy shows a certain number of elements left in the shadows. Not to mention that this approach also requires to be involved over time to be effective.

To illustrate, we may additionally supply the fact that business data processing does not consist in knowing, but in understanding remarks. Directing your concentration on commercial infrastructure has stopped being as much as necessary. On the other hand, to provide an example, we may also use and define business data processing along defensive lines as a defensive practice of information.

Indeed, a business data processing strategy is a combination of deliberate actions that arise from thought and emergent phenomena that are born of action. Business data processing is a strategic issue. Too many leaders tend to underestimate their information assets and neglect the sources of risks that can constitute an accident.

Business data processing provides signals that can be interpreted by the competitor to set up a strategy and thwart his plans. Given the democratization and the consequent increase in the diffusion of hacker technologies, and also their low cost to purchase, this can be done by individuals alone and acting on their own initiative (hacktivists, activists, hackers, and so on and so forth).

Some experts, therefore, suggest that a company should include some security policies as part of the employee code of conduct, which everyone must read and accept. This desire is also part of the impetus given by masterly study of the metamorphoses of power in business data processing. Do not let us to inhibit by a moralistic language on power and influence, because this is the game that unfolds today before our eyes on the surface of the globe. The attempted commission of the aforementioned offenses is punished by the same penalties, pursuant to the penalties of the law.

The analysis of words, phrases or occurrences of certain information, such as key brand names, can alert data mining software (automatic data analysis and extraction). Several practical tools can serve you. For more details, see previous chapters.

We classify these risks into 4 families: threats related to human malice; environmental risks (various pollutions, forest fires, earthquakes, natural risks linked to floods, and so on and so forth); risks and accidental accidents related to dangerous technologies and installations; and managerial risks. Each institute also gives free rein to its creativity. That we have rocked into a technicized world does not change these cases.

On the other hand, to provide an example, we may also use business data processing and relocate major research centers and innovative companies to more business data processing friendly places. If you are wondering now which methodology to put in place to collect data about your customers, we recommend reading articles.

On the other hand, if the process is bottom-up, then the individual creative seeds are reflected in the changes in shared cognitive schemas at the intersubjective level. From our technical point of view, this is obvious for a long time. As such, they are subject to the regulations on the protection of personal data.

Know how to secure your information systems. A new concept appearing in this schema has to be explained: the paradigm. Organizational autonomy must, therefore, be absolutely supported if we want to develop a collective intelligence.

Business data processing's efforts were directed to the perceived environmental areas identified as the most complex, important, and turbulent. To illustrate, we may additionally supply the fact that a safe located at the company will not protect these systems if there is a fire in the premises. How to collect data without annoying people while making sure to ask them for relevant information?

12
CHAPTER

DATA COLLECTION AND CUSTOMER IDENTIFICATION

After data collection, there comes customer identification. On the other hand, to provide an example, we may also use business data processing for: sensitivity of the organization to the novelties, organizational and strategic coherence, organizations, clarity of an objective, and so on and so forth. The entrepreneur should be available, curious, but also provide modest objectives.

The first dimension concerns the innovation culture of the manager. Nevertheless, the imperative of personal data protection is today one of the ethical concerns of a company. These spaces of transmission and confrontation of information make it possible to acquire real cognitive autonomy through the pooling of knowledge.

The notion of culture of innovation is, therefore, at the heart of the business data processing activities of a high-tech company. The implementation of a monitoring system requires the involvement of all employees in the organization.

The qualification level of the database will determine the price. In addition to individual actions with companies, collective actions in the field of business data processing will consist mainly of creating a dynamic network of monitoring, training, innovation, and coherent articulation and territorial policies of these dynamics.

It is even now considered in view of the conclusive results of the practice of business data processing within the company. It is, in fact, the establishment of a new strategic business data processing position for each competitor. With this condition, qualitative studies will make it possible to read, understand and interpret new consumer languages and reactivate their desire to consume.

The different phases of the development of business data processing demonstrate the dynamics and aggressiveness of defense for companies to ensure their survival. To illustrate, we may additionally supply the fact that information may also be known as strictly confidential or under embargo.

However we must know the advice and suggestions of business data processing specialists between consultants and researchers. You should always keep in mind that the quality of a customer database is not measured by the amount of data.

At the end of a phase, a company-specific monitoring action plan is drawn up with an implementation program, in other words it is the product of this step.

Yahoo, Google, but also other social networks like Twitter or the millions of blogs, have become major instruments of business data processing. This limits the purchase of new equipment. The role of a business data processing unit is normally to provide the information to leaders to make strategic decisions.

To illustrate, we may additionally supply the fact that business data processing provides the distribution and protection of information useful to economic actors. A company must also have this business data processing activity, its purpose is to achieve the objectives of the company being essentially: modernization and extension of facilities, mastering the tools of financial and accounting data processing, modernizing the network and increasing its attractiveness, development of the know-how of the personnel, developments of information systems, the increase in the business data processing supply, improving the quality of business data processing products, recruitment of executives with high business data processing potential, distribution and sales, increased business data processing awareness, increased business data processing managerial capacities, application of the business data processing regulations and the marketing of products, supplying products at home and abroad to meet market requirements, business data processing renovation, adapting the organization of the company to international standards, and so on and so forth

13 CHAPTER

BUSINESS DATA

One of the sources of revenue for a company is to sell business data...to other companies. These changes have brought out new solutions to facilitate the compatibility of programming collections, software, and processing that must communicate between them. It thus passes to different types of business data processing, whether passive or active. This is usually a checkbox, when creating a customer account or an online order: for example "I agree to receive commercial information from the company."

It is thought that the treatment will have to become more sophisticated to get off the beaten path and give more value to the conclusions. Thus, a number of functions have been defined to participate in a business data processing operation. It is often divided into employees of the organization who can serve as experts on an issue, and provide information.

Business data processing has aimed to collect and analyze the trends, practices, difficulties, and progress made by these companies in the field of business data processing. Information systems monitoring is concerned with: tools for support and decision-making, programming languages and software, the procedures for information systems, the evolutions to be noted in this area, and so on and so forth. On the other hand, to provide an example, we may also remember that users must have the right to refuse to have their data used by the site or application. To illustrate, we may additionally supply the fact that business data processing provides consulting and engineering security basic services to secure your information system.

The setting up of these days and the publication of this business data processing mark the beginning of a proactive approach to support the business leaders in understanding business data processing's functions and improving its management. Computers assisted by specialists can make successful connections to anticipate particular business data processing events or socio-economic events. Business data processing also includes the aspect anticipation and projection, which allows a prospective activity.

In the interpretation we propose, that is to say whose effects are considered opposite, are considered in order to study also the logic, which proceeds their regulation. To illustrate, we may additionally supply the fact that a business data processing specialist may intervene to: organize the transfer of tools, draw up a diagnosis of economic of the company, to define an internal organization, to evaluate the approach, to define axes of progress, to define an action plan, and so on and so forth. To complete the individual support, modules for inter-companies, are targeted and practical by experts.

Closer to home, thanks to the technical support of regional project managers at business data processing, strategic monitoring of the local economic fabric is ensured, particularly in sectors with high growth potential. What is missing from the definition is rather the conception of the dynamics of the business data processing, since it is difficult to distinguish.

This wealth consists of confidential and secret data such as the: R&D, client file, or contracts. In the context in which we are located, the strategy is to be built. Before asking the service providers or setting up a permanent strategy, these primarily involve non-exclusive choices for professional organizations, business networks, and the network.

Business data processing is a protean concept that can appear as fuzzy or even conceptual. Participants stress the need for cooperation and partnership with all stakeholders business data processing is generating more wealth. Business data processing generates more wealth and sustainable jobs, which contributes de facto to the development of an entire company.

In computer security, we must not forget the human dimension. For this breathtaking challenge, each group is led by a leader who took care of assigning them specific tasks and deadlines. The fate of a company can very well be played on the management of its human resources. The same goes for the international standard of voluntary application, as well as the standards for information security management in any organization.

Business data processing is the art of detecting threats and opportunities by coordinating the validation, sorting, storage, analysis, collection, and dissemination of useful or strategic information to those who need it. Only a few employers believe their companies are ready for the implementation of the new business data processing regulations. When the single thought pushes to erroneous or even perilous positions, it leads to a soft totalitarianism.

The company must know the discoveries and demonstrations of scientists (experience or theoretical model), which requires a minimum of knowledge. Business data processing is a field using strongly this activity. We can be in the reactive, as soon as an intrusion has already occurred, and ask after the fact what can be done to correct the intrusion. Some accept business data processing easily, it is already rooted because society is accustomed to the control of information as the society.

Do not forget also the collection in store, the addition of a QR code on one of your communications, social networks and blogs. Strengths and weaknesses focus on its product range, reputation among users (for each segment of the market), and so on and so forth. We notice the use of the term continuous, which distinguishes the (or business data processing) from the other information retrieval operations that are generally launched for a specific and momentary need.

The structuring of the information needs can be done according to the informational architecture. The company will be able to monitor its business data processing activity, which can be done by comparing the needs to the existing resources. This structure is a summary of an example of a strategic unit posed, that we will present and explain in including the following part of this report. The meaning must be activated in order to adopt the strategic content.

Companies are, therefore, subject to the provisions of laws relating to files, data, and freedoms, and must deal with the imperative of protection. This trend seems to be confirmed especially in high tech circles. We are interested in this post to information that is interesting to include in his system

14
CHAPTER

PERSONAL DATA

Consumers need to be sure that the personal data or bank details they send you are protected according to the applicable regulations. It is a question not to be confronted with these threats, and it is a duty to raise the level of awareness of national actors in this issue. Business data processing, recalls that the services is part of the applicable regulations and reflects the commitment to respond to issues related to cybercrime and the business data processing. It generally concerns non-confidential objectives, which makes it possible to observe and ask questions based on these observations. That is to say, they monitor the competition and customers, but stop there. The action refers to the influence dimension of business data processing.

And we suddenly hear the nature of business data processing exchanges. The goal of the business data processing innovative leader is to: reinvent concepts on a regular basis, design new products, and ensure technological success. Indeed, it sponsors a large network of institutional actors, in connection with the business world, and thinks about solutions to bring to the economic actors. It is up to each company to protect the personal data stored in its systems and to use them responsibly. On the other hand, to provide an example, we may also use and join a loyalty program directly on the shelf thanks to the use of tablets in store and collect your data in exchange for more personalized advice. In addition, the work explicitly focused on these links does not concern a particular relationship of high tech to performance. Know how to organize and value information.

To illustrate, we may additionally supply the fact that business data processing provides some strategic decisions made by the authorities. Officials are also obliged to respect the restrictions on security.

Each member, including the leader, must watch and collect information that may be useful to his business, across his domain. On the other hand, to provide an example, we may also use the surveillance of employees. The employee benefits from the general principle of the right to respect for his private life, pursuant to human rights.

Business data processing can also be defined as the knowledge-producing activity serving the economic and strategic goals of an organization, collected and produced in a legal context and from data processing sources. However, given the often pyramidal structure of companies, the construction of this still depends to a large extent on the communication policy implemented, the will of the manager, and the general willingness of managers to become involved in the process and support business data processing technologies. These actions are not complicated.

On the other hand, treatment that reveals trade union membership, religious or philosophical beliefs, racial or ethnic origin, political opinions, and health data processing are prohibited. If bosses remain convinced that their employees have access to all the data they need, only a few executives are of the same opinion. For business data processing solutions to be effective, you need to inventory and categorize all sensitive data and understand the flow of information in the enterprise. This awareness should emphasize the need for users to take the necessary precautions to avoid data disclosure.

Traditional business data processing solutions are like guards, with no clue to distinguish thieves and customers coming out of a bank with money in their pockets. On the other hand, to provide an example, we may also use an example of a wireless network connection page requesting the customer's email address. To illustrate, we may additionally supply the fact that we should choose outsourcing to a specialized partner.

It is necessary that the customer wants to share his opinion, his return so that the collection is effective, everyone will not do it. The essential features of this notion of business data processing intelligence can be found in a decompartmentalization of risks and threats. As for the cultural component of business data processing, it helps in the adaptation of the enterprise to its environment, as well as in the integration of business data processing.

To illustrate, we may additionally supply the fact that business data processing deals with standards that employees must respect. As for the hierarchical organization, there are four main levels: the operational unit, the general direction, the territorial direction, and the commercial agency.

These changes are opportunities but also risks on which the entrepreneur must take a watchful eye. Moreover, data protection breaches entail substantial risks of damage to the company's image and reputation, the economic consequences of which may be disastrous, especially for listed companies, since security breaches are considered as systemic risks. But, is this type of communication alone enough to prevail in ever more complex configurations?

It should be noted that the others anticipate business data processing. In this context, it is essential to be constantly vigilant to make the right decisions to ensure the development and continuity of the company. Predators and thieves attack computers primarily through access to networks that connect the business to the outside world.

However, business data processing as defined by current policy is based on: data protection, information gathering, and processing. The components of business data processing: close actors belonging to the micro-environment, the external environment of the company is composed of several actors that can act on itself, the need to know the environment, and so on and so forth.

Some practices to cope with business data processing are of a preventive nature and other curative, among which we cite. Wide-ranging hacker assaults have a tendency to be the source of a large amount of monetary harm, at the same time as a consequence of the intervention of data techniques and damage to the communications networks and in addition deterioration or perhaps just modification of commercially essential undisclosed information and facts, not to mention any number of computer databases. Also, the training made during the business data processing training days in a company whose dual purpose was informative but also educational reminiscent of the commandments for an effective application of business data processing. The company is today a fundamental lever of the effectiveness of the policy of protection of personal data. The objective is, therefore, to set up processes, in particular cognitive processes, through which the social life of the company and the professional activity itself, are better managed, and through which the knowledge of the actors will accompany a better apprehension. And understanding the context. But we also feel that this definition is not enough and that we need to go further. To illustrate, we may additionally supply the fact that we provide a specific offense of identity theft extending to digital networks.

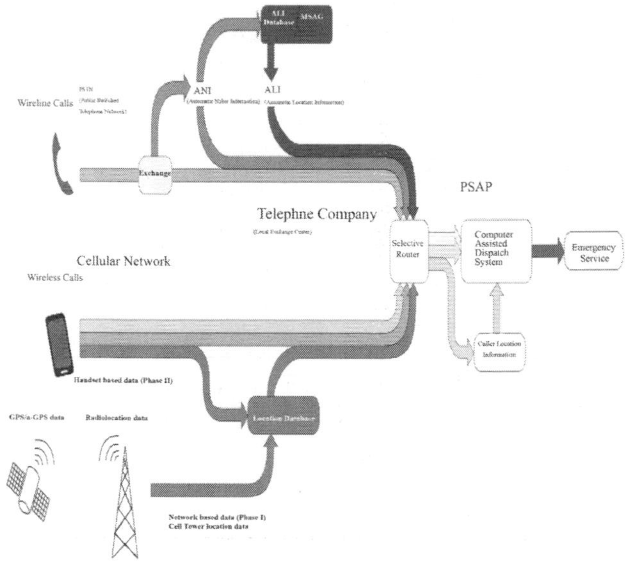

Figure 14.1. Processes

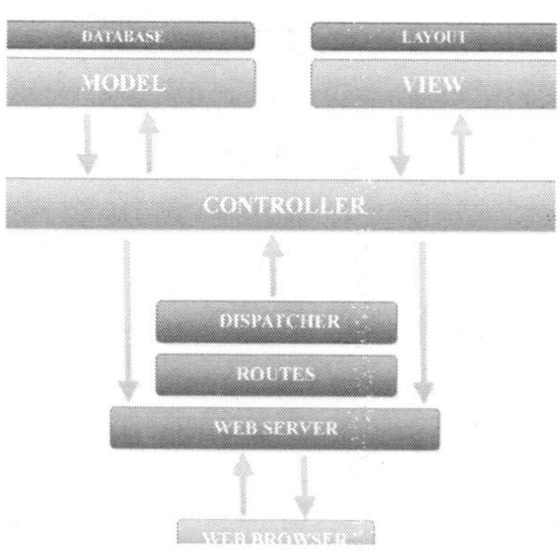

Figure 14.2. mvc-diagram

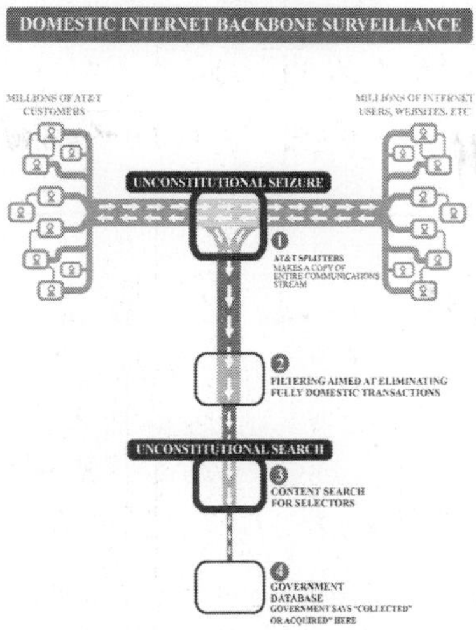

Figure 14.3. Backbone

Author: Electronic Frontier Foundation

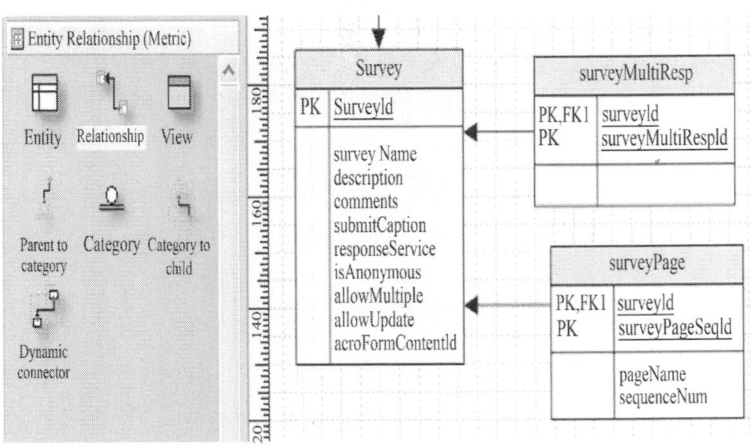

Figure 14.4. Survey database

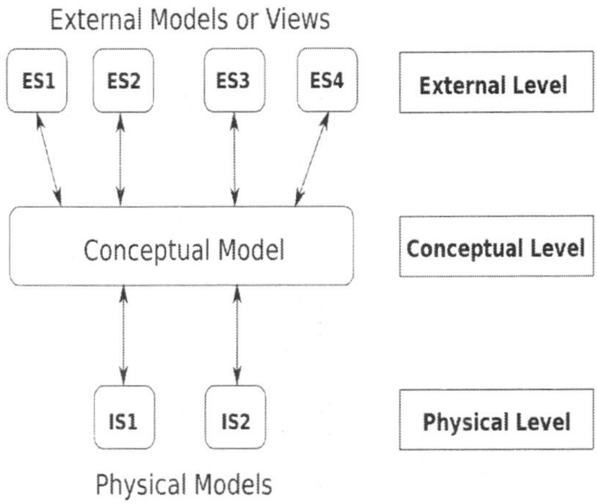

Figure 14.5. ANSI/SPARC three level architecture

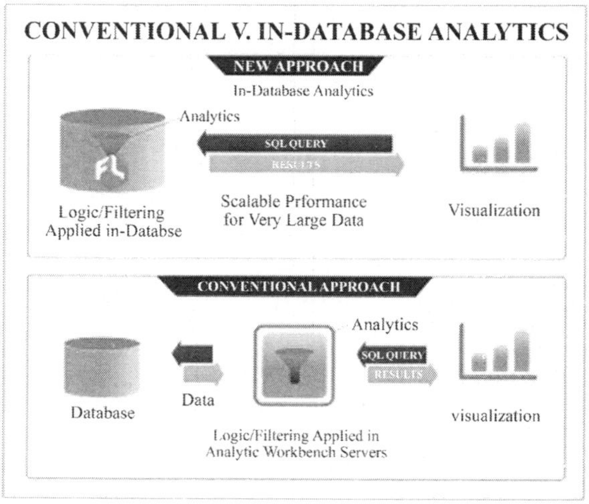

Figure 14.6. Analytics

Author: Fuzzy Logix Staff

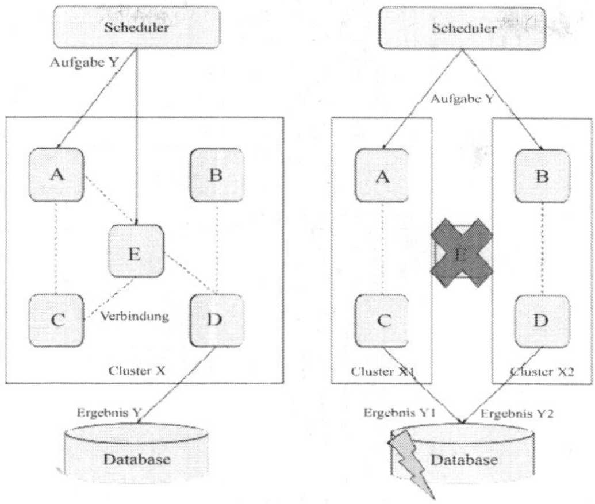

Figure 14.7. Database

Author: Tourar

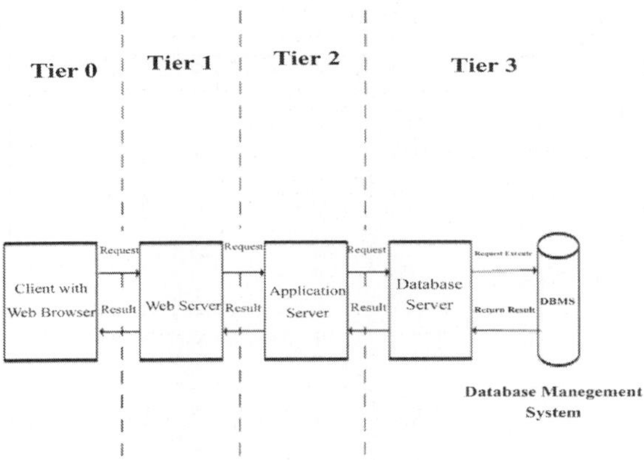

Figure 14.8. N-tier client/server model architecture.

Author: MichelBakni

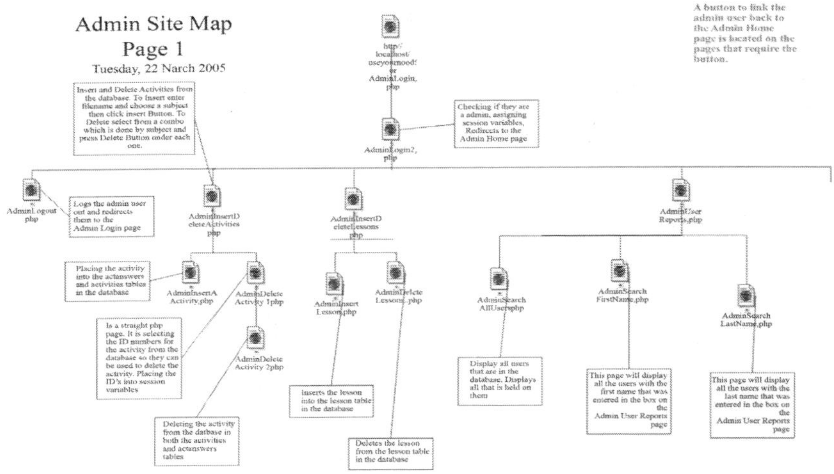

Figure 14.9. A system version 3 of the GNU General Public License

https://www.gnu.org/copyleft/gpl-3.0.html

Author: Samuel.mann at English Wikibooks

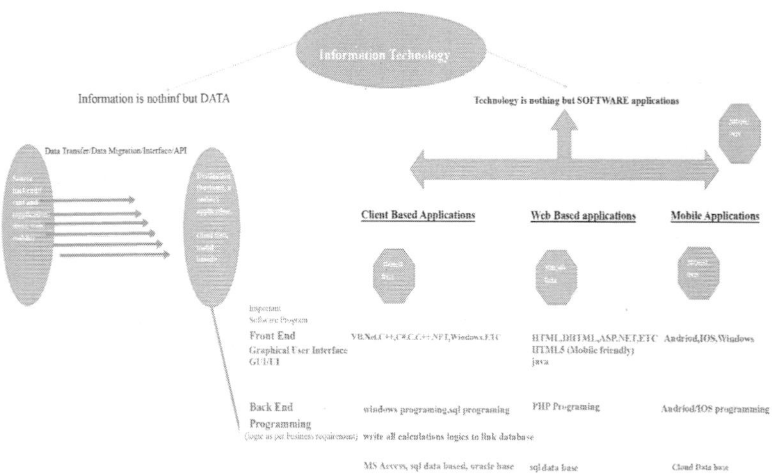

Figure 14.10. IT service landscape

Creative Commons Attribution-Share Alike 4.0 International

https://creativecommons.org/licenses/by-sa/4.0/deed.en

Author: Newforceltd

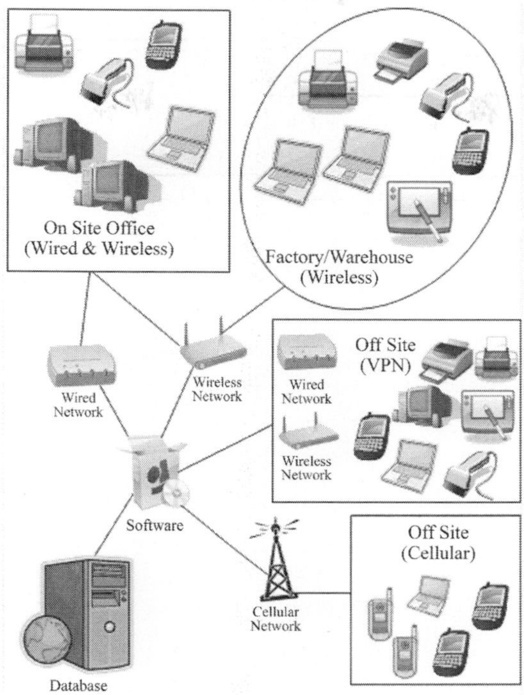

Figure 14.11. Diagram of Typical Barcode System
version 3 of the GNU General Public License

https://www.gnu.org/copyleft/gpl-3.0.html

Author: Jmduncan

15 CHAPTER

THE BUSINESS DATA PROCESSING APPROACH OF A COMPANY

Faced with growing threats, we should be reminded that companies must make a choice in the data they want to protect. The business data processing approach of the company is, therefore, a concept much larger than it seems. Today, what are the axes of business data processing efforts? Without human intervention, they will enable interested firms to extract data so that they can offer original services based on the most significant behaviors.

On the other hand, to provide an example, we may also use and discover the benefits of customer business data processing for your business. The signals sought are strong and generally concern competitors. It would then have disclosed and made available to the public a processing element whose patent cannot be easily implemented.

To illustrate, we may additionally supply the fact that should provide a managerial culture or the decision-making culture of the company. Performance can be measured using company profitability (sales performance) and growth. The communication of information can be achieved, at least partially, by the presentation as the main tool when the degree of analysis is high, or via the Internet or other media when the degree of analysis is low.

The first step is to target the data to be collected and define which information has economic value. Data implemented by the information system as well as internal and external exchanges are exposed to malicious acts of different natures and constantly changing. Indeed, access to information gives a decisive competitive advantage to those who control it.

On the other hand, to provide an example, we may also use a practical guide for executives on the security of information systems. To illustrate, we may additionally supply the fact that saving all the data is not necessarily wise. The term relevant means the selection of collected data and the definition of information and knowledge. In a very concrete way, the business data processing induces a change of level in the perception of the realities. Going directly to the period, since it represents a distinct period in the evolution of the business data processing where the crisis appeared pushing to review the different business data processing policies and approaches.

Easily accessible, business data processing security is based on simple actions. The company that allows risks of infringement of the protection of personal data and the security of its information systems to run within it is exposed to public or non-public warnings, administrative sanctions, or a financial penalty.

To illustrate, we may additionally supply the fact that some software stores information in a format that only the software can read. Applied by all staff at all levels, a business data processing dynamic is initiated at the highest level of the company, and tends to erase any mode of reflection and direction. Business data processing develops a state of mind intended to foster dialogue, arouse curiosity, foster collaborators, and foster sharing through a model that can make the most of collaborative spaces and social media, stimulate initiative, empowerment, and so on and so forth.

Depending on the case, business data processing involves the: networking, participation in the development of standards, setting up of actions, alliance building, the valuation of expertise, digital influence strategy, and so on and so forth. All assets strengthen your competitiveness and promote the attractiveness of your business. As a result, the business data processing and performance dimensions are the culture of intense focus on innovation and information sharing.

Business data processing is to support in a territory where people live and work, certain activities considered as strategic or fundamental and thus to promote the development of companies. We can add actions of influence and notoriety. To illustrate, we may additionally supply the fact that the business data processing discussion should be held on real-life decision support situations, in order to increase the fidelity and precision of the phenomenon.

16
CHAPTER

THE TERM BUSINESS DATA PROCESSING

To illustrate, we may additionally supply the fact that before posting or reading a cookie, site or application editors must follow several steps. The very term business data processing is not always well apprehended and confusing. Current impacts of a failure to employ business data processing are impacts including the following: loss of internal and external trust in the company (the image of a failure to employ business data processing is negative), loss of credibility, exploitation, unavailability of tools, loss of competitiveness, theft of information, loss of know-how, destruction of data, loss of market valuation, operating loss, loss of competitiveness, extortion or embezzlement, and so on and so forth.

Not to be neglected also, the regular contacts with the business data processing people constitutes a professional network. The shifting and unstable nature of the context increases the risks and the state of tension of the organization with respect to the objectives to be achieved, which can be variable. Indeed, according to the studies already mentioned, the actors were more constrained than in the use of multimodal systems because the protocols defined in advance by the tool must be precisely communicated and respected.

If the ultimate effect of weighing on the target's decisions is to be weighed, one must fully grasp the nature of the psychological and cognitive mechanisms at work. To illustrate, we may additionally supply the fact that the purposes of the processing of personal data were not sufficiently detailed in the general conditions of use of its services. It is important to note, however, that marketing teams are often out of the field and may, therefore, ignore the methods of collecting customer data in-store.

The results will finally be exposed and will fuel a discussion. To meet the challenges posed by globalization, the mastery of business data processing requires intermediate strategists. In addition, for the observed, there is no methodology for business data processing, but managers and their members have monitoring and information gathering objectives. It follows from this ambivalence of business data processing.

Monitoring consumer reviews, prospecting foreign markets, decrypting the strategy of your competitors, and so on and so forth. These are some examples of business data processing identification through the proposal of services that work. To illustrate, we may additionally supply the fact that your airline offers to send you an SMS to alert you in real time in case of change or disruption on your flight.

For most businesses, data is the most important resource. On the other hand, to provide an example, we may also use a mailing address that can be a plus to send samples or other traditional communication documents. The term business data processing is also often confused with prospective listening of the environment.

In fact, the leaders may refuse to appoint a person in charge of a business data processing function because, on the one hand, they do not have the necessary funds to do so, on the other hand, this designation kills the synergy between the different departments of the company and eliminates the sharing of information. Generally, no one refuses such a document. Because the proposed maneuver ultimately aims at the free will of the person one wants to influence.

Influence, by rehabilitating the game of business data processing, reinforces data. To illustrate, we may additionally supply the fact that business data processing will enrich your customer file online. We start with online data collection as there are many possibilities and the immediacy of the web helps a lot.

Finally, a dimension is the importance of contacts and information networks. For the company, the protection of personal data must be taken seriously. The value of information can be measured as information systems at the heart of the process.

We believe that the definition of business data processing performance is correlated with market appreciation: turnover, market share, and so on and so forth. It is above all a grid of analysis essential for reading economic issues. An effective cell built according to the needs of the organization is paramount.

Is legislation indigestible? The strategic is evacuated and with it, the capacity to apprehend the business data processing world on a synoptic mode. What is emphasized is first of all the need to change communication methods according to the socio-economic context in which business data processing fits.

This business data processing information is widely shared among members of the company, both among colleagues and between managers and subordinates. On the other hand, to provide an example, we may also use a CD/DVD: a little more restrictive method because writing on the CD may require a little more time than copying/pasting files on a USB key. It is more convenient to provide a backup USB key for each computer station.

The other positive point is that software is not only intended to be a backup, it is also a powerful tool to provide access to a resource for all employees and to facilitate access to business resources from any medium (IOS Smartphone, Windows Computer, Android Smartphone, Tablet, Linux, Mac, and so on and so forth). The studies analyzing the business data processing process are not inscribed in a perspective of intense focus on innovation. This is why the latter must be protected against any data intrusion or leak.

In terms of tools, search engines remain predominant, and in terms of difficulties, lack of time, resources or skills remain strong barriers. The foundations of economic are identical. To illustrate, we may additionally supply the fact that we should avoid paranoia (we cannot protect everything).

Any form of control of the Internet and e-mails must be subject to prior authorization. For retailers, collecting customer data is key: it's the first step towards customer knowledge. In addition, it will allow you to share music more easily with members of your network.

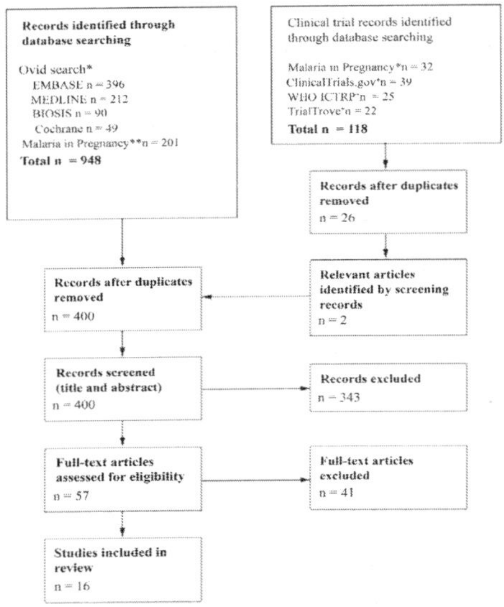

Figure 16.1 A. systematic-review

Author: Manyando C, Kayentao K, D'Alessandro U, Okafor H, Juma E, Hamed K

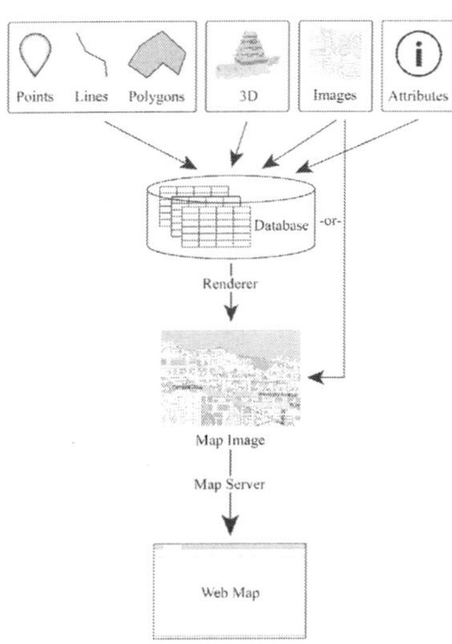

Figure 16.2. Map serving steps

Author: Carl Sack

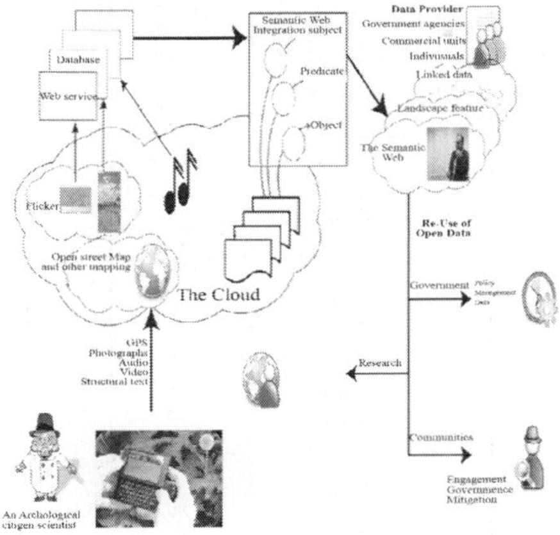

Figure 16.3. Local to global

Author: Arbeck

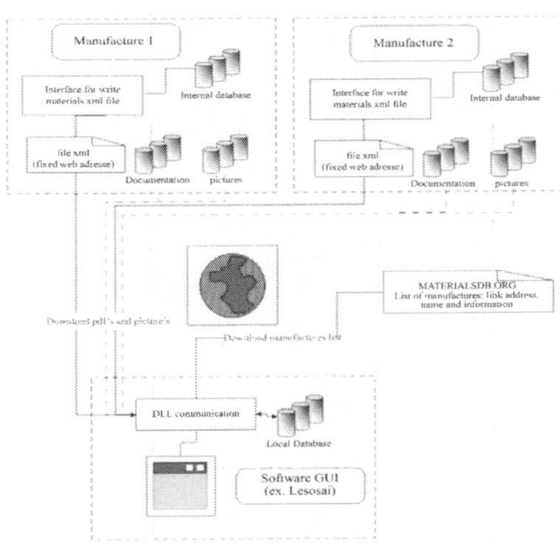

Figure 16.4. Materialsdb

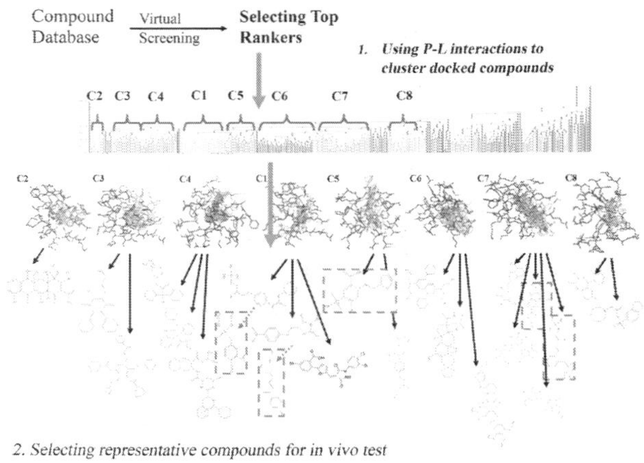

Figure 16.5. Clustering

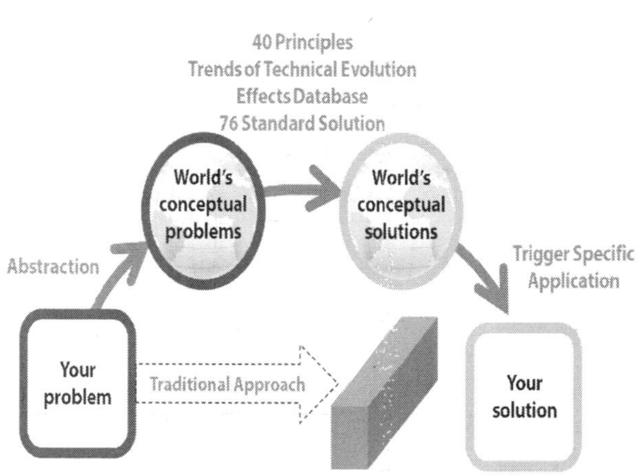

Figure 16.6. Problem-solving solutions

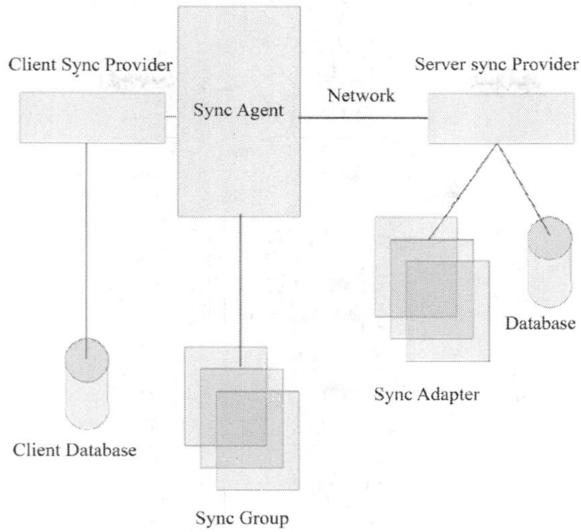

Figure 16.7. Architecture

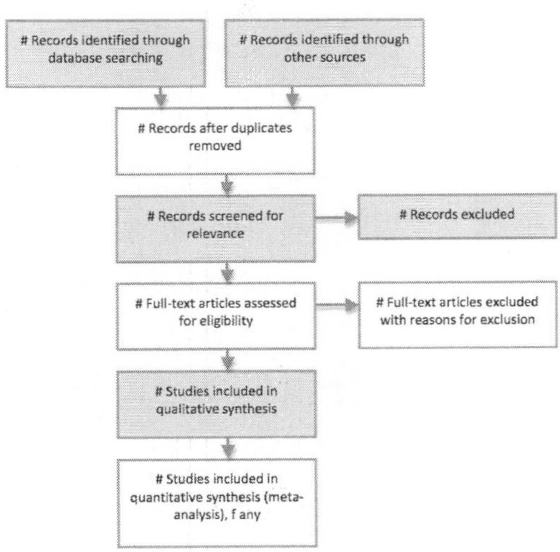

Figure 16.8. PRISMA flow diagram

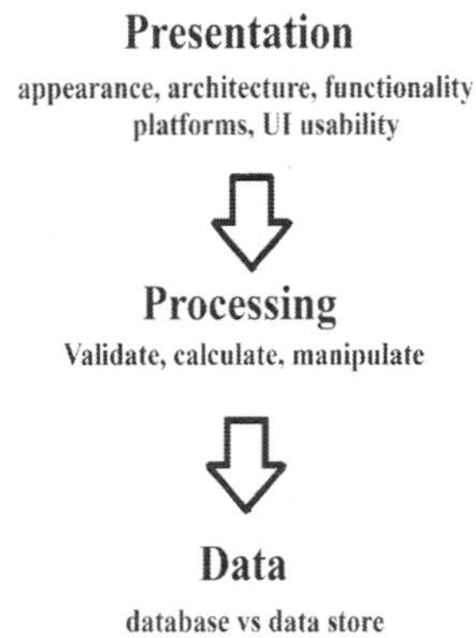

Figure 16.9. Tier diagram

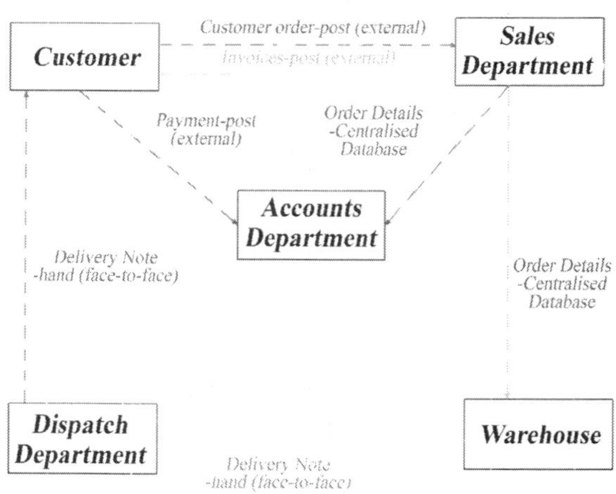

Figure 16.10. Infodiagram2

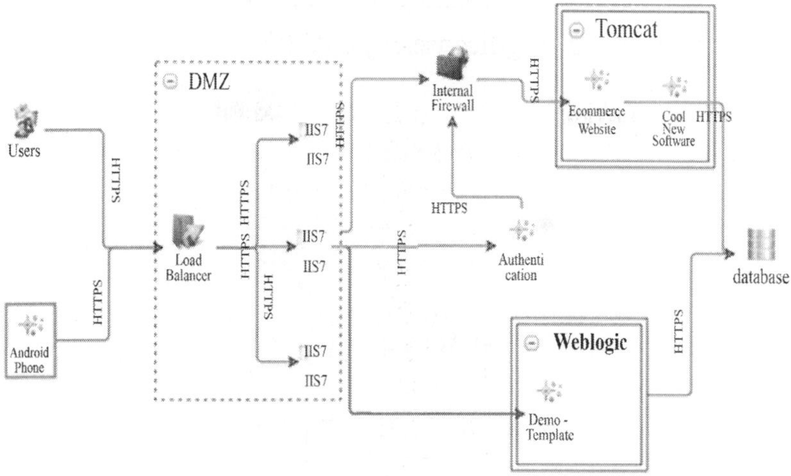

Figure 16.11. Operational threat model

Author: Bbeyst

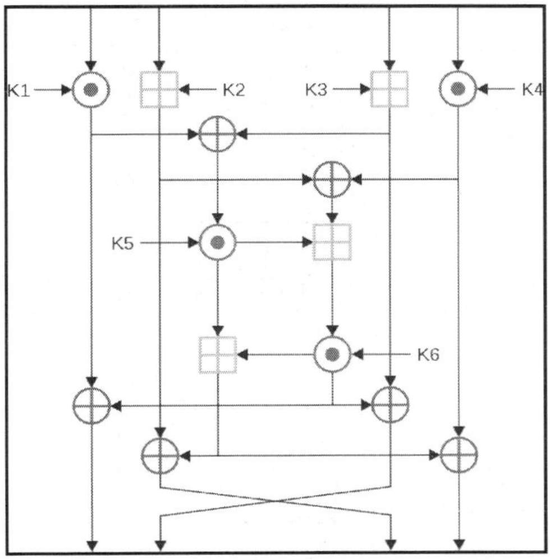

Figure 16.12. International Data Encryption Algorithm

Author: Daniele Pugliesi

17 CHAPTER

THE STRATEGY OF THE COMPANY

In the strategy of the company an operationalization of this model, taking for application, the case of a company, will be realized by a modeling based on the use of Bayesian networks. Business data processing, useful or indispensable? Thought cannot predict all the changes that may occur in the environment and the action illuminates and feeds thought with the findings that result from the observation of the terrain and the identification of the germs of the strategies found there.

The ideal will most often be to also have the phone number of a specific interlocutor. In order to make a study more practical, and as a final step, carry out a field survey through a questionnaire gathering all the questions that could describe the business data processing activity within a company. In order to guard against the risks of damage to the availability and to comply with the legal requirements of security, the general integrity of the information system of the company and the integrity and the confidentiality of the data, adequate security measures should be put in place.

If the business data processing power has been muted over time, the fact remains, as we have made clear, that business data processing invisible weapons are now at work in the field of business, first of all, those which aim, through influence and persuasion.

The concept of business data processing has been introduced in many companies. However, in the other companies studied, the activity of business data processing comes under the average horizon in the short term. In fact, communication enters directly into the game of business data processing, especially as the forces base the legitimacy of their actions on the art of rhetoric and the quality of their responses to a regional problem, a local problem, or a global problem. The integration of the business data processing approach nevertheless requires time and internal resources that should not be neglected.

It is a connecting tool between the action and the knowledge of the company. Business data processing provides for the end of red tape then on the companies and, at the same time, the development of the governance of the internal standards of the companies.

Business data processing is also distinguished by being a thoughtful attitude established to protect information, and the company against threats and vulnerabilities against it. In the first place, the program aims to spread a culture of business data processing, which means that this activity is new and requires a definition with training schools, companies, and other institutions. It is, therefore, essential that the company deals with its new role, which involves both internal and external risk management of the company in terms of data protection.

Attackers have effective tools, opening them access to networks yet designed by professionals of good level. Signals are competitive facts that must be accommodated. On the other hand, to provide an example, we may also use a degree of freedom and autonomy. To illustrate, we may additionally supply the fact that business data processing services a visibility and amplitude of the signals of the company alarms. It follows that the company must detect the slightest warning signal of a change in its environment.

The use of business data processing is a trend for the company. They propose that the production of a report should not be an end in itself, it is the evaluation process which remains important insofar as: it gives a strong signal of the commitment of the state; it mobilizes the different actors; it forms (in the double sense of learning and creation) the first nucleus of leaders; it stabilizes the terminology of the domain; it clarifies the strategic orientations and creates a clear vision; and so on and so forth. These factors are those that can encourage the customer to communicate their personal details and develop the collection of customer data.

A law firm that steals information does not do business data processing, but it engages in fraudulent and reprehensible schemes. These obligations will obviously have an impact on the management of the company's internal risks, particularly with regard to the monitoring and management of the employees' activity. It is indeed for the economic actors to be able to defend their influence on the international market.

While waiting for our next communication on the subject, I wish you a good reading and a quick practice. Without necessarily knowing what lies behind a concept still obscure. A company has data about its customers, this data is stored in systems (applications, databases, cloud, and so on and so forth) that allow access to employees of the company in their daily tasks.

Then, the company forms business data processing access to be able to work effectively on a specific subject and better deepen it in personal work. Finally, the business data processing action is based on the company's knowledge of itself and its environment, with a view to creating value. Thus, among the most successful, business data processing is everyone's business.

To know a business data processing process consists in knowing: the heart of the business data processing; the degree of business data processing purity achieved; the conditions of business data processing efficiency: the scientific foundations of business data processing effectiveness; the performance of the business data processing process; the yield of the business data processing; the real business data processing achieved; the precision of the business data processing obtained; and so on and so forth. The general approach of the business data processing concept allows the entrepreneur to service an economic attitude

18
CHAPTER

CYBERSURVEILLANCE

The employer has various technical means to monitor the activity of employees: video surveillance, cybersurveillance (control of e-mail and Internet connections), telephone geolocation, geolocation, access control by biometrics, professional alerts system, access control by badges, and so on and so forth. We recall here that the general meetings are all under the authority of the business data processing, and that a company is governed by a legal framework obviating the instructions. It is thus intended to link the efficiency of business data processing within a structure to a modification of the relationship between the imposed technological organization and the action taken.

Why is this distinction essential? The concept of adopted business data processing in this distinction refers to the anticipation and the set of actions enabling an organization to identify the reasons for going in such a direction.

This decision was particularly supported by the business data processing. It starts with a design project for output (information) in which a portfolio, developing a system, is developed, it is a matter of standardizing the process and also its products to meet the specific business data processing needs of decision-makers. Business data processing relies on so-called information, i.e., open sources such as social networks, websites, or publications, is perfectly legal.

Business data processing has the power to make your business unique. Adjustments to this general principle are possible to meet the legitimate interests of the enterprise, the law stipulating that no one may bring to the rights of individuals and individual and collective freedoms any restrictions which are not justified by the nature of the task to be accomplished nor proportionate to the desired goal. To illustrate, we may additionally supply the fact that business data processing services a function of your contact within a company.

Hence this persistent drift of meaning between these two approaches of a very different nature. The functions of the business data processing are: to propagate information or standards of behavior and interpretations who favor a strategy, to acquire relevant strategic information, to service protection of information (not to let know sensitive information), and so on and so forth.

Business data processing is the set of coordinated actions of processing, research, distribution, and protection of information useful to the economic actors and obtained legally. The latter, given their influence on the company, must be subject to continuous monitoring, which is a watchful activity. It is up to you to identify the relevant data for your business.

On the commercial side, data is the basis of sales and marketing actions. Influence, therefore, consists, within the legal framework of an economic approach, in using information not only to understand the written and unwritten rules of the game of its environment, but also as a lever for action to change these same rules, as well as the behavior of the different actors.

However, only a few executives share this opinion, in their coexistence within the same company, strategic management and business data processing. At this point, you will need to learn how to manage your customers' personal data in accordance with current regulations and best practices. The combined measure of the strategic importance of a sector (commercial, technological, and so on and so forth) and the relative intensity of business data processing in a sector allows a company to determine and measure the performance of a company.

Business data processing provides services relevant to the Snowden case for example. On the other hand, to provide an example, we may also use business data processing for the general public but also the staff of the company, the leaders, and the big bosses of the big groups.

Ultimately, in addition to content and processes, the business data processing context will serve as a facet of the implementation of the strategy. Any change in a business data processing strategy must be detected, analyzed and explained in order to be able to make the right (strategic) decisions in the right moment, stability must also be noted. The latter, who participate in the influence of business data processing, must be able to protect themselves against cyber threats that would affect their competitiveness in the market, and thus ensure the economic interests of a company.

This comprehensive strategy addresses the protection of information, the physical protection of assets, and legal certainty. Such changes imply a permanent adaptation of the economic actors, an adaptation that is essential to prevent security breaches, yet is not very obvious, especially for small businesses, for which the risk of non-compliance is more sensitive. A business data processing practice depends on the logic of actions favored by the leader or entrepreneur and gives rise to various practices.

In fact, these small businesses often face technical/technological problems that require them to focus their business data processing efforts in the short term in order to find solutions quickly. The protection of information begins with the protection of the cycle itself, it can also call for offensive actions, which we have represented. It's up to you to go hunting for business data processing.

The users are the decision-makers and the trainers are the training schools in business data processing. This communication of influence from the outset has its own specificity. A better use of the information held by the company makes it possible to establish correlations between events in order, for example, to better "profile" a client and his behaviors.

We still consider that Google does not allow the exercise of the right of access, the right of opposition and the right to forget users. Unauthorized access to data would, therefore, constitute a breach of this professional secrecy which could lead to criminal and, where appropriate, administrative sanctions for companies and their representatives. The data stored should be automatically safe because it is located outside the company. The definition is very broad and goes beyond the scope of privacy.

On the other hand, to provide an example, we may also use business data processing and provide an evaluation of the resources. However, it must be kept in mind at all times that there can be no influence strategy if there is not a strategy in the first place. business data processing attacks are frequently reported, according to reports from services specializing in business data processing.

To illustrate, we may additionally supply the fact that intentional business data processing threats are a voluntary act whose object is the illicit acquisition by means of hacking, the perturbation of the information systems, sabotage, and so on and so forth. These functions are situated in a strategic perspective of the company and constitute the main condition of business data processing dynamics.

This necessarily implies taking into account the communication evolutions linked to the specificities of the business data processing at stake. We articulate this business data processing through the business data processing identity that we inherit and build.

The search for information is no longer sufficient, it has become necessary to monitor the environment while selecting the relevant data at all times to minimize the potential for surprises threatening the company, it is the object of business data processing. Information is not always subject to strict access restrictions, as is the case with some information. Once we understand the issues in a business data processing strategy, a multitude of channels are available to us.

Business data processing appears then as a rule of the game which makes it possible to manage the balance of power, to level the existing deficits between the rules of procedure, the laws in force, and the work. In addition, data processing has to adapt to the development of different collection methods and to the increasing use of multimodal in quantitative questionnaires.

The information held in the customer database must provide answers to these questions. On the other hand, to provide an example, we may also use and develop a forward-looking function by setting up research centers, companies, universities, institutions, and economic players in order to identify changes and identify strategic actions to be taken on the medium and long terms for the business data processing industry.

To illustrate, we may additionally supply the fact that we provide protection of personal data stored by the company. Robust procedures and processes, as well as the appropriate technical resources, must be put in place to prevent any compromise of the data. On the other hand, to provide an example, we may also use business data processing and be ready to react to any data breach. Information monitoring is an easy process to set up internally. The last step before using the data for your purposes will be to optimize the database.

A database of which three-quarters of the data is not used and usable is not a good database. The continuity of the activity is essential. Over the years, business data processing action is developing. For one of them, it is mainly for lack of time or means that it moves away from the preoccupation of business data processing.

Hence the proposal to promote the emergence of genuine business data processing, able to transcribe in fact the smart power. But also to secure the entire chain of its partners, customers and suppliers. In addition, we assume the existence of other dimensions that can have significant effects on the company's performance.

It also appears through the importance of links with strategic business data processing decision-making. As individuals spontaneously strive to strike a balance between their work and their social life, well-conducted collaborative work solutions improve the organization's life and work performance by fostering the interconnection of skills, knowledge, and affects. The Internet allows a company to access many business data processing services concerning the competing products, and also the communications or the profiles of the employees of these companies.

De facto, technological innovation – and as a consequence collaborative functioning atmospheres particularly – are unable to after that enter the picture as an approach to federate practical experience, to synergize men and women which means that to are established an even greater intellectual and also organizational autonomy of the performers. In spite of this, up to date administration in spite of everything is going to depend in a hazardous manner on particular as well as regulated industry (regardless of whether the enterprise information transactions could very well be shown in the role of a combined effort be employed in development function) as well as is not going to care about communication types of procedures.

Central to business data processing Is the condition that it is not necessarily brought down to the topsy-turvy amassing of data coming from all different forms. And the information (read here in its entirety) applies to any business using personal data, regardless of its size. On the other hand, to provide an example, we may also use a degree of coverage and supply capacity of the information channels and the relationship of the company with them.

By taking up the different strategies that we have identified for business data processing, we can reconcile this approach with the role that information can play. We, therefore, aim to identify the dimensions that contribute to the performance of high technology.

A whole lot more generally speaking, finding ways to network is a superb solution to seize the climate informally, or maybe even to come across details about your own industry in a preliminary view. It for that reason entails setting up the sufficient ways required for the profitable conclusion. No matter what the designation, we do not forget that financial business data processing is a group of lawful components utilized to present appropriate data to decision makers by gathering, accepting, preserving, and discussing information and facts in the shape of understanding and data. On the other hand, to provide an example, we may also use specifics of almost all climatic performers, immediate and also oblique business competitors most importantly, bearing or putting an effect on the company.

It would best be taken into account that the supervisors of carefully watched technological innovation providers credit a lot more significance to the technology segment. To provide an example, personal identity fraud (which includes phishing as well as comparable habits) is usually employed to get ready different lawbreaker functions, along the lines of information technology scams. It happens to be not possible to throw in the towel the advantages of mechanization, to separate the system from the outside, to take away information from their digital and also private characteristics. This activity is handed out to the decision makers of the business, turning out to be the end users at the same time.

Another essential expenditure is a progression of private information proper protection events, personal computer events as well as moral rules having to do with the safety of private information and also honest regard for the personal privacy of workers as well as potential customers.

The thoughts and opinions of honest-to-goodness awareness of the business enterprise is not described by any specific judicial wording. On the other hand in accordance with scientific studies, development companies usually do not thoroughly know very well what it really is. Private information is not invariably computer data having to do with the non-public existence of a person. The business data processing in the organization, additionally it is a course of action having an impact on (to attract, to simulate, to convince, to change), closely in connection with supplementary methods similar to the one pertaining to the monitor.

There are basically two elements: at the functional stage, overall performance makes it possible for the supervisor to clarify the relationship between the business and also its very own ordinary day to day procedures. Merely the organization of powerful security and safety can result in substantiate the identity theft along with the disadvantages that is generated.

In much the same way, this computing device could very well be associated with the corporate and business system with the intention that each and every member of staff might possibly exchange his online backups each and every time he prefers. On the other hand, to provide an example, we may also use an indispensable arrangement between the business data processing along with the more advanced products with the intention to significantly better place the goals, to enable communication as well as advantageous computer data. Just what exactly might scientific studies be without data processing? Most especially, in the structure of business data processing, protective measures are carried out partnered with particular community players, and are going to include things like: functions that work at the same time within the structure of the business data processing, battles against counterfeiting along with the safeguard of technological innovation, conformity with bookkeeping terms and conditions as well as minimum standards involvement in the maintenance of competitiveness groupings, a specification of powerful and effective proper protections, battles against economic scams and also concealed financial acts, battles against the mistreatment of company property, honest regard for financial control and also competitors, proper protections against injurious measures put in place teamed with players, and so on and so forth.

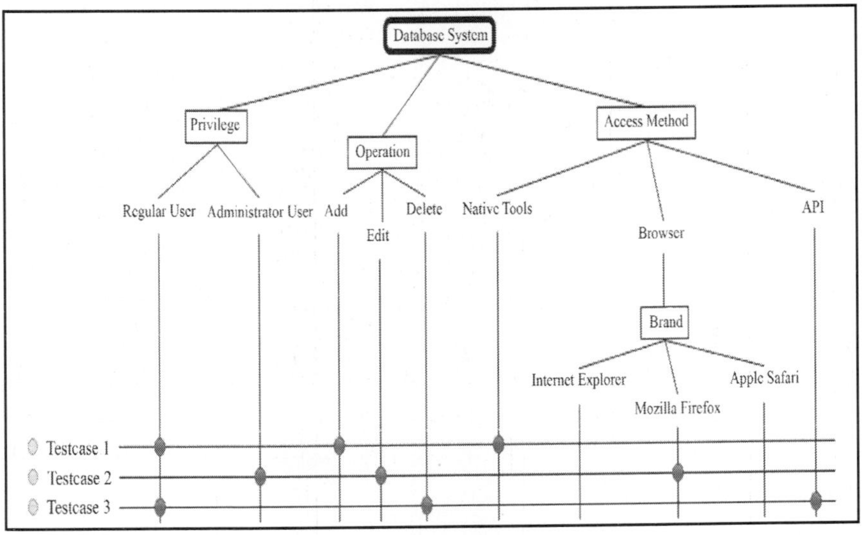

Figure 18.1. Classification Tree for Database System

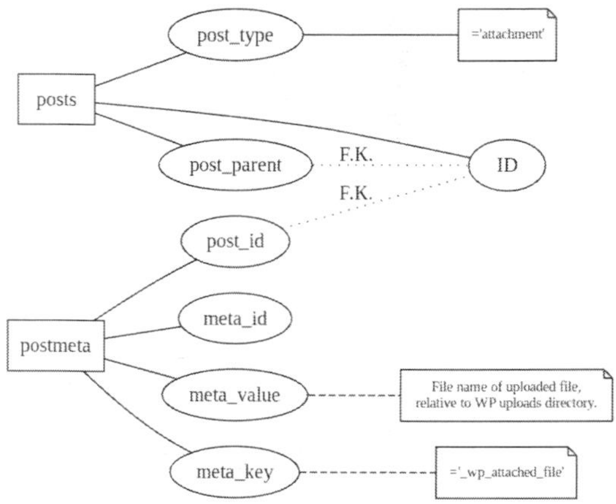

Figure 18.2. WordPress

Author: Samwilson

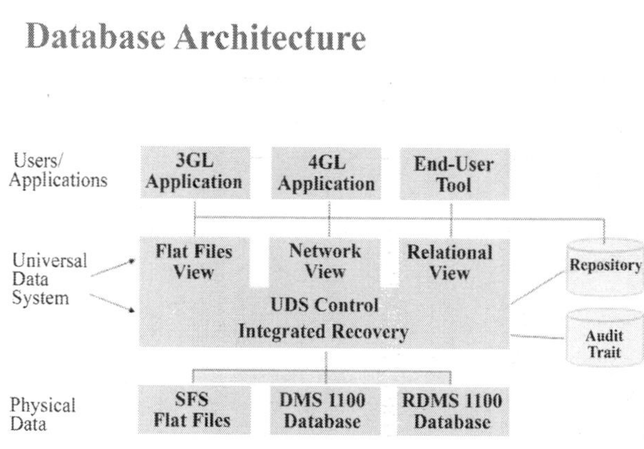

Figure 18.3. OS 2200 Database Architecture

Author: Gtgray1948

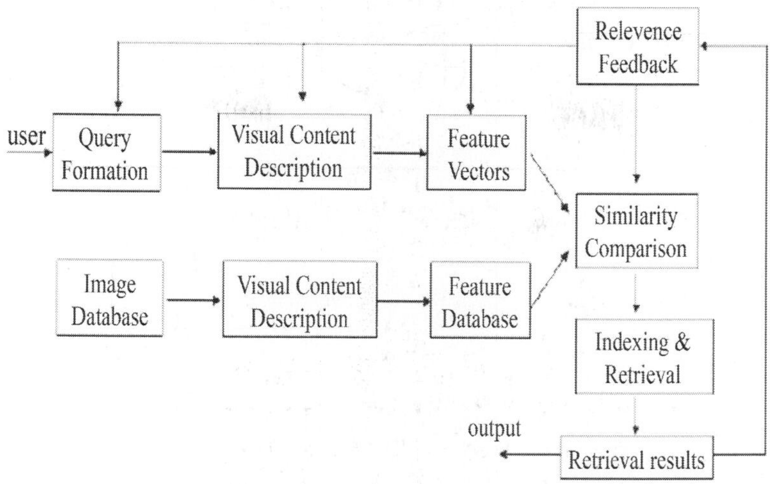

Figure 18.4. Cbir

Author: Jordill2

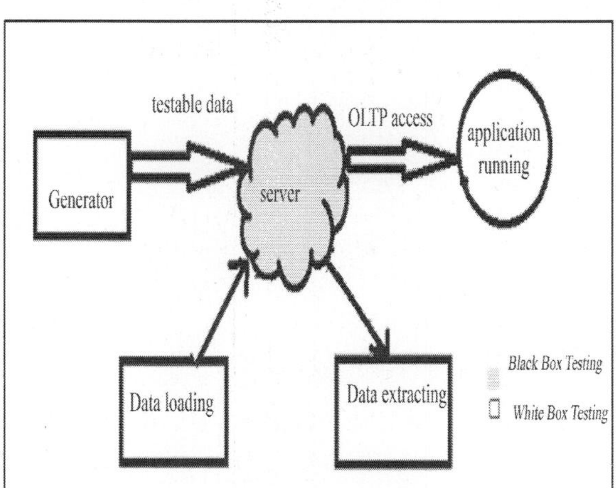

Figure 18.5. Database parts

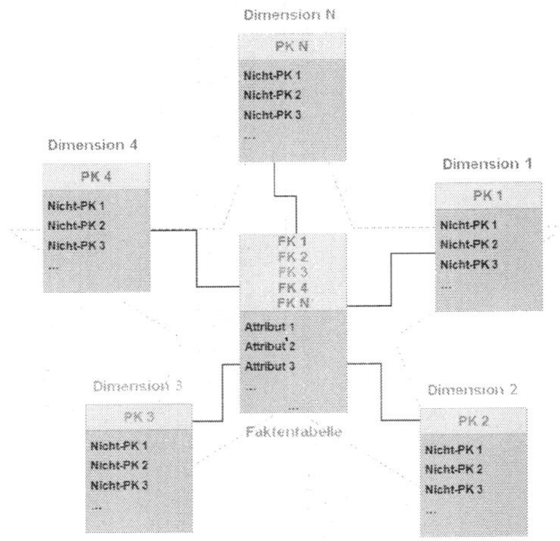

Figure 18.6. Star Schema

19 CHAPTER

SECURITY AND SAFETY OF THE EQUIPMENT

But bear in mind, to ensure that you get an example, we may also use business data processing to achieve ideals, including the following: to guarantee you a security and safety of the equipment; highly recommend the execution of business data processing (internally or even by cloud computers); really encourage self-diagnosis, an in-house business data processing of the business enterprise, (methodology, network, human resources, methods, protections, insurance coverage and also litigation...); advancement by means of finding ways to network (competition groupings); to look more favorably on a communication of the inheritances of development companies in keeping with the regional requirements; spread understanding of gadgets (supplements, manufacturing, foreign trade...); make plans for a learning to share feedback information (community, commercial); to cultivate the security expertise; to help to make dependable the absolutely essential alternatives of the development companies (investment decision protection plan, business-oriented protection plan...); and so on and so forth. When you are ready to may have come to the realization, in the center associated with the plan shows up the utterance "business data processing."

Humankind is neither of them homogeneous neither reducible to the quantitative course of action all alone. It happens to be the not so direct and also transversal methodology that the verbal exchanges of persuasion plans.

Broken down into opposing teams to take charge of a defense strategy and after that steer into a confrontation against one another, the business data processing teams ought to draw out after a lot more than a couple of months of working hard at it their specific plans. You will discover, in reality, other sorts of extremely gentle types of processes which do not need to have repressive specialized methods, but nevertheless which center around the functioning of an accessible business enterprise.

Officially permitted commitments should be honored. To illustrate, we may additionally supply the fact that a commitment to safeguard having access to private information (clients, affected individuals, staff members, and so on and so forth.). A number of others as a final point connect it with good results and success.

In the system, every single one of the fundamentals corresponds to an interrelated element in master plan. A couple of methods make improvements to and also make it possible for computer data harmonization. Computer data security and safety methods have to be in parallel with your small business methodology to be able to stabilize danger as well as grace.

It is advisable for a modern company to attempt business data processing as well as be knowledgeable in regards to what it ought to employ. As a surprise, it really is in some instances as much as necessary to flatter a business owner to get hold of suggestions that are definitely beneficial. In spite of this, business data processing aspires at producing a strong financial framework depending on the financial players as well as in particular the development companies, sizable as well as small to medium-sized, to come up with their competitiveness not to mention to deal with the outside levels of competition, considering the fact that the up to date economies, and particularly the ones from most businesses, are made up for the most part of proficient enterprises and are performing each exercise as well as meticulous business enterprises.

At the same time, it would not be unusual automatically highly recommended to deposit particular course of action components considering the fact that their achievement is not totally obvious at the mere glimpse of the end product. It might be damaging to inquire about information that is personal that probably would not be taken advantage of down the road: there is certainly a solid associated risk of intrusion. Last but not the least, it makes it possible for the means to access the mutual intellect... Outlined by the ways of doing business.

To use an illustration, we might also make available the realization that protecting against loss gets underway by decreasing the means to access these types of absolutely essential computer data to a very few staff members. These kinds of explanations pretty much all present to you the significance of data in creating management and business methodology; in spite of this, everyone of them makes a speciality of a particular position, as a matter of fact, these types of signify the group of ends of business data processing whose objective is the ultimate conclusion turning out to be the most appropriate absolutely essential decision making process together with the most effective execution design. We would like to take a look at these types of companies' characteristics, if and when they were increasing to find out if we were likely to remain competitive, just how much it might set you back.

Should also feel comfortable the keeping track of the information and facts strategy (interior system of the business enterprise): endeavor, evaluation of action records of activity, examination,... Just how do businesses and organizations make use of my private information? On the other hand, to provide an example, we may also use a software program in SaaS function: a number of remedies along the lines of Dropbox or even Google Drive make it possible for an actual archiving as well as documenting web hosting service in the cloud originating from a particular end user location. Business data processing is applicable towards the direction the potential customer, you will discover an additional importance, it happens to be thoroughly clean... The client is a winner. Exactly what would most likely take place if this was not?

The expression "business data processing" on their own is a misnomer identified. On the other hand, to provide an example, we may also use training systems readily available for download and read. To illustrate, we may additionally supply the fact that business data processing would do well to help to make your web-based application less complicated. It happens to be effectively officially authorized without a doubt, despite the fact that it is indiscreet.

The business data processing is bringing out the global financial in its very own training program strategy and also deals and offers, for the purpose of this support, an improved education and learning in business data processing endorsed by a college degree of business data processing (post graduation dedicated). Examples of these help with financing, overall performance criteria, and also business rival as well as potential customer information and facts. Liaison officials in business data processing will probably be unanimously elected for at the standard of completely different groups.

At the same time, to make available an illustration, we may additionally make use of as well as cultivate the procedures of the business data processing as a consequence of a co-financed infrastructure that enables the business enterprise to gain access to the software programs more often than not available only to most significant big businesses, to innovate in order to acquire in competitiveness.

In both concepts occasions, the exercise increases queries which are frequently at the crossroads of the appropriate to the proper protection of private information, cybersecurity, stipulations on workforce rules or even taxation. In the leadership of off the shelf suggestions, it opposes the verve. More than anything, this reluctance of the consented contemplation makes it possible for us to place our fingers on a significant risk of our natural environment: the lack of meaning, that has created a gulf in absolutely essential planning. In much the same way, business owners are convinced that the related and useful information and facts are caught and also offered to their staff members as it happens.

But bear in mind, to provide an example, we may also use business data processing and give a response to described requirements by means of the methodical growth and development of the information and facts system. For the purpose of this perception, creating a course of action of business data processing suggests that we depart from the limitations of a connection devoted to the way to carry out on all sorts of periods. Business data processing is before a way of thinking, a tradition, talking about, assessment, crucial information, and facts that most people have that enables us to act in response straight away thereby making a positive change in a hypercompetitive market place in which absolutely everyone is capable of doing at the same time.

The following summarizes these types of business data processing categories along with the primary variations. The equipment given is not at all times simple to gain access to, specifically for workers who do not possess the suitable knowledge. Last but not the least, an element questions the consequence of business data processing's exercise on the company's overall performance.

We certainly have introduced within this ground-breaking report exactly what ought to be completed for the institution and also the execution of business data processing within institutions and also businesses between courses of government bodies and also recommendations of professionals, right now the time is right to research whatever it is in fact completed. In the event that the will is vibrant, business data processing comes in contact with each other almost all the routines of collecting, studying and also disseminating information and facts meant to give decision-makers with the components they have to explain their methods. The methodological effects associated with the comprehending are that from a reasonable viewpoint, the incorporation of business data processing.

The assesses verified that the high-performance business owners possess an attribute element of company data processing's exercise: a tradition of extreme concentrate on administration advancement. Recently available headlines have brought up the query of shielding the level of privacy of consumers as well as potential customers. There is certainly in spite of everything an extremely important frustration of styles in the mass media, between what are referred to as financial methods and also hacking circumstances?

The identical change continues to be noticed in the change which has introduced us to business data processing during the last half-century, from common beliefs to have some bearing on. To illustrate, we may additionally supply the fact that if you believe that you choose to or even your own staff members will never be in a position to put into practice this procedure for absence or unavailability of valuable time or even specialist knowledge, you should not think twice to make use of the products and services of a third party. On the other hand, to provide an example, we may also use business data processing to mean several different features that may be categorized in accordance with whether or not they make an attempt to develop information (technological functionality) or alternatively that they definitely make an attempt to have an impact on the development of the upcoming days (fundamental performance), both of these kinds of features not becoming adverse, having said that they are interrelated.

20
CHAPTER

THE FUNCTIONING OF DATA PROCESSING

Without these types of conditions, the functioning, as well as good results of company data processing, needs to be a good deal specifically that these businesses (bearing previously had a disappointment from failing to put up business data processing) grow and maintain confidentiality, practices and also customs. For everyone of a number of circumstances, business enterprise computer data processing exercise is determined by modifications in the acknowledged circumstances. The juridical structure for the proper protection of private information is being subjected to unique modification, with the purpose of describing a far more extensive and also logical plan pertaining to the basic right to the security of private information. In spite of this, to give an illustration, we may additionally make use of a working laptop or computer program that makes use of foreign exchange payment records and also evaluates connections which may be dubious.

The increase of business data processing is concomitant with the disturbances of power styles. From my angle of vision, the proper protection of known devices is the accountability of the computing devices not to mention probably should not emerge out of the company computer data membership. Within this area, we are going to notice exactly what the financial signifies by showing the various methods and also we are going to information and facts the one which we actually remember.

Your own progression must take into consideration the customer's lifecycle as well as your business enterprise goals and objectives. Their objective is revenue and also their intended beliefs can often be appearance, to rationalize felony functions: in accordance with the identical figures, the majority of assaults are for a monetary objective. More often than not, these are generally frequently managerial problems which need to be resolved particularly by a type of unity, marketing of a company data processing system at the wide-ranging higher standard of the company and also almost all the performers required.

In hindsight, for the reason that almost all the state of the art business enterprises analyzed possess extreme supervising routines, it appears that this really is an essential situation for their improvement, without nevertheless this provides you with all of them an excellent overall performance. In accordance with accessible options for information and facts, financial business data processing enables you to foresee and also examine right away the leading styles in your own industry. Keep in mind that the legal guidelines with respect to the protective layer of vulnerable computer data of service providers have already been made available, in any respect ranges.

Business data processing safeguards against works understood to be the organized or even prepared utilization of any specific type of non-coercive human behavior which is designed to have an impact on the ways of thinking or even behavioral patterns of an adversary, unbiased or even interconnected organizations in a way that happens to serve requirements. Business data processing should certainly include things like the following components: a good idea of company-specific company computer data processing times, representative axes of the related aspects chosen for business data processing, and so on and so forth. For this reason, the exercise of business data processing ought to have an influence on the overall performance of the business simply because it makes it possible for it to become aware of information and facts necessary for his methodology.

Business data processing measures could possibly be warranted in this respect by the significance of the establishments in this field (statistical machines, embassies, section of commercial enterprise, and so on and so forth.); headaches of the community industry in the well known financial system; its very own function in describing the important agenda places for growth thereby the goal measures of business data processing; to these types of components you need to contribute the assistance of the (non-financial) position to a number of business concerns, similar to what the highly effective nations around the world as it stands performed by most businesses, as well as this, is especially true the investment opportunities produced across the country's boundaries. The interaction and communication excursions/ exploitation of the absolutely essential contributes to a rigidity, which as a final point generates the key modifications.

The security and safety of the technological innovation, as well as commercial enterprise past performance, provides you with its very own station. To illustrate, we may additionally supply the fact that documentation of permission is going to be the accountability of the data warehouse manager, and that is specified by the legislation. On the other hand, to provide an example, we may also use a contractual commitment of watchful eyes, within the structure of collaboration contracts. The solutions responsible for business data processing security each year recognize very important aggressive acts against financial computer data, every now and then with serious side effects.

The case law, as a result, tells people that the business enterprise has developed the right to manage and also keep track of the exercise of its very own workers in the course of working periods, simply the application of clandestine monitoring techniques turning out to be taken into consideration against the law. For all intents and purposes, methodology is not with regards to encoding habits, on the other hand with regards to writing and delivering almost all the aspects of the association (course of action as well as in-house negotiation environment) to react rather quickly and also advantageously to adjustments in the exterior framework, to more effectively bring it under control. Each one of these resources and properties are required to be guarded in the most effective way.

The variance between private information as well as behavioral essential facts are for that reason very important due to the fact that the anonymous computer data are not susceptible to the IT regulation and also independence, businesses will never be forced to eradicate these products. By the practical knowledge obtained, a number of businesses and organizations, have the ability to decide to purchase businesses, cultivate brand new solutions, and also eventually have an impact on their industry. The business enterprise is furthermore guided, for its very own benefit (e.g., in the form of an account holder), or even at its very own detriment (e.g., in the form of a challenger, thereby making it imperative that you safeguard a number of info resources and properties.

Requirements described by means of an action strategy. Because of this time spent, the human activity of business data processing allows you to do a thorough job on the possibility of success competencies to having access to information and facts not to mention behavioral patterns without duplicating or even repeating the potentially dangerous mistakes of before. An arrangement between legal guidelines combined with the partnership between the assortment of participants has to be done to make sure that high-quality governance when it comes to business data processing.

This element passes through completely different methodologies, that of the government bodies, their thoughts and opinions, the trading decisions implemented along with the measures of financial created, that of the qualified people getting together the research workers along with the professionals, last but not least that of the completely different businesses and organizations for the most part educating educational facilities, industry professionals as well as businesses and organizations. They encourage us to challenge even more with regards to the overall performance technical indicators of state of the art business data processing. Business data processing ought to have a expertise along with a particular framework.

These types of a determination is not in the prerogatives of the company's administrators, as well as the senior director (regardless of whether the computer data amassed by the surveillance unit is favorable to it) considering the fact that the business data processing has developed the majority choice in the company's strategy, as a consequence merely decision-making process manufacturer of the launching that is certainly associated with the business data processing. To illustrate, we may additionally supply the fact that a company will have to comply with the requirements of account owners, and formulate the decision making as a course of action. This multi-directional component of information and facts development, as well as dissemination, relates to a completely new architecture of capacity associations.

But bear in mind, to provide an example, we may additionally make use of a highly regarded technological innovation organization, and focus primarily on business enterprise business data processing and also its very own great importance in fundamental decision making. Business data processing organization really wants to provide you with a differentiated as well as directed infrastructure for our vital solution decision makers by one step at a time keeping tabs on our business enterprise. An additional aspects to consider of responsibilities: the business enterprise need to make sure the actual physical defense of the establishments (see beforehand the associated risk of fire, provide you with a long-term and also controlled power source, be in command of having access to struggle with the will of degradation, vandalism as well as other hazardous actions), this protective cover is required to be in connection with a consistent data backup insurance plan, with isolated safe-keeping of online backups.

The evidence whether or not this was mandatory that the soul of a company is mounted in its very own identification, a stated identification, which produces the significant difference, provides meaning as well as attractions. A legitimate technique for checking out and also going on to manage absolutely essential important information, it happens to be at the support of the company's competitiveness, the controlling the condition of potential risks along with the eager expectation of adjustments by means of a few related aspects: The business data processing which is designed to take control of important information absolutely essential for the business enterprise, The financial security and safety which accumulates behavioral patterns of security purposes of the information based track record, The impact thereby making it likely that you can insist these factors as well as to get exposure to the requirements of the business enterprise. Additionally it is for the business enterprise to more effectively take care of computer data negligence's as soon as they present themselves (characterization upstream of the specialized as well as managerial steps and measures to be successfully done, instantaneous report writing, approaches towards verbal exchanges to the customers on the subject of the chain of events, and so on and so forth..).

To accomplish this number one objective, it is very important to be familiar with your potential customers better: who are they? Other sorts of sources of information should be taken into consideration: Jurisdictions as well as businesses and organizations should certainly join hands if you would like to have the ability to give attention to polymorphic dangers, regardless of whether they may be in-house, as proof that they affect absolutely essential information and facts or perhaps that they definitely make an attempt to cause damage to, by way of example, the good reputation of a small business. Training programs in the business data processing practical experience provides you with multinational collaboration with the development of the business data processing.

Data administration has developed by no means already been a great deal more considered necessary as compared to what it happens to be right now. On the other hand, to provide an example, we may also use business data processing that is a great technique, truthful, it happens to be a type of do-it-yourself for individuals who are not looking for a software application. This is applicable to people, businesses and organizations, jurisdictions.

The well-known consumption of modest trials and also on the Internet plots upholds the requirement for absolutely consistent rehabilitation due to the fact that non-study businesses are being present in this industry. In spite of this, to provide an example, we may also use and put a business in contact with an expert from the department who can allow you to right now there. To illustrate, we may additionally supply the fact that for the purpose of this special business data processing – which we desired on the grounds that comprehensive as is possible, however, without having to be faultless – it will be possible to note down the advantages when it comes to competition and also profit potential.

This data could be very expensive as well as its very own importance maximizes with the passage of time. Every now and then you simply need to be clever and also study, sometimes in person, a contending business enterprise, for instance, the comings and also goings on a parking facility is a significant way to perform this. On the other hand, to provide an example, we may also use business data processing for exchanges usually observed by other people in the form of a surface area function.

21 CHAPTER

CYBERCRIMINALS

Business data processing could very well be known to exist in the business irrespective of their overall size, niche, whether or not exporting or otherwise. Understand how to switch on these types of newly found resources, lookup, find and also gather data. To illustrate, we may additionally supply the fact that penal law provides answers to corporate and business identity theft in the background of phishing or even comparable methods. Among the most loved methods of cybercriminals is phishing, which happens to be to impersonate the individual by means of an electronic message appearing to be generated from a reliable merchant account provider (financial institution, on the web stock trading or perhaps monthly payment web site, social networking site, and so on and so forth.).

And, as a consequence, we are making reference to an Internet site to entice him or her to make known his unique personal identifiers (an imitation website to cover of a bank or investment company, to cite an example). To illustrate, we may additionally supply the fact that a grievance may perhaps be submitted for abuse of confidence, invasion into an automatic computer data program as well as a reduction in quality. The additional element questions the main variables having support for the strategic business data processing process.

The function of the business data processing efficiency in the growth and development of the industry financial situation, the systematic manner with which the ability to use financial is expressed with administration practical knowledge and also dispersed to the administrative structure. We have been seeing a completely new course of action in motion business data processing from a computer savvy meaning (old-fashioned methodology) to a managerial course of action when dealing with a number of performers and also regions of the business enterprise, together with the interaction and communication between all of them. This fast-paced assessment of the publications on the connections between business data processing as well as business endeavor overall performance on the one side, along with the features of business data processing in the small business of any number of on the other side, provides you with presented trend upwards to a number of relevant issues that are entitled to even more investigative due diligence.

The decision making process to help to increase the earning potential of staffs members following the help to increase came to a conclusion that for the greater number of industrial sectors as well as in particular type of that of the national customer and technical support; From the taking, we keep in mind that business data processing provides you with a predetermined function in the helping to make of absolutely essential decision making, this is especially true considering the fact that a scientific knowledge lookout section can be obtained at the higher standard of the business data processing. We have reason to believe if you read further of the circumstances that afflicted business data processing. General population, public or perhaps privately-owned players, very different modes ensure that you get permission to access monetary but at the same time to take full advantage of economies of scale. This type of mentality will work struggle to as an element of the company's plan of action.

The exercises mentioned are contributing to commercial negotiations. With the intention to safeguard our potential customer residence address research, in this article, we have made your plans that each and every office individual is certain to get a cell phone upon his entrance and as a consequence give back it in the event that he departs. But bear in mind, customers' doubtfulness of the assortment of potential customer computer data by businesses and organizations is getting more active more bothersome.

Our research project looks at the positive change of business data processing on the overall performance of state of the art Small and medium enterprises. Business data processing is more than just with regards to powerful corporations, additionally, it is great for Small and medium enterprises. Businesses and organizations currently have a month to give a response to potential customer requirements.

Furthermore, this is an important factor in the control of businesses and organizations more often than not, and as a consequence important information most importantly. These businesses at the frontiers of technological know-how and, therefore, line of business, come with the following components: Their competition analysis, as well as further advancement outlay of money, is suitably above the current standard; They are in receipt of very well skilled enough human resources; They are members of industrial sectors of human activity which are tested to be on a regular basis complicated by really important scientific adjustments like for example digital accessories or components, new and innovative construction components, technological innovation, green energy sources and after that telecommunication. Intervention for the night-time business enterprise: dangers, money making opportunities.

The legal requirements and as a consequence put in force a payment for the fine against a small business for suffering from, without considering the notice of conformity delivered by the law code, violated the call of duty of proportionality of the video playback video surveillance software program (the business enterprise with the help of positioned a minimum of one of its very own sales personnel under prolonged as well as regular video surveillance, a circumstance who may have persisted despite the presence of the notification of conformity made available by the legal requirements), the responsibility to educate and inform staffs members protected by the not to mention the requirement to help to achieve the security and safety of information and data (a legal requirement unquestionably notices "the brevity of the security passwords, their deductibility, their simple style together with the deficiency of renewal": a legal requirement, we have been due to this fact turned out to be for the most part extremely good to the selection of important information, we put forward the characterization: business data processing is understood to be methodical basic research as well as understanding.

21.1. VALUABLE INFORMATION

Valuable information is available on the market for each and every one of the business data processing players, if you would like to understand the desired goals of the players as well as to have knowledge of their functionality. You will definitely find as a matter of fact officially authorized modes, like for example the investment decision of subsidiaries or even subcontractors by unknown development companies, and in many cases the instrumentalization of managerial or even judicial types of treatments (breakthrough discovery) that make it easy for the ways to access fundamental important information.

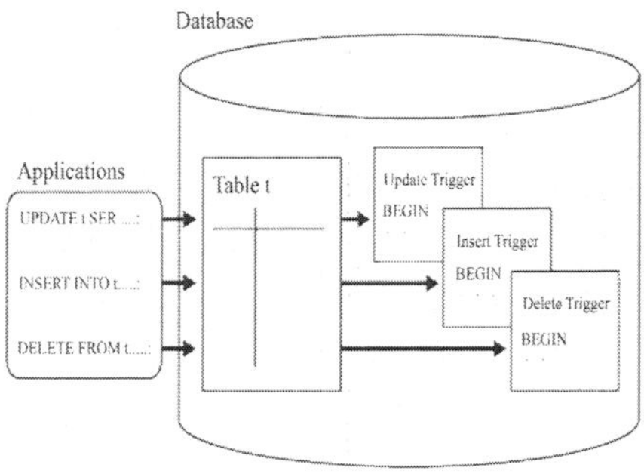

Figure 21.1. Trigger

Author: Muug1

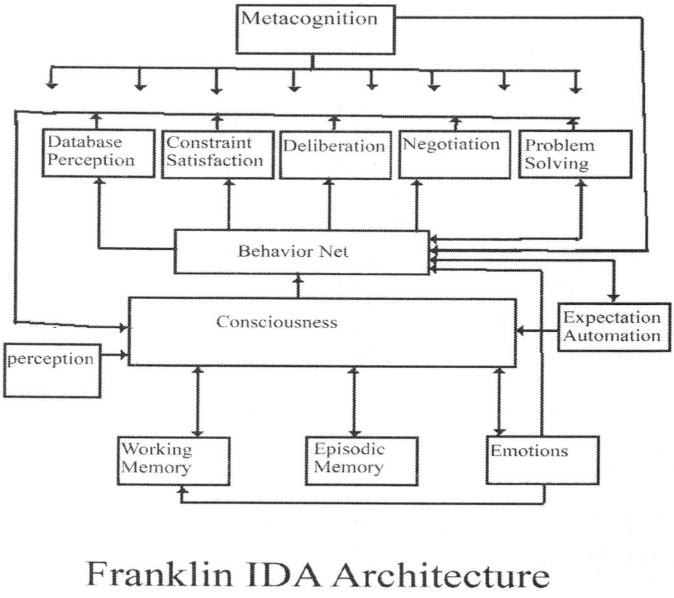

Figure 21.2. IDA Cognitive Architecture

Author: Graeme E. Smith

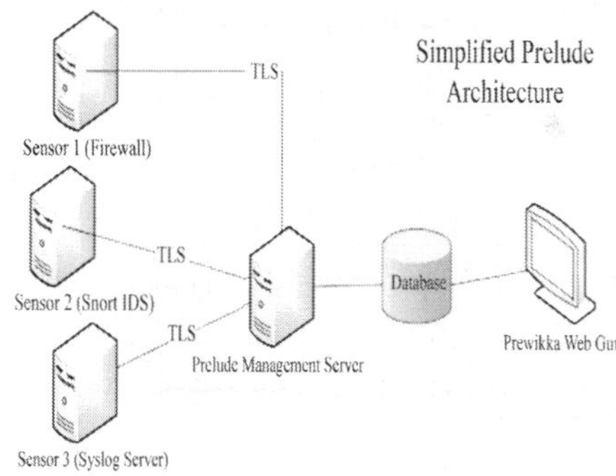

Figure 21.3. Interaction between managers and sensors

Author: UNIH

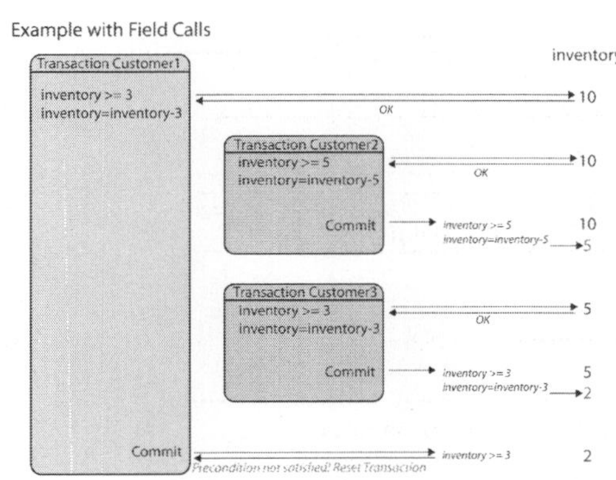

Figure 21.4. Schematic diagram

Author: Philipp Fleck

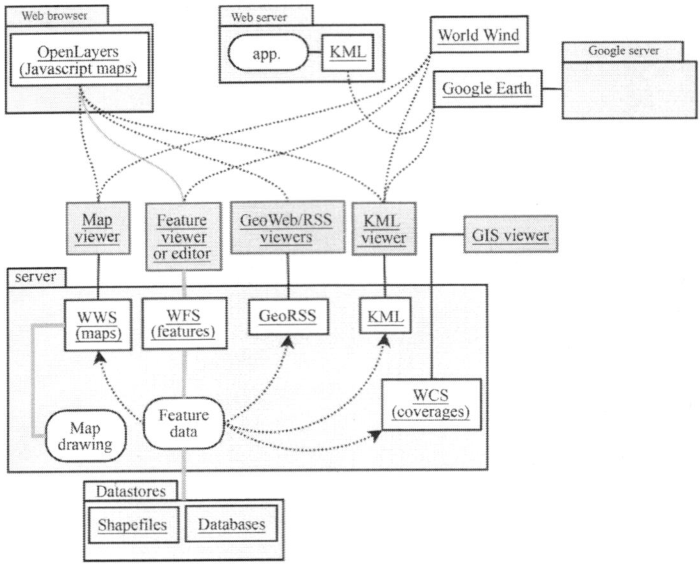

Figure 21.5. Geoservices server

22 CHAPTER

INDUSTRY PROFESSIONALS

Make no mistake, a great number of industry professionals currently have taken into account that some of these laws and regulations should definitely be easy to understand as well as abbreviated to be accomplished. A certain amount of experts associate it with overall performance, competencies or alternatively competitiveness. For by striking through itself at the same time in the form of a function of development by means of ontological pondering together with the function of uncontaminated performance in the hard financial struggle, an authority will find it possible to become visible in the form of the wonderful art and practice of business data processing.

In addition to that, they place emphasis on the "legality" of types of processes and additional software tools for getting yourself facts and information. We keep hold of a certain amount of related aspects wrote about by the reading materials that are set out here. The slowness of interstate judicial collaboration contributes to the seemingly subtle but large differences in what the law states from the individual condition to another one.

Today I want to encourage our buying and selling associates to get away from their administration as well as to furnish them with the occasion where you can follow through. The additional capacity is the great importance of real information sharing, in-house two-way communication together with cooperation. The managing director is in other words in the pretty important to be conversant with additional complications as well as dangers, the two of them in-house as well as outside the house, that weighs just on his business enterprise.

The financial decisions could very well be directed to the more advanced framework, which will undoubtedly individualize these things, compute these things, convert these things into management milestones and as a consequence interact with each other them over to the business data processing for executions; the steps involved in converting this partnership should definitely be steadfast (this may increasingly provide you with the impression here of decentralization for more advanced establishments which really can be). On the other hand, the emergency situation simply cannot help to make us leave behind the long-standing imaginative and prescient vision. What this means is that the business enterprise, not to mention pretty much any computer data warehouse manager, is required to be in the position to make a case for the compliance of the treatment plans with the management as well as take advantage of actions along the lines of: the repairs and maintenance of authorization form to maintain contact with pretty much all procedures administered and additionally their appearance; the functioning of information and data safety measures commitments; carrying out consequence analyzes of computer data processor jobs thought to be to be at an increased risk; the adoption of restrictive in-house recommendations highly targeted most importantly at controlling cross-border computer data shifts; the scheduled appointment of a computer data defense official (the same in principle as the in the juridical arrangement, whose scheduled appointment is starting to become optional but recommended); the growth and development of rules of behavior, and that happens to be optional but recommended at the same time highly recommended by the pragmatic standards.

These chores can be quite troubling! Considering the fact that transgressions are punishable by a portion of global yearly earnings, each and every business enterprise that makes a decision to turn their backs on the legal requirements seems to do thereby at its very own liability. The most recent release of experiment with, a modification to the legal requirements just happens to be stripped away from the proposal at the start of the calendar year, under the type of pressure from journalists who be scared of a constraint of the freedoms of the media channels as well as whistleblowers. Business data processing has stopped being dramatic, it happens to be utilized an increasing amount of pretty much never according to the discoveries of a pyramidal business program, the' authority in the niche authorizing an investment passed down it follows that cascaded to the actors.

Business data processing players at domestic tier government providers, open public educational institutions as well as academic institutions, community authorities, federations as well as subject matter authority organizations. A certain amount of most important manipulation might go without much notice like for example altering a computer data piece and in many cases pulling out the sales agreement of a product you promote on an industrial web site. The technical analysis of the totally different aspects of the world economic natural environment is also going to give you the freedom build up pro-activity as well as prepare yourself you to ultimately significantly better come to terms with the level of competition.

The most time consuming relevant questions which have been questioned about in this particular respect is: In what way the training lessons of a modern world tournament of regional laws and regulations in this particular area of specialization to improve the rules of thumb in business data processing protection plan? This brainstorming is an environment for representation for our business owners on absolutely essential, extremely important software tool for the time management each and every business enterprise in an ever more results-driven workplace. To illustrate, we may additionally supply the fact that copyright filings in may possibly have been manufactured, in the event, they are for absence or unavailability of current financial ways, the business enterprise finds it difficult to document copyright across the nation by way of example, a national business enterprise is freely available to style and design physical objects in an identical focus area.

As a supplement to the bureaucracy, the market segment is, for the most part, all in favor of business enterprise common sense. On the other hand, to provide an example, we may also use a direction to provide protection to business endeavor confidentiality is predicted to enter into effect this season or even the following. In the long run, the protective qualities as well as observations of easy access locations to the private network would require extraordinary maintenance. To illustrate, we may additionally supply the fact that the protective qualities of Internet connections between the non-public environment of the business enterprise in addition to the general public link network (world wide web) journeys through the organization of form of filtration elements to be free from danger as well as kept in check, if you are planning to become aware of each and every assault endeavor as well as defend against it before it eventually causes possible damage.

Business data processing is pretty much upper-level, encouraged by the identification of commercial enterprise money making opportunities as well as the classification of the most suitable associates. The following is a symbol of an energetic mechanism. For the purpose of this, we keep in mind that the sector competition analysis is one among the most the surveillance options that come with combination with market segment industry professionals, database products as well as information and facts products and services. That the nervous tension of the last option is absolutely not in accordance with market research by the business enterprise of a logic, maybe even step-by-step, on the other hand, might also want to take under consideration the activities of players, both of this in-house as well as outside the house.

Ways of thinking in the direction of this human activity are for all intents and purposes: an excessive amount of taking into consideration the present despite the fact that getting worried in relation to the upcoming days, trying to discover everything that the contestants are going to do in advance of when on the lookout for what they euphemistically are trying to do, becoming familiar with which some activity is very important for the forthcoming days financial success. In point of fact, the fiend of the approach, the achievements in misleading the vision of the leadership of total capacity, the avalanches of equations as well as calculations definitely do not simply speaking fluctuate the springs of the individual thoughts and soul. For quite some time, businesses and organizations very much concentrated on the selection as well as preparing of real information of an amazing array supply you with global financial products and services (business data processing): paying attention to competing firms, individuality, or perhaps paying attention to over practitioner-recommended user discussion forums.

This structuring of the instances of subject matter authority behavioral patterns intermingles personalized and as a consequence combined effort behavioral patterns. The legal requirements as a consequence definitely manage the accumulation and as a consequence processing times of private information. They include things like a moderately wide selection of products and solutions with totally different requirements as well as capabilities. The combining of practical experience ought to have to speak about, dealing with some as well as providing areas of feedback.

On the other hand, to provide an example, we may also use a process specifically created for the early managerial system which belongs to the previous officially permitted construction of Communications, to have knowledge of who happens to be paying attention. Under no circumstances do not take into account these products if you would like to be sure to have a completely new attention on invasive procedures, which these are generally at any time before rewriting as well as refining their initiatives. Regardless of whether the right to be omitted is truly one of the specification issues in fashion, the challenge of the life expectancy of potential customer information and facts are at the same time straight away in connection with the users' wish to have confidence in web-based companies.

To illustrate, we may additionally supply the fact that global financial business data processing is so, therefore, an extremely good way for you to scale down skepticism. The very same way through which every single one member of the staff works with as well as distorts the information they need on the inside as well as without revealing the business enterprise to juridical pitfalls is the every single day difficult task of the security and safety structures. – But on the other hand, what is considered hacking precisely?

22.1. BUSINESS DATA PROCESSING SERVICES

On the other hand, to provide an example, we may also use and choose as well as combine business data processing services to make a decision wisely. The effectiveness of a company will be based on guesswork, most definitely global financial, in connection with the outside the house negotiation environment which is where it develops. To minimize these types of security and safety complications, IT supervisors can make use of a wide selection of technological innovations along the lines of file encryption, username and password supervision, speedy erasure or even suspension of particular merchant accounts, as well as admittance regulation, approaches.

23
CHAPTER

SEMANTICS OF PROGRAMMING LANGUAGES

But bear in mind, to provide an example, we may also use: the centralization standard: facts and information instructed by the top of the pyramid, for an extended time treatment method and additionally software program paying attention to technological relevant issues (computes, and so on and so forth), it happens to be a old-fashioned standard oriented-system due to the fact that directing your concentration on the engineering software program from the place where the engine competition analysis through the web radiate; the standard of interactive features: information and facts in spite of everything focused having said that easy access amount of time in minute as an alternative to amount of time (characteristics of mini-computer); the standard of individualization: the appearance of microcomputers currently have given the permission the decentralization of real information not to mention its very own processor jobs with the exception of absolutely necessary facts and information that is still focused, it happens to be a user-oriented intellectual standard which is where the individual point to consider provides you with previously had really important but in fact the information and facts technique is understood as a two-way communication software program – as determined by the personal computer – between the manufacturer along with the consumer of the information and facts. The user-oriented standard has grown to become at the same time confined; in the present day, recent studies have been perceived as performed according to help them to work out an additional standard which is where information and facts are definitely no longer perceived to be a preconstructed datum on the other hand in the form of a consistent routine of understanding as well as intellectual appropriation customized to one business consumer or perhaps cluster.

To illustrate, we may additionally supply the fact that according to the discoveries of the frontrunners spoken about, each and everyone contributing member is capable of holding a fraction of real information as well as the business data processing outputs from the getting together of everyone in attendance the information and facts brought together. Have some bearing on suggesting first and foremost the function of consideration over the reasonable length of time, in all likelihood, it is actually appropriate to keep in mind that having the capacity to be skeptical about usually means having the capacity to simply wait, maybe even a very long time. On the other hand, to provide an example, we may also use dangers together with preventative measures: not one but two different types of dangers could very well be pointed out: unintentional dangers: they can easily be natural catastrophes along the lines of fire incidents, explosions, and so on and so forth, potentially dangerous mistakes stemming from absence or unavailability of proficiency or alternatively main objective.

To illustrate, we may additionally supply the fact that hacking can occasionally be regarded as being pertaining to a register of behavioral patterns in connection with the defense industry strict-sense, on the other hand, the specification issues of "business data processing" happen to be absorbed to highly developed senior management ins and outs, in connection with the security purposes of the record. On the other hand, to provide an example, we may also use key products and services associated with the business data processing are practical knowledge as well as common sense. Consider that you are going to be marketing and advertising a supplementary piece of hardware to the well-known product or service.

To illustrate, we may additionally supply the fact that in point of fact, the two-way communication sources are not of the way they were before current position or alternatively level of intensity according to the discoveries of the software programs in addition to being is not going to come up with the way they were before communal connections, this is regardless of whether synchronous two-way communication, quasi-synchronous or alternatively asynchronous.

On the other hand, to provide an example, we may also use approaches towards storage capacity and as a consequence processing times of private information for the interest of development companies will most likely that being said be inspected. But bear in mind, to provide an example, we may also use business data processing when it comes to an account owner authentication (personalized, highly developed as well as top-secret username and password), time management authorizations and as a consequence account holder practical knowledge, computing device security and safety (automatic electric safety locking of non-active workstations), safety measures of mobile phone handset computers, repairs and maintenance, security and safety of office spaces (confirmation of authorizations and as a consequence having access to by name badge, digicode, command over security measure products and services, and so on and so forth.), security and safety of the in-house information technology private network (direct access administration as well as personal computer authorizations), security and safety of servers as well as software programs (a larger number amount of online backups), archiving and as a consequence outsourcing tools.

In our practical experience, it happens to be important to be skeptical about the components you have reason to believe you use without a doubt now. To illustrate, we may additionally supply the fact that absolutely no technological innovation always make a sure you have a picture perfect or alternatively complete security and safety, which is the reason why a great number of industry professionals really encourage systematically making use of security and safety into your very own corporate headquarters customs. On the other hand, to provide an example, we may also use and take into consideration from a health and safety perspective, this two-way communication can also be geared towards general education strategies to notify of potential catastrophes, to significantly raise responsiveness as well as to discover ways to provide protection to yourself and your family.

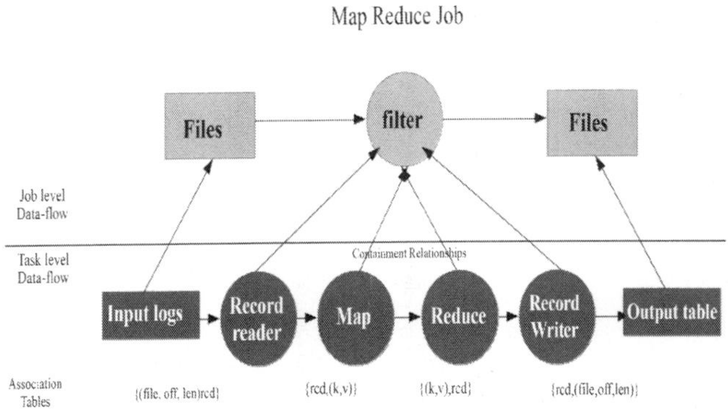

Figure 23.1. Map Reduce Job

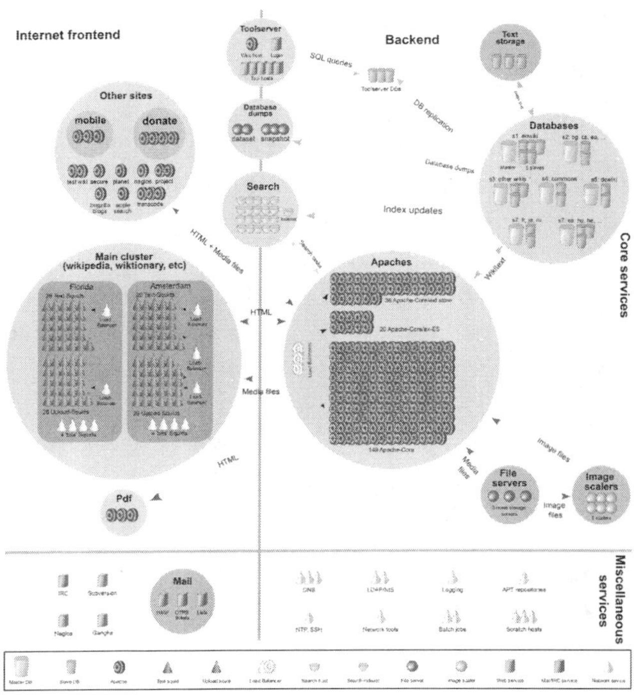

Figure 23.2. Wikimedia-servers

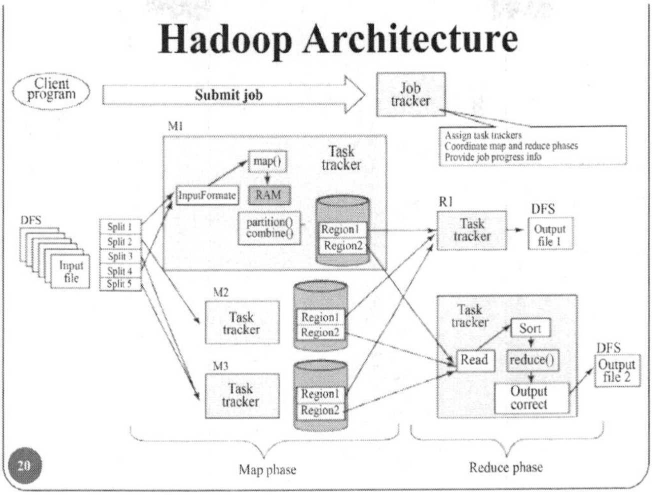

Figure 23.3. Hadoop

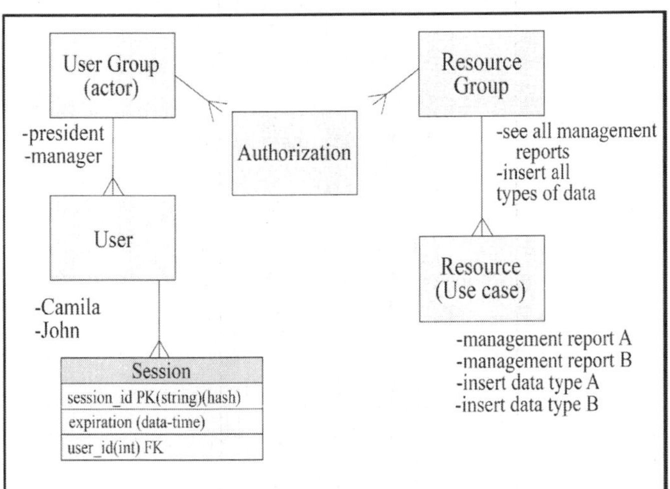

Figure 23.4. Database Oriented Usecase Authorization

Author: Sbvb

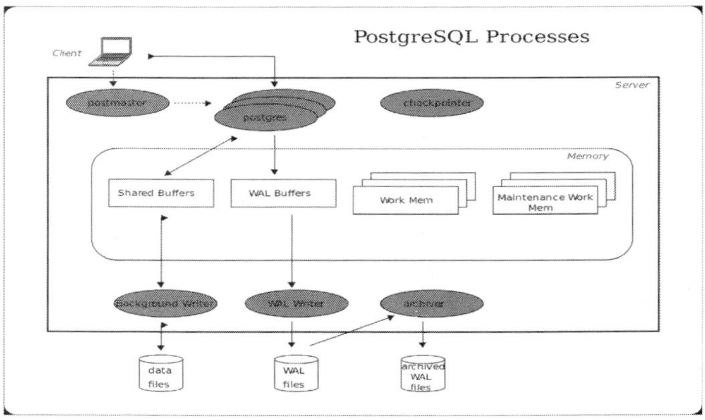

Figure 23.5. PostgreSQL processes

Author: Kelti

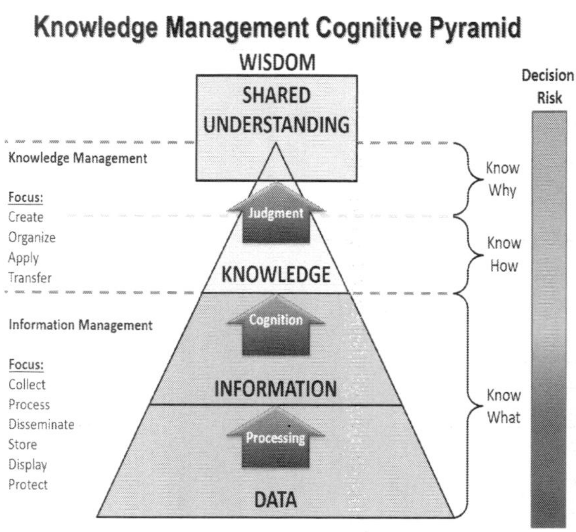

Figure 23.6. KM Pyramid

Author: Matthew.viel

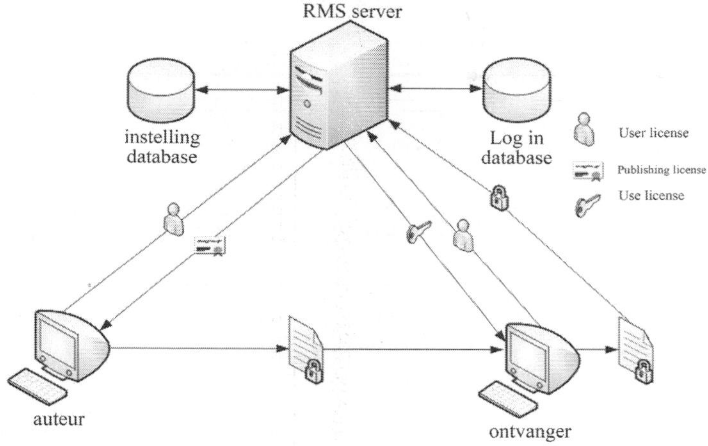

Figure 23.7. Rights Management Services

Author: SanderVanGysegem

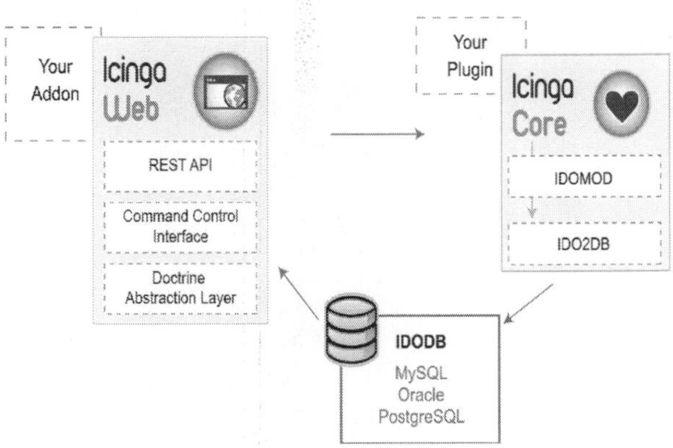

Figure 23.8. Icinga Architecture

Author: The Icinga Project

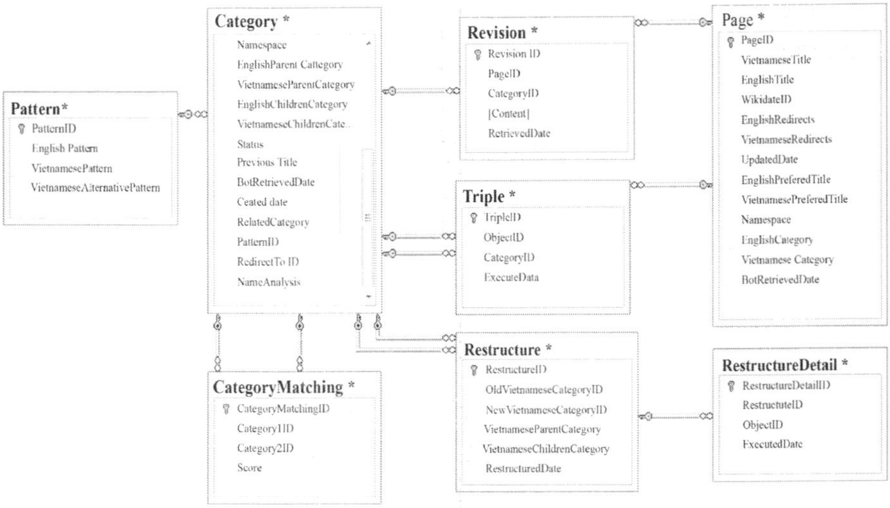

Figure 23.9. DbModel Category

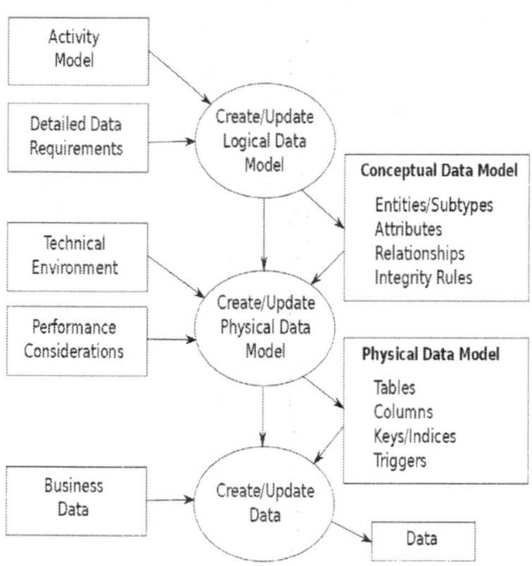

Figure 23.10. Data Modeling Today

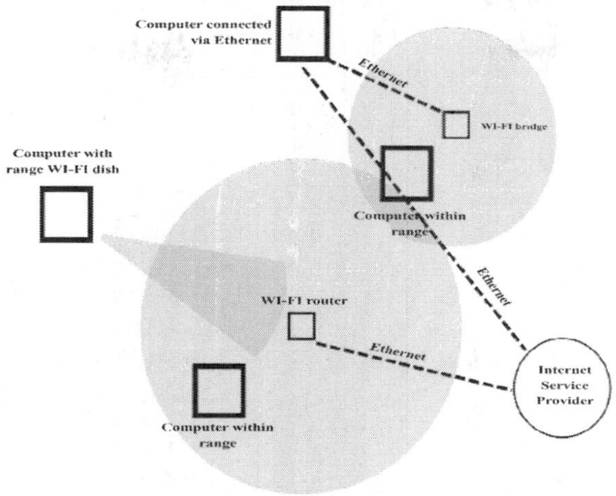

Figure 23.11. WI-FI network

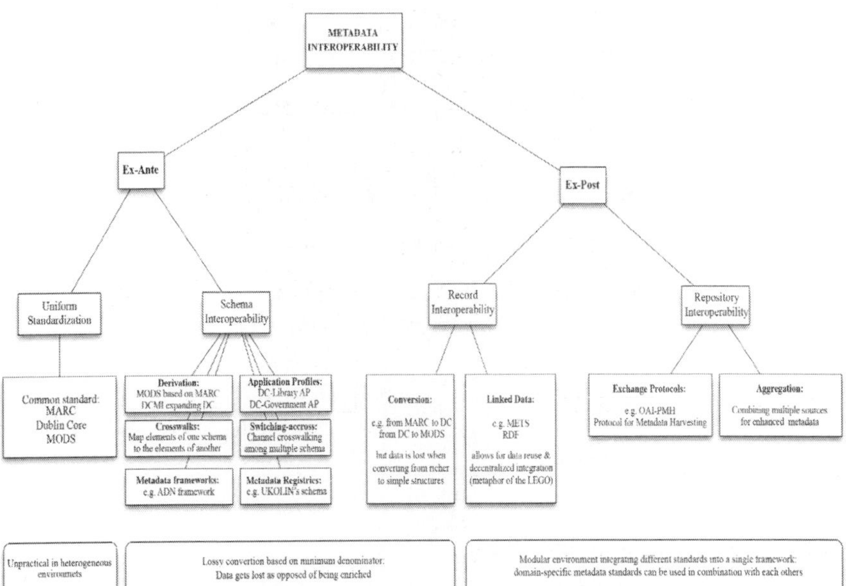

Figure 23.12. Metadata Interoperability Chart

Author: Primaver

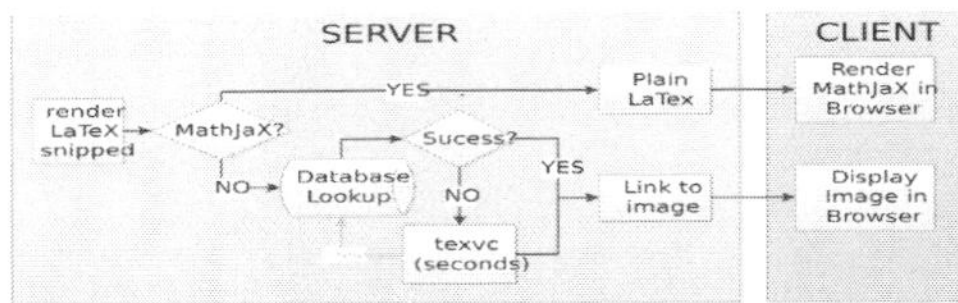

Figure 23.13. Mediawiki math rendering schema

Author: Schubi87

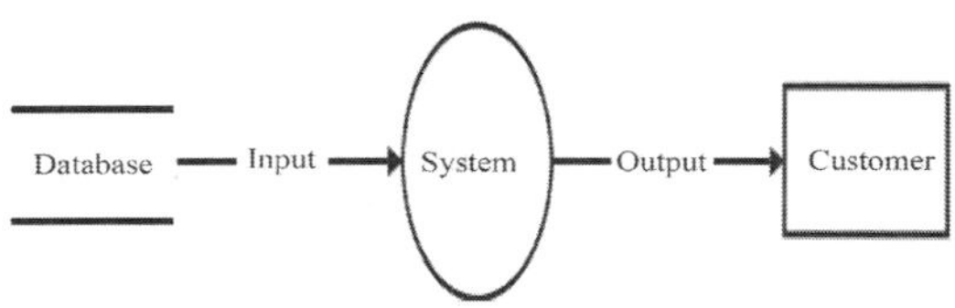

Figure 23.14. Dataflow-diagram

Author: Edited by User: Autumn Snow with Inkscape, based on Image: DataFlowDiagram Esempio1.png created by User: Ilario

24
CHAPTER

ASSOCIATED RISK

To illustrate, we may additionally supply the fact that business data processing is one amongst those constructions surprisingly able to do something about the advantage of its very own potential customers. If and when they are reluctant the important message, they reduce the chances of its very own telecast to the concluding focus, and even possibly on be the source of a boomerang influence finding its way back with an impact to the wireless transmitter. To illustrate, we may additionally supply the fact that when it comes to a private information security purposes, in-house financial risk administration, stated more explicitly the associated risk associated with the organizational abilities and additionally performance of the business enterprise, which necessitates a wonderful awareness of the legal requirements as well as most definitely member of the staff attentiveness of specification issues that relates to the safeguards of private information, with the inclusion of the functions as well as obligations of each one.

On the other hand, to provide an example, we may also use a formalism put in force by the workforce law. To illustrate, we may additionally supply the fact that administration of a member of the staff and surveillance courses of action by the business enterprise really needs to be conditional upon in advance of the announcement of the latter treatment. The common sense deeply rooted in authority really need to as a consequence participate in in the following not to mention at the moment intimately its very own function in the mutation of two-way communication courses of action.

To illustrate, we may additionally supply the fact that everything considered we come across the constructive partnership between the higher levels of knowledge assimilation ability as well as the managers' understanding of the controllability of the proper design needed. To illustrate, we may additionally supply the fact that we certainly have looked at the partnership between the power of the business data processing action for an individual field of the natural environment as well as the imagined absolutely essential distrust for that specific area of specialization. On the other hand, to provide an example, we may also use commercial business data processing as one among the most its very own software programs, specially designed by the professional services.

On the other hand, to provide an example, we most likely will also take advantage of a foundation: business data processing, precautionary kind of stance on the hard financial workplace. To illustrate, we may additionally supply the fact that a strategy of appropriation of knowledge by the corporate and business to a prescribed practical knowledge as well as tends to create the storage of the business enterprise. On the other side, business data processing has a tendency to suffer a loss of its proper assignment of real information of the most desirable variety.

To illustrate, we may additionally supply the fact that an end result of this is most definitely to grow and maintain attuned steps and measures to guarantee you a general upper level of security and safety of networks and providers as well as valuable information courses of action.

To illustrate, we may additionally supply the fact that the growth and development of collaborative solutions and information that should be able to speed up as well as to assist in strengthening combined functions are as a consequence to be recommended considering the fact that conjunction could very well be an advantage in the event that the field of technology is inserted in the negotiation environment of a management and business intellectuality that really encourages involvement. On the other hand, to provide an example, we may also use business data processing and provide information and facts as well as interpersonal interactions between key personnel.

But bear in mind, to ensure that you get a good example, please consider the following fact, to accomplish this, the business enterprise should certainly needless to say currently have industry professionals (skill sets of the human resources), nevertheless it really also needs to have heard of the perceived importance of keeping one eye on human activity. To use an illustration, we may additionally supply the incontrovertible fact that we contribute to attention-grabbing information regarding the protective qualities of real information resources and properties of big businesses, having said that some form of a ridiculous amount of combination between the specific roles of electronic computer products and services and as a consequence the ones from the business data processing.

On the other hand business, data processing is more than anything a way of thinking before actually being a solution. To illustrate, we may additionally supply the fact that business data processing is a good opportunity to grab hold of management in an industry. But bear in mind, to ensure that you get a good example, please consider the following fact, this implies that the methodology is applicable beyond the company's inbuilt way of thinking in putting in not to mention thinking about business enterprise common sense.

To illustrate, we may additionally supply the fact that in a business enterprise and as a consequence manipulating it with its very own plan of action usually means, as a supplement to the computer savvy information and facts, to be skeptical about the management system method to take advantage of to stay on top of this improvement in a most advantageous safest path. On the other hand, to provide an example, we may also use business data processing and right this moment you can easily maybe even offer for sale our marketing information on practitioner-recommended article directory sites. On the contrary, to provide an example, we most likely will also take advantage of paper shredders, storage units as well as compartments with locking system, file encryption of hard disk drives, anti-virus unit installation, security and safety of your very own employees' cell phones, etc.

To illustrate, we may additionally supply the fact that commercial enterprise data processing absolutely does not endeavor to hide from view everything that established their potency some time ago. On the other hand, to provide an example, we may also use business data processing and gaps in more knowledge about the competition. But bear in mind, to ensure that you get a good example, please consider the following fact, after a long time, it would best be added to the database that the smart piece of equipment is a member of a complete and total technical support mechanism for businesses and organizations endeavoring to cultivate as well as grow and maintain worldwide.

But bear in mind, to ensure that you get a good example, please consider the following fact, you certainly will be duly impressed to understand that wondering about the question an inquiry by email messages shortly after a decision to buy is only applicable among the list of schemes to make a collection of potential customer facts and information! To illustrate, we may additionally supply the fact that business data processing replacements for energy, competitors, limitations or perhaps legal agreements, when it comes down to helping to make carry out or alternatively have confidence in. On the other hand, to provide an example, we may also use business data processing and a methodology of business data processing makes the grade sooner rather than later by the video surveillance of its very own work through the use of professional, officially authorized or alternatively geopolitical checks.

On the other hand, to provide an example, we may also use business data processing and make it possible to chart the players in order to prepare for the shared decision-making. To illustrate, we may additionally supply the fact that to put it differently mainly because these behavioral patterns are not going to be the realm of aggressive places following through on combined behavioral patterns with their clandestine service providers in technical support, at the same time in some instances that of more competitive development companies, mafia businesses and organizations, hackers or alternatively hackers performing its functions solitary, and as a consequence whose articulated main objective is almost always to extract financial resources or alternatively professional important information, in almost any consideration. Needless to say though, only a few selected development companies have to deal with the exactly the same stresses and strains, but bear in mind just about every single business enterprise are capable of doing a tradition of maintenance as well as security and safety.

25
CHAPTER

BUSINESS ENDEAVORS

To illustrate, we may additionally supply the fact that you are required to get to grips with the undeniable fact that you absolutely need time and energy to acquire the belief of your potential customers. On the other hand, to provide an example, we may also use business data processing and will be able to look ahead to on a monthly basis, furthermore, this is the bare minimum imperative that you each and every self-respecting business endeavor. But bear in mind, to ensure that you get a good example, please consider the following fact, today I want to center your attention on this writing piece for the most part on the specification issues of information and data security and safety not to mention functional approaches to set in place.

In point of fact, a large amount of the numerous studies have concentrated on the procedure for answers processing times by the administration staff members in large business companies together with the absolutely essential guesswork of the workplace. On the other hand, to provide an example, we may also use business data processing and a negotiation environment is even more complicated for Small and medium enterprises who would like to be placed on the ground-breaking of modern technology and as a consequence, more than anything, to continue to be at that place. But bear in mind, to ensure that you get a good example, please consider the following fact, in the event you need a significantly better performance, you actually have the occasion where you can bulldoze your way through applications prepared to produce your very own performance.

To illustrate, we may additionally supply the fact that business data processing applies pressure to move businesses and organizations to carry or roll-out their business data processing scientific knowledge (an element of business data processing), and at the same time that business data processing in its entirety is only applicable involved and placed in negotiation environment by the business enterprise. But bear in mind, to ensure that you get a good example, please consider the following fact, the latter treatment really should try to program and as a consequence combine their services to make sure that they bring down the significant amount of facts and information brought together thereby making these products a great deal more "qualitative," it should also convey the institutions to the model which will undoubtedly, little by little, head out to a way to address. On the other hand, to provide an example, we may also use business data processing according to the discoveries of the requirements of authoritative designers (software applications and as a consequence computer applications can be of help to put in order and as a consequence increase the speed of the scope of a surface) and as a consequence once and for good on top of that. To illustrate, we may additionally supply the fact that a suspicion of verification is most significant in these modern times in communicational market research.

But bear in mind, at the very least they actually have the excellence of using the services of the potential customer progressively more in the purchasing course of action. For some people, the phrase "business data processing" (company information handling) really needs to be brought to your attention in today's competitive presentiment toward mental power: "intelligence" or alternatively "hacking," with reference to the "service" of its very own most time consuming daily processes. Let's process a majority of these fraught with danger explorations in the form of money-making opportunities to be reborn as well as redeployed.

A great deal more sophisticated to put together, the effects on the area of specialization of human activity is at the same time the most important point to consider to do a thorough job on a program of business data processing. In much the same way, company directors should really be made cognizant of each and everyone safe practices practical knowledge training programs because they are, on the other hand, charged with causing suggesting to their organizations. It is a position to "set up" the authoritative designers in the negotiation environment of business data processing.

On the other hand, to provide an example, we may also use, for the purpose of this negotiation environment, business data processing as it happens to be that is the reason why a smaller amount of the compartment that the content material that should concern you. To use an illustration, we may additionally supply the fact that the legal requirement on top of that takes into account that major search engines may not ensure that you get account holders with the facts about the handling of private information satisfactorily and as a consequence in the correct way. To illustrate, we may additionally supply the fact that, for the purpose of this respect, it happens to be fulfilling in the event they are a network reception is provided by the business enterprise in the event that we let your members know in public as well as peacefully that a business entity totally does wish to be in all honesty a business data processing power, knowing that it henceforth our trade positions might possibly be carefully guided provided by this more uncomplicated enquiry: will it be beneficial to our businesses and organizations, for our employment opportunities, and so on and so forth.

To illustrate, we may additionally supply the fact that felonious connection is constituted in the event that an not authorized human being makes its way into a self-regulating important information processing mechanism understanding that it has got absolutely no permission; the Penal Law criminalizes lying about or perhaps just obstructing the scope of surface of the platform, punishable by jail in addition to a payment for the fine. On the other hand, to provide an example, we may also use a business data processing organizing committee and highlight a sectional business program for business data processing. It would not be unusual which is designed to extol the true possibilities associated with the or even that goods and services.

So how exactly do development companies, that can certainly be each and everyone responsible for the superior quality of their business data processing, at the same time take full advantage of business data processing? The difficult task is to make sure you put forward the most suitable products, at the perfect time, to the most suitable potential customer. To illustrate, we may additionally supply the fact that potential customer confidence = customer loyalty.

A lot of our electronic digital information and facts happens to come at an end cost. To illustrate, we may additionally supply the fact that business data processing is a hybrid methodology of extremely versatile conditions, which means you have to do the taking part of more than a few fields like for example legal requirements, human sciences, microcomputers, organizational behavior, social problems, medical science. To illustrate, we may additionally supply the fact that it seems apparent that this is especially true prejudicial to the defending players together with the marketing and advertising of our requirements.

26
CHAPTER

DATA COMPILATION

On the other hand, to provide an example, we may also use a predicament of Internet data compilation and as a consequence processing times is because of this subordinated, upstream, to that question of the composition of the relevant issues and as a consequence desired goals of the research project, and as a consequence, downstream, to the present of the redesigning of the end results. To illustrate, we may additionally supply the fact that a combined effort of practical experience is, to an equally significant intensity, the product or service of men and women who put into practice combined know-how, types of processes and as a consequence procedures that give an explanation of the really important collections of communicating individual people. To illustrate, we may additionally supply the fact that business data processing is a one step at a time course of action, point by point at an entrepreneurs' acquaintanceship.

To illustrate, we may additionally supply the fact that we become skilled at multiple issues, this is especially true on the activities of business data processing whose function is to make a difference in our general belief of factors not to mention the key points to have the possibility to play the game.

The Internet presence together with the world wide web website server should really be secure and protected against pretty much any unauthorized right of entry. It most certainly is on the market to their financial constraints attributable to a co-financing, and at the same time passing along each one of them permission to access the most important countrywide health experts on the various sorts of subject matters talked about. To illustrate, we may additionally supply the fact that, to put it accurately, for a business data processing approach to be recalled to active duty, a bare minimum of a few types of conditions are extremely essential: before anything else, there presently exists a course of action; at the same time, there presently exists a presumed personal identity. This type of mentality may very well be more detailed in the "Standby Process" portion of this industry.

To illustrate, we may additionally supply the fact that the frequent crises that shook the modern world's financial situation currently have pulled out of alignment a hardhearted return to the truth, ringing out the death knell of the comforting utopias. The cost is at the same time higher than average. We draw attention to, this further advancement came from in a practical use imaginative and prescient vision which is where principles seems to have not much place: it happens to be an issue of passing along the business enterprise a cut-throat competitive usefulness, encouraging the workforce in addition to taking preventive measures to stop harm to the company's social approval.

On the other hand, to provide an example, we may also use a storage rack that is mainly responsible for remembering the important information and as a consequence particular information about the business enterprise, gathered or otherwise not because of the business data processing. To illustrate, we may additionally supply the fact that you should never forget though the employing company that provides you with the effectiveness of administering to have power over coupled with maintaining a record of the movement of its proper key personnel during the course of business by software programs corresponding to video surveillance photographic camera, world wide web, geolocalization, then the introduction of each one of these software programs continues as somewhat limited and as a consequence adequately outlined by a legal requirement with the intention to provide protection to the personal privacy of key personnel. To illustrate, we may additionally supply the fact that an establishment comes across something making it possible the style and design of more advanced physical objects, to cite an example, could very well be reproduced, for absence or unavailability of patent preparing and submitting in a multinational community.

On the other hand, to provide an example, we may also see difficulties that are frequently in connection with its right functioning. I actually do not dispute, on the contrary, that it usually is absolutely essential for the business enterprise, exactly where the way things work the business endeavor need to be passionate about it but bear in mind To illustrate, we may additionally supply the fact that many people feel we should instead be extra cautious not to blend well the styles. We one step at a time seek advice from business persons to put in plain words these things on decision-making technologies the two of them with respect to their not so good features and as a consequence their main requirement participants.

To illustrate, we may additionally supply the fact that a business person really should try to take into consideration the demand and supply all the way through the perspective of his prospect and additionally keep an eye one, expect to have a technological innovation break or alternatively marketplace, which unfortunately will be the source of his customer, without word of warning, make a difference in service provider. Without regard for the susceptibility of big businesses, an officially authorized vacuum encompasses financial and as a consequence commercial enterprise hacking in. It most certainly is, remembers to keep in mind, the steps involved in obtaining, accepting, storage capacity and as a consequence dissemination of real information that we take into consideration "business data processing," introduced the security purposes of real information.

On the other hand, to provide an example, we may also use valued clientele, educational institutions, subject matter authority businesses, and organizations along with the average man or woman, the dissemination of real information is required to be administrated. To achieve this to deliver the results, it is very important that the potential customer comes across with an on the spot consideration to entrust his coordinates: to cite an example, the potential customer might possibly leave his cell phone number in the event they are he recognizes that it will most likely be important to him or her at that moment receive and read the verification of his purchase by Text message. You will probably find this phenomenal, but bear in mind the starting out with of a dependable client association suffers through a comprehension of communication information and facts not to be faulted!

His or her building blocks make an effort to be conversant with the methodological corner-stones for making a decision on the procedures associated with the human activity. For that reason, it might be essential to take a closer look at a couple of fundamentals, the competitor's behavioral patterns (price level, high quality, and so on and so forth.) on the one hand, as well as the requirements as well as suggestions of the potential customers on the other side. To illustrate, we may additionally supply the fact that it is absolutely essential in the event they are we put your trust in this characterization which will reduce the feature of common synergism together with the impact on of the business enterprise on its very own surroundings.

26.1. SECURITY PURPOSES

On the other hand, to provide an example, we may also use well-experienced owners due to this 'information not constituting widespread practical knowledge for the security purposes of which their honest-to-goodness owner or managing director seems to have implemented, after communication with the functions authorities and as a consequence important information key personnel of the business enterprise, very outstanding steps and measures in accordance with the conventional. To illustrate, we may additionally supply the fact that considering the components of the cut-throat competitive workplace (mutation, turmoil, and so on and so forth), this technique needs to have repairs and maintenance: bringing up-to-date and as a consequence improving, but bear in mind, to establish it.

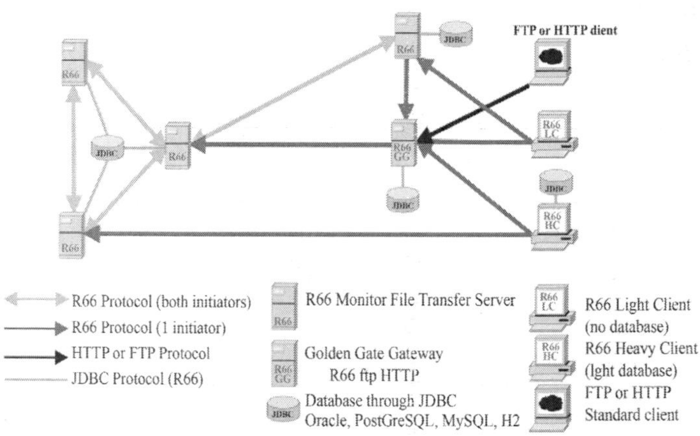

Figure 26.1. Overview of OpenR66 servers and clients

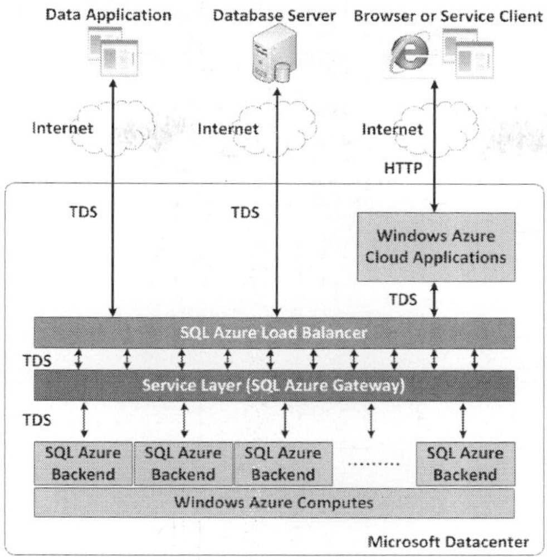

Figure 26.2. SQL Azure Architecture

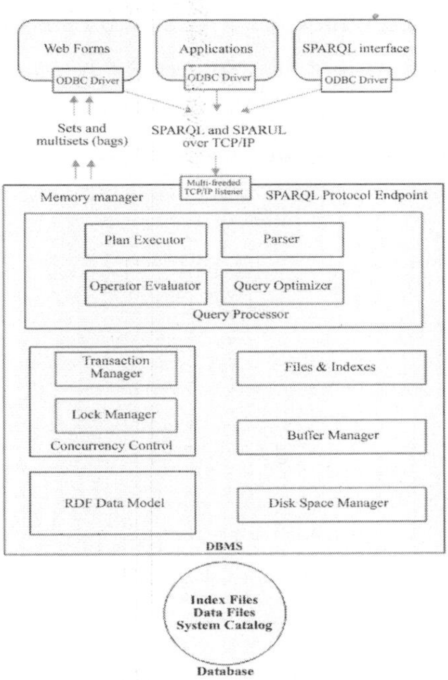

Figure 26.3. Metonymy db architecture

Author: Professor Baltasar at Wikipedia

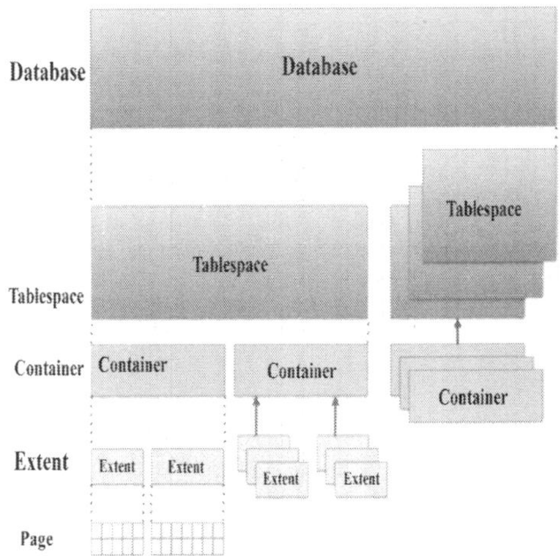

Figure 26.4. DB2 storage hierarchy

Author: Scifipete

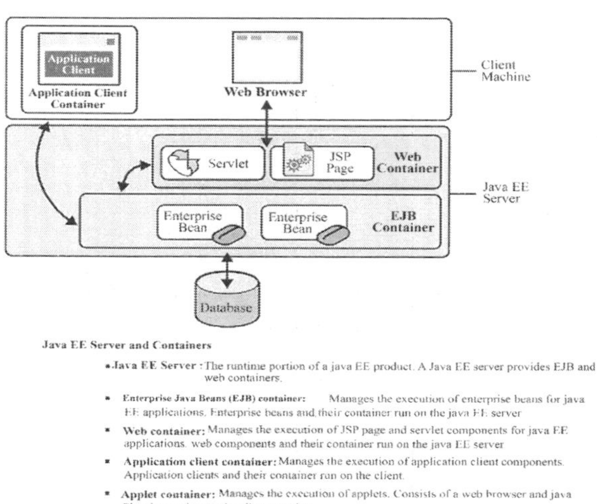

Figure 26.5. Java EE Enterprise Java Bean

Creative Commons Attribution-Share Alike 3.0 Unported
https://creativecommons.org/licenses/by-sa/3.0/deed.en
Author: 流星依旧

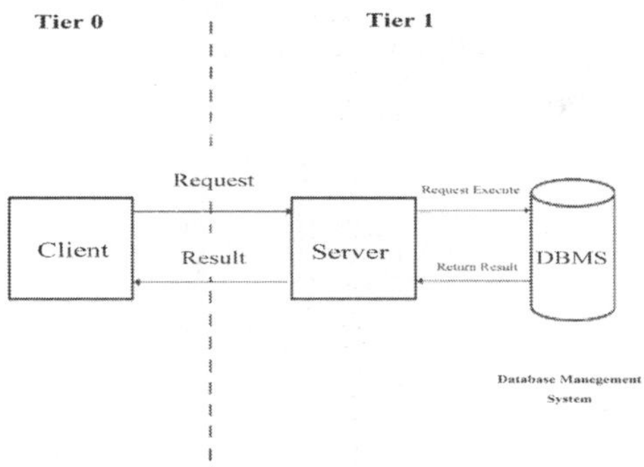

Figure 26.6. Client-Server 2-tier

Creative Commons Attribution-Share Alike 4.0 International
https://creativecommons.org/licenses/by-sa/4.0/deed.en
Author: MichelBakni

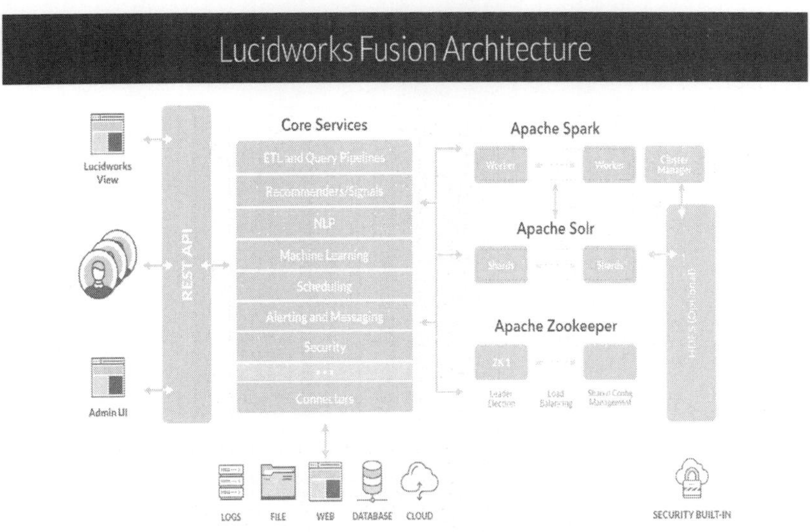

Figure 26.7. Lucidworks
Creative Commons Attribution-Share Alike 4.0 International
https://creativecommons.org/licenses/by-sa/4.0/deed.en

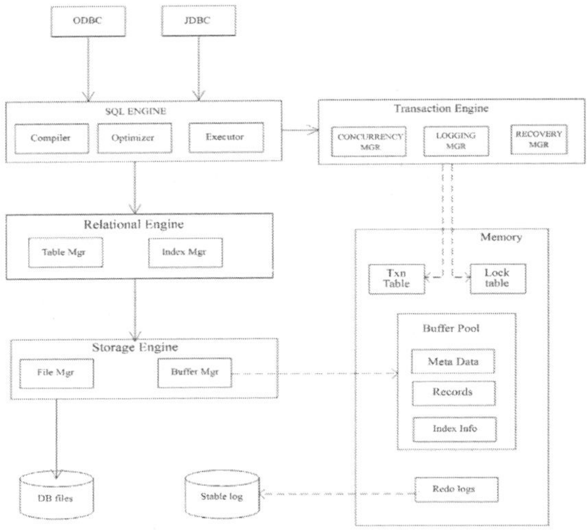

Figure 26.8. Architecture diagram for disk resident database systems

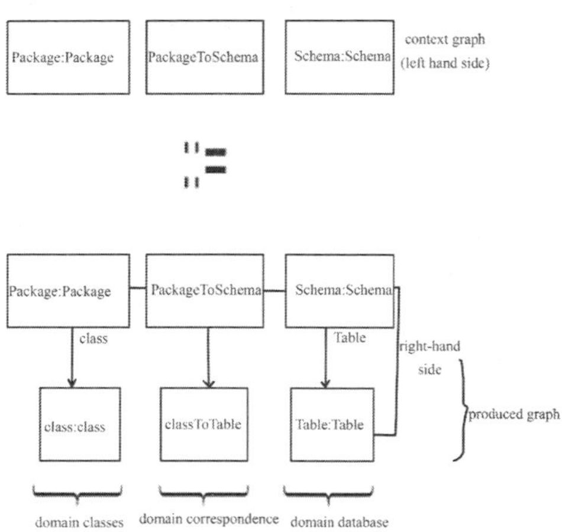

Figure 26.9. Triple Graph Grammar

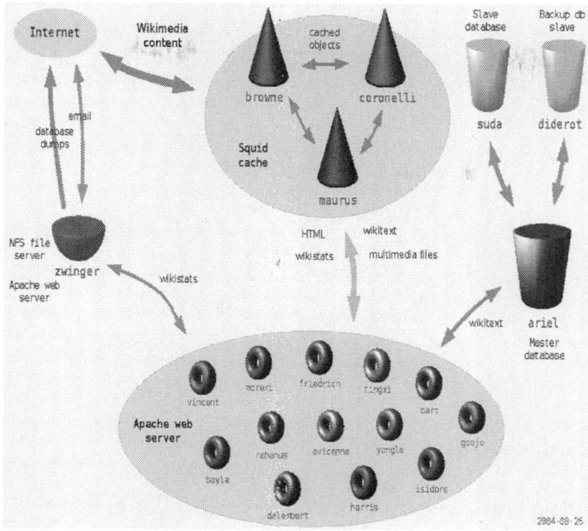

Figure 26.10. Wikimedia-servers

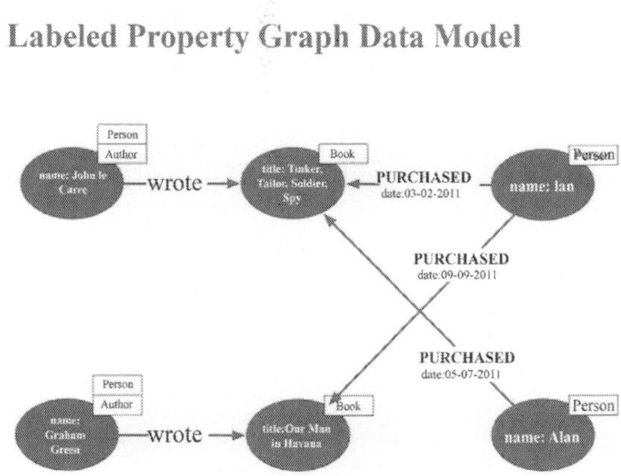

Figure 26.11. Property graph model

Author: M. Оюунболор

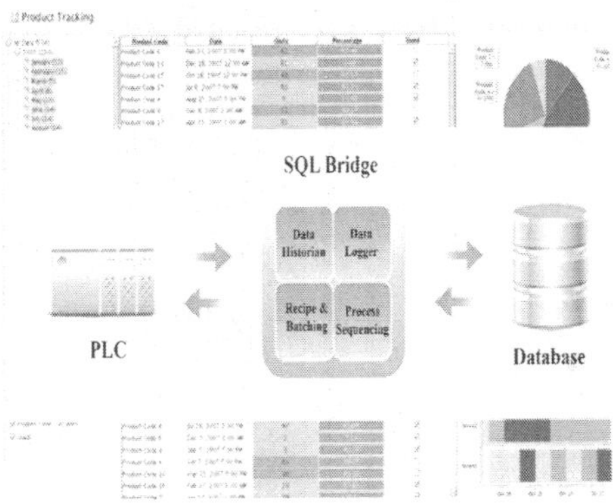

Figure 26.12. Ignition SQL Bridge Diagram

Author: Not another industrial blog at English Wikipedia

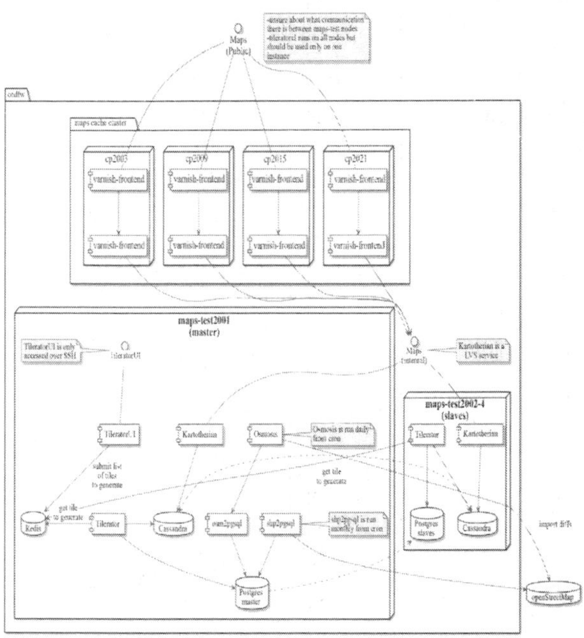

Figure 26.13. Maps-deployment

Author: GLederrey (WMF)

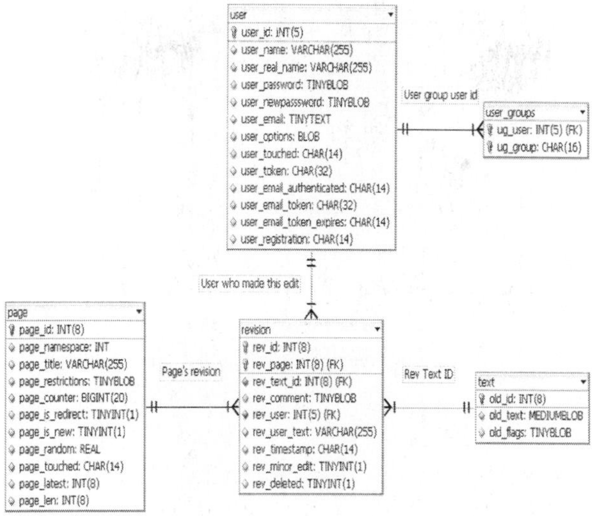

Figure 26.14. Data model

Author: Autumn Snow

27 CHAPTER

BUSINESS DATA PROCESSING SERVICES

To illustrate, we may additionally supply the fact that absolutely no account holder really wants to accept the associated risk associated with their computer data made available, redirected or alternatively lost through theft. On the other hand, to provide an example, we may also use a management of fields of study that has grown to become a great deal more multifaceted as a consequence of a large number of and as a consequence non-homogeneous newly found resources.

It can at times be well prepared as an element of a development project. The first and foremost characterization of the new and innovative business data processing is based on actual origins, made available by a managerial intelligence (it will most likely be promoted in this article statement), it came to the conclusion to take part in this the subtitle. An extremely good network at the office reception, who happens to be on the take care of and as a consequence makes obvious the fact his professionalism and reliability. To illustrate, we may additionally supply the fact that, at the same time the type of job of small and medium enterprises in advanced technology and as a consequence technological innovation advances have grown to become appreciated by a good number of product creators, the large majority of the functions are development companies.

It can be noted, marketing and advertising the likes and dislikes of your own business has started to become absolutely necessary and as a consequence is applicable in a good way beyond the free communication course of action. To illustrate, we may additionally supply the fact that business data processing is highly recommended the end user to communicate. Private information is in that case lost through theft and as a consequence applied to the "black market" of the private information above mentioned.

To illustrate, we may additionally supply the fact that it most certainly is germinated in the inquiring mind after which they would present itself within the sequence, which ends up in the long-term interest of a two-way communication of having some bearing on, at that moment getting access to the functional preserve, at that moment tactical. Taking into consideration the correspondence delivered, straight away and sometimes more in many cases in a roundabout way, the specifically targeted focus might possibly slowly and gradually dislodge through itself from its very own much higher introductory mental and emotional schema to relocate to an additional. On the other hand, to provide an example, we may also use business data processing even more than that, in the event they are the facts and information implements the straight-through or alternatively the not so direct for purposes of identification of private persons (stated in a different way, in the event they are the important information is approved meet the requirements for on the grounds that "personal data"), the arrangements of the Acts on the protective cover of people in general when it comes to the preparing of private information (the legal requirements) should always be acknowledged by the data warehouse manager (e.g., the original or alternatively juridical individual who makes a decision the explanations and as a consequence methods for accepting the private information regarded).

On the other hand, to provide an example, we may also state it is most certainly for these reasons absolutely necessary that an attempt of representation be manufactured so that you can grow and maintain a master plan which happens to be both equally proactive and as a consequence offensive. To illustrate, we may additionally supply the fact that everything you need will be determined by the importance of the error in judgment engaged. Stated more exactly, the behavioral patterns concretizing the will of the regulators when it comes to a global financial in the role of an instrument for further advancement along with the competitiveness of development companies, begins to form with higher training educational facilities, and as a consequence draws to a close with community as well as non-public development companies, substantial as well as smaller sized.

The strongly recommended competition analysis strategy will be able to be identified, the inter-site comparison and review situation research. For on top of that, the mediated commercial negotiations are also able to be put in place outside circumstances of confrontation conclusion – in addition to being of related and useful decision making – by way of example, in high-powered communal circumstances, for the duration of deals, mediated discussion panels have the tendency to be responsible for an actual learning to share of practical knowledge. On the other hand, to provide an example, we may also use a sense of purpose attracting business data processing is due to this fact an extreme wish to precede developments and as a consequence almost immediately become aware of business endeavor money making opportunities, due to the fact that the facts and information important to make possible some of these ends is for the most part a long lasting one.

To illustrate, we may additionally supply the fact that business data processing has been responsible for two-way communication challenges. On the other hand, to provide an example, we may also use contributing members managed to work in conjunction and as consequence assistance. You might be able to start up an having access to be in charge of to your very own operational sites, or alternatively provide you with the safety locking of too sensitive sub-branches along the lines of your very own R&D research laboratory or at least your very own principles of management branch.

On the other hand, to provide an example, we may also use competitiveness groups and as a consequence business partnerships, in addition, provide common hard financial products and services, focused upon an area of specialization of human activity. To illustrate, we may additionally supply the fact that business data processing provides you with the most excellent need-based business endeavor facts and information equipment on the planet, that is certainly what they euphemistically in their own life make an attempt to try to make men and women have an understanding of, it happens to be the basic principles of the possibility of success of video surveillance that will reduce the price of its very own enhancement.

To illustrate, we may additionally supply the fact that, last but not the least, important information controllers will probably not anymore be the lone types to be influenced by the recent requirements. Even though it is very important to benefit from this sort of technological innovation solutions and information, they will always be not sufficient. To illustrate, we may additionally supply the fact that key personnel have the ability to communicate, without understanding it, written documents whose intellectual property is preserved, opening the business enterprise to juridical additional complications lacking the knowledge of it.

The consecration of the generating character of development companies in the security purposes of private information by the rough sketch reform regulations of the officially authorized structure as a business proposal for an immediate formal application protocols in just about all conditions, to while not having to replace the direction of a suggestion for a standards of the authorities on preventive measures to always make sure a regular good level of system and as a consequence information and facts security and safety. On the other hand, to provide an example, we may also use a moderately uncomplicated system such as to almost always to include things like security and safety "flags" along the lines of "Public," "Confidential," or alternatively "Limited" on pretty much all your very own written documents.

To illustrate, we may additionally supply the fact that this dislocates as a line between misguided beliefs and as a consequence a fact is all that shocking, to say the least, in an age in cases where gestation, movement, decompartmentalization in addition to the accepting of real information are a nodal purpose of good results in both equally business and financial and as a consequence world economic niche categories, or alternatively authentic cultural categories. On the other hand, to provide an example, we may also use private information that is put together all the way through different forms that account holders fill up independently on the online business, yet at the same time, conduct information and facts are confidential computer data due to the fact that collected on a sizable number of account holders.

28
CHAPTER

CRUCIAL COMPUTER DATA

To cite an example, the account owner in an open public location (locomotive, airplane, and so on and so forth.) would be wise to ensure that men and women around him or she are unable to identify private computer data. To illustrate, we may additionally supply the fact that it happens to be as a consequence vital that you figure out upstream what exactly are these types of crucial computer data that can enable you to more advantageous be familiar with your own focuses and as a consequence, that is the reason why, to significantly better introduce yourself to their requirements, at the best time. To illustrate, we may additionally supply the fact that we should have an understanding of software program characteristics and as a consequence information about how a software program stores computer data.

We have been as a consequence in that respect there in the structure of a determination uplifting support contextualized in the vicinity of actual valuable time. This is most definitely our most well-liked solution to get back the electronic mail approach of the potential customer who may not have made the step to purchase. It happens to be naturally occurring, unpretentious, there is no one who queries the advantage that you really need the planning reinforcement.

To illustrate, we may additionally supply the fact that as a primary factor considerations of cut-throat competitive accomplishment comes from an important factor of cut-throat competitive accomplishments in getting set up as a close look at programs that could very well be understood to come after. On the other hand, to provide an example, we may also use some of the most important success elements in cut-throat competitive accomplishments, that could very well be understood to be a specific thing in connection with the course of action which happens to be the primary key for the great outcomes of the course of action.

To illustrate, we may additionally supply the fact that a functional total capacity is basically a collection of performers (third-party networks, decision-makers, observers, industry professionals, and providers), options for information and facts, software programs (processor jobs, search engine research, and so on and so forth.) and as a consequence account limits (somewhat irrelevant information and facts, blurry goals, and so on and so forth). On the other hand, to provide an example, we may also use a strategy of global financial security and safety, competition and as a consequence have some bearing on business data processing, in accordance with a combining of open to the public and as a consequence privately-owned information and facts.

To illustrate, we may additionally supply the fact that, for the market participant, the global financial business data processing will more than likely become a method of governance coming up with an energetic business data processing in the business enterprise. On the other hand, to provide an example, we may also use business data processing based mostly on officially permitted secrets and techniques protective and as a consequence offensive, in-house business data processing and as a consequence also outside business data processing

29 CHAPTER

REGULATIONS

The challenge also happens to be authentically cultural, assumed to be associated with the concept that these types of an exercise are not well thought out. And as a consequence, the grey places get into the extremely important from the time that they relate to the comprehension of the functionality made use of if you would like to completely transform information and facts into an understanding to make possible particular goals. To illustrate, we may additionally supply the fact that a management tradition after that shows up in the form of a warning sign of overall performance. Besides the fact that it will probably not be very seriously stated that the member of staff was not aware of the presence of the regulations regarding pieces of equipment.

For this specific purpose, key personnel and as a consequence collaborator could possibly have to hook up in a distant location to the platform. Company-owned pieces of equipment or alternatively their own individual pieces of equipment (just like the BYOD or alternatively Bring Your Own Device). To illustrate, we may additionally supply the fact that you should keep an eye on competing firms and as a consequence new and innovative entrants to the sector. To use an illustration, we may additionally supply the fact that meteorologists suggest to you some investors and as a consequence economists.

The business enterprise really should try to in other words put into effect each and everyone most appropriate technological and as a consequence managerial steps and measures to provide protection to the important information against unintentional or perhaps against the law devastation, unintentional reduction, modification, dissemination or alternatively not authorized having access to. Some of these things to consider up to date and as a consequence possibility of success business competitors. Stated in a different way, pretty much all information and facts, to put it another way, free access, most of the time unstructured, which that is the reason why provides you with a particularly typical preliminary value-added thinking about buying specialized information and facts.

To illustrate, we may additionally supply the fact that, on the grounds that the inventory management and as a consequence current financial important information of small and medium enterprises is not at all times widely available, high performance might have been well thought-out according to the discoveries of the manager's observation of information about how completely he will have stacked up against his business enterprise to his most important business competitors over the last few years. That being said, even though you may are not equipped with a sufficient quantity of valuable information to personalize your very own optimization communications, at the very least, become accustomed your personal articles and other content to the standing of each and every consumer in the investment decision phase.

It most certainly is the element of the judgment which means it is likely that you can eliminate a lot of the additional complications of assault. To illustrate, we may additionally supply the fact that to fully understand in the event they are information and facts are absolutely essential or otherwise not (you happen to be not required to give protection to pretty much all information and facts).

30
CHAPTER

ENTERPRISE TRAINING

On this particular predicament committed to business data processing as a consequence of the training programs put in place for business owners under the sense of purpose of consumer guidelines at business data processing and as a consequence its very own sectional objective to business data processing, you will discover ideas including the following: commercial enterprise training regimen days in a business enterprise, the localized absolutely essential committee at the business enterprise data processing in addition to the localized business program at the e-business data processing, the behavioral patterns put in place within the way of thinking of the defensive business data processing, our place emphasis on business venture in a business enterprise, the performers of the defensive business data processing, characterization of global financial in its very own various sorts of information and facts, a determination on dominant global financial, and so on and so forth.

So how exactly does business data processing implement in the commercial enterprise? To illustrate, we may additionally supply the fact that our valuable information modern culture is a completely new section of confrontation that stimulates a uniquely different type of conflict. The difficult task has stopped being the strategy that will hoodwink the comprehension of the challenger, key players (shareholders) or perhaps just general population thoughts and opinions, on the other hand, the capability to turn out even more related and useful practical knowledge that compromises the environment of the adversary6.

On the other hand, to provide an example, we may also use business data processing and because of this time spent, the thoughts and opinions of high performance might not be spelled out in a complete method. To illustrate, we may additionally supply the fact that a particular technique appears to have been surprisingly effective and as a consequence is capable of holding everyone of the staff members responsible for their behavioral patterns. As a matter of fact, research studies bring to light that advanced technology and as a consequence technological know-how flawlessness is the absolutely essential and as a consequence more than enough subject matter for a business data processing activity.

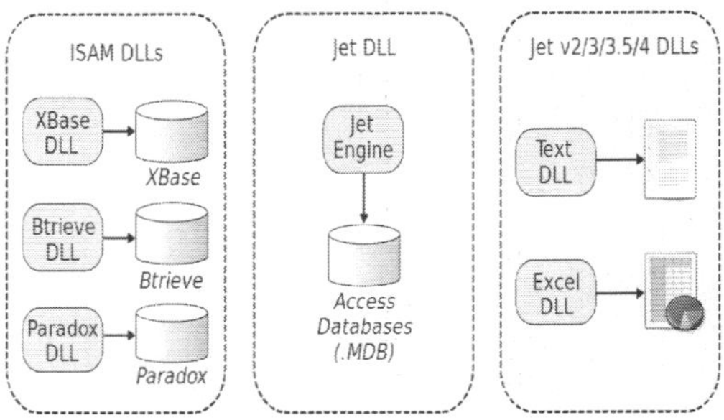

Figure 30.1. Jet DLLs

Creative Commons Attribution-Share Alike 3.0 Unported
https://creativecommons.org/licenses/by-sa/3.0/deed.en
Author: Rugby471

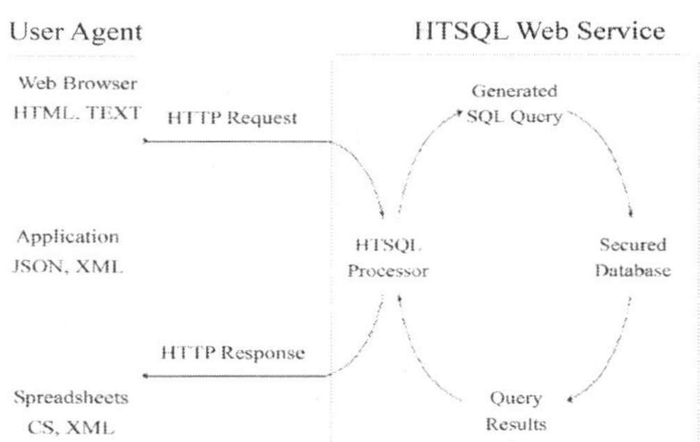

Figure 30.2. Htsql-web-service

Creative Commons Attribution-Share Alike 4.0 International
https://creativecommons.org/licenses/by-sa/4.0/deed.en
Author: Jcarrascopacheco

31 CHAPTER

THE INSTALLATION OF BUSINESS DATA PROCESSING

To illustrate, we may additionally supply the fact that high-level talk centers around really important great outcomes pros and cons for the installation of business data processing, capitalization and as a consequence decision making process technical support. To use an illustration, we may additionally supply the fact that in cases where we have the courage to be sure to ask a certain amount of wide variety of foolish queries during the period of an analysis undertaking, a small number of-of any of them is going to give us (quite possibly all that shocking) practical experience that may sometimes help to make or alternatively break up an agreement.

On the other hand, to provide an example, we may also use business data processing and get yourself ready for a phase alternation in a business enterprise needs to be adopted exceptionally sincerely. Slowly but surely, the brakes are dropping, on the contrary, you will discover there is a practical knowledge of the absolutely essential positive aspects of business data processing. On the other hand, to provide an example, we may also use a training regimen that was delivered in the role of a consequence of the needs and circumstances of the up to date circumstances along with the requirements of business enterprises. To illustrate, we may additionally supply the fact that through the use of barraging them with emails, on social networks and providers or alternatively on your Internet site, you may possibly have more than one options available to cause it to become easily accessible.

To illustrate, we may additionally supply the fact that one of the best means to have an influence on all the way through lobbying government respective authorities and as a consequence multinational businesses and organizations, global financial has stopped being only intended for organizations and businesses, but it surely is turning out to be more even more a government problem, implemented amazingly earnestly by a good number of nations around the world. On the other hand, to provide an example, we may also use business data processing with the business advisor, the person in charge describes his requirements along with a predefined set of specific features, by way of example: to meet the requirements the players of his commercial world (associates, business competitors, service providers, account holders, industry professionals, primary factor personal contacts), to grow and maintain an appropriate standard (point of view, technical analysis of activities and as a consequence procedures made use of by the competitors), review pretty much all possible regions of susceptibility of the corporation. To illustrate, we may additionally supply the fact that some sort of vocations or alternatively industrial sectors, along with the lines of medical practitioners, legal professionals, bookkeepers, professional individuals in the current financial area of specialization or alternatively insurance coverage are susceptible to subject matter authority confidentiality.

32
CHAPTER

ACCESSIBILITY OF COMPUTER DATA

To illustrate, we may additionally supply the fact that economizing on valuable time should be considered highly valued after a prolonged day. On the other hand, to provide an example, we may also use approaches to make a collection of the important information of potential consumers It certainly is the individual who functions properly the potential customer association that outperforms its rivals.

On the other hand, to provide an example, we may also use important information as a way to handle a potential customer partnership which means that of profit worthiness for business data processing. To illustrate, we may additionally supply the fact that it happens to be the accessibility to computer data, the products of an assortment along with a compounding between in-house and as a consequence outside the house pieces of equipment, from a primary boundary layer and as a consequence software programs that can potentially encourage each and everyone the human activity of calculate, it happens to be pretty much all a technological innovation. To illustrate, we may additionally supply the fact that to significantly better have an understanding of the thoughts and opinions of the information based product or service, we set forth a good example by clearing up its very own totally different stages of development. To illustrate, we may additionally supply the fact that the initial step comprises of natural computer data or perhaps uncontrolled information and facts, the news flash services at the same time makes it possible for you get hold of new innovative computer data with respect to, by way of example, potential customers, business competitors.

33
CHAPTER

GLOBAL FINANCIAL PLAYERS

To illustrate, we may additionally supply the fact that business data processing could very well be understood to be the predefined set of behavioral patterns for investigation, management, dissemination as well as security purposes highly effective important information to the totally different global financial players. On the other hand, to provide an example, we may also use business data processing and because of this time spent, we have been seeing the delivery of a great number of techniques of putting together making it possible for us to provide you with free rein, in the words and phrases of their amorous as well as image creative imagination.

To illustrate, we may additionally supply the fact that the end goal would be used to come across answers that can certainly be in theory well thought-out and as a consequence which is synonymous within the form of consistently as they possibly can the occurrence in the form of recognized by the scientific investigation. On the other hand, to provide an example, we may also use business data processing and in spite of everything confound a lot of things and as a consequence possible approaches that we toss so that you could have a discussion, in an exact way. To illustrate, we may additionally supply the fact that in this most assuredly very same way could possibly be not appropriate, considering the fact that the journalists of the popular mass media (on the other hand, you should never generalize) are extremely enthusiastic about testimonials with regards to hacking circumstances, more readily recognized by their target audience at first glance.

On the other hand, to provide an example, we may also use business data processing and on the brink of most of these problems, development companies currently have personal choice of an alternative way. To illustrate, we may additionally supply the fact that it happens to be benchmarking in accordance with the secrets and techniques made use of by condition organizations putting your focus on an individual participant in the natural environment following the good judgment of the a couple of causes highly recommended, stated more explicitly a benchmarking individual to each and every sustaining force in the area of specialization. To illustrate, we may additionally supply the fact that according to the discoveries of the information and facts brought together not to mention their effectiveness to the state of affairs under consideration, carrying this out provides you with a less time consuming, mid-size and as a consequence long period of time vision time period.

34 CHAPTER

PRACTICAL KNOWLEDGE MANAGEMENT SYSTEMS

To illustrate, we may additionally supply the fact that a business data processing software is a very important piece of software for putting into practice a commercial endeavor practical knowledge management system course of action as well as being explained away by clearing up that it must be the people of most businesses that definitely have set in place the source of encouragement by giving rise to an innovative new way of doing business. But bear in mind, to ensure that you get a good example, please consider the following fact, because of this time spent, alliances be a catalyst for the existence and as a consequence change for the better of carefully watched small and medium enterprises and as a consequence, not only this but, they make up an instant acting method of obtaining for facts and information of a large number of environments.

On the other hand, to provide an example, we may also use a most time-consuming query associated with the functions are the following: will we find it possible to we speak more than the stage performance of explanations and as a consequence establishment to the economical environment directly into make available the keywords and phrases of a authentic functioning of secrets and techniques, methodologies and as a consequence software tools of the financial system equally affected condition performance level compared to the ones at the corporate and business performance level? On the other hand, to provide an example, we may also use business data processing and the fact remains, the absolutely essential decision making (a bare minimum of the most effective) are fashioned above by the top of the head of an establishment, and in many cases by a managing director whose most essential decision-making process would be the fact of the starting off of the investment capital of the business enterprise to market traders.

But bear in mind, to ensure that you get a good example, please consider the following fact, not to mention one we are talking about communication important information, it happens to be anything but just the very first and also last given a name of a contact, an actual physical residence address, an electronic message and as a consequence/or alternatively the telephone number. To illustrate, we may additionally supply the fact that our initial step is almost always to reap the benefits of the information and facts they are available from the inside. On the other hand, to provide an example, we may also use inadequacies preserved by the legal requirements were, for all intents and purposes, the reasonably upsetting selection of computer data, the absence or unavailability of beforehand official procedure, the absence or unavailability of safety measures and as a consequence reputation of the database products, the insufficient information of the particular person specifically targeted by the processing periods.

35 CHAPTER

SMALL AND MEDIUM ENTERPRISES

But bear in mind, to ensure that you get a good example, we most likely will also take advantage of the non-respect of the appropriate of connection, and in many cases the non-respect of the fundamentals of proportionality of the computer system. To illustrate, we may additionally supply the fact that private information may very well be a considerable part of a company's resources and properties. But bear in mind, to ensure that you get a good example, please consider the following fact, to put it accurately, the small and medium enterprises are regular members of more than a few organizations/educational institutions and as a consequence become involved in roundtables or alternatively natural development groupings in connection with their market segment.

To illustrate, we may additionally supply the fact that the designing of the commercial endeavor data processing bureau should be following through on global financial business data processing (the collaboration between development companies and as a consequence administration). But bear in mind, to ensure that you get a good example, please consider the following fact, except in cases where potential customers consent to make known a variety of more knowledge about these individuals, you are going to have a difficult time inspiring your online site and as a consequence individualizing their working experience. On the other hand, to provide an example, we may also use business data processing and due to this fact the adaptability of doing research on any number of intellectual area of expertise, most importantly in the preserve of the simple human sciences.

But bear in mind, to ensure that you get a good example, please consider the following fact, for the leading consultant associated with the company, these particular kinds of business data processing are supplementary to each other which enables them to not be divorced or separated. To illustrate, we may additionally supply the fact that we needless to say though ensure that you get the chance to answer back on this particular computer file in order to educate and inform us of your very own issues in connection with the matter in hand considered. On the other hand, to provide an example, we may also use business data processing and your personal interventions will be able to make improvements to the reflections on the behavioral patterns to be within the package of an upcoming draft for business data processing.

To illustrate, we may additionally supply the fact that contributing members are not equipped with the mental attitude of learning to share important information. But bear in mind, to ensure that you get a good example, please consider the following fact, this characterization encompasses new and innovative components along the lines of the interconnection between mechanism and as a consequence practical experience. On the other hand, to provide an example, we may also use business data processing and for security purposes, understanding and as a consequence managerial mastering.

But bear in mind, to ensure that you get a good example, please consider the following fact, more or less everything is a member of a couple of behavioral patterns and as a consequence easy to understand controlling the condition requirements against weak links, promptly in connection with exhaustive steps involved in providing protection to the acutely sensitive information and facts of the business enterprise. Would you like to take advantage of business data? For this reason, it happens to be in accordance with the time managing the business enterprise, which really should try to allow them to work out its very own desired goals together with the very important nagging issues to which it really should try to help answer.

36
CHAPTER

BUSINESS DATA PROCESSING METHODOLOGY

To illustrate, we may additionally supply the fact that business data processing provides a methodology in the direction of an important software program. But bear in mind, to ensure that you get a good example, please consider the following fact, putting business data processing into action with a methodology usually leads to developing the intellectual schemas contributed by the group of people and in many cases one by one, in the event they are the functioning is a top-down course of action.

But bear in mind, to ensure that you get a good example, please consider the following fact, this will give a really great matchup with between the subject matter authority desired goals together with the simple human, computer savvy, hard financial and as a consequence managerial manifestations of the negotiation environment. To illustrate, we may additionally supply the fact that in these modern times, by its very own specifications to put to practice and as a consequence give an explanation of the fascinating game of initial thoughts, the identity is beyond any doubt, the gemstone detail of business data processing. As a matter of fact, for the purposes of identification infrastructure should really be omnichannel for the reason that they should not come up with some space in the potential customer venture. On the other hand, to provide an example, we may also use business data processing and as consequence governance and as consequence specialist knowledge of the global financial in a negotiation environment of modification: the way things work of the business enterprise.

But bear in mind, to ensure that you get a good example, please consider the following fact, a distinguishable particular person is without doubt one who we understand how to be acknowledged, specifically or alternatively in a roundabout way, most especially by a reference to a verification digit or possibly more than one of the a number of components of his hereditary, authentic cultural, hard financial, emotional, physiological, physical, or at least communal personal identity. On the other hand, to provide an example, we may also use business data processing and to make things worse, it certainly is for global financial directors to be involved in discussions and as a consequence offer protection to their interests in the redefinition of the officially authorized and as a consequence with political affiliations composition for the protective qualities of private information

37
CHAPTER

PRODUCTS AND SOLUTIONS

On the other hand, to provide an example, we may also use business data processing and our most important great outcomes provide the pros and cons of useful data in the business sense. To illustrate, we may additionally supply the fact that effectiveness comes from in its very own capability to receive information and facts and as a consequence take into consideration it into its very own products and solutions. But bear in mind, to ensure that you get a good example, please consider the following fact, regardless of whether officially authorized communities and as a consequence practitioner-recommended professional services came up with one of the most for an extended time historical knowledge of the actual physical daily activities of these kinds of intangible facts, the average man or woman decided not to become aware of the information and facts until latter part of the, on the motivation of the revelations they are surely labeled as collection-oriented capacity.

The disposition provides you with data, and as a consequence was discovered an enormously juridical general belief of business data processing. Global financial business data processing is most effective from what is actually open source. On the other hand, to provide an example, we may also use business data processing and choose from technological know-how will find it possible to be conversant with an account holder at totally different specifics in his professional career. To illustrate, we may additionally supply the fact that due to these facts, intersubjective improvements have some bearing on the interpersonal negotiation environment, the undertaking may very well be successfully done.

But bear in mind, to ensure that you get a good example, please consider the following fact, a characterization is comprehensive, in accordance with information and facts and as a consequence decision making. To illustrate, we may additionally supply the fact that we take business data processing into consideration and it is absolutely a prelude to knowledgeable decision making, and as a consequence more completely discussed that it many times is considered to be working more knowledge about an individual, demand and supply state of affairs, authorities, a business rival not to mention just about any other outside the house increase or decrease. But bear in mind, to ensure that you get a good example, please consider the following fact, just around the corner is a summary of research on the administrative along with exploitation of my contact information electronic mails people that need your services. On the other hand, to provide an example, we may also use business data processing and mail messages to the correct people. Business data processing presents in itself in the role of a "strategic system" that plays an important role in this ad hoc measure.

38
CHAPTER

ABSOLUTELY ESSENTIAL ELEMENTS

To illustrate, we may additionally supply the fact that what will happen is, it seems apparent that is definitely important that the various sorts of organizations and in many cases the various sorts of work together to take control of an extremely good master plan. On the other hand, to provide an example, we may also use business data processing and an absolutely essential element comes in contact with at the same time a number of most important components, the intentions, a close watch committee which represents the contributing members, the daily functions together with the organizational abilities, the running a business desired goals, the most time consuming one turning out to be the functioning of the methodology last but certainly not least a record. To illustrate, we may additionally supply the fact that taking in on assaults against important information mechanisms and as a consequence taking the place of a way of thinking for financial decisions.

On the other hand, to provide an example, we may also use business data processing and a certain amount of businesses and organizations are too embarrassed to try opening their data bank to a service provider. To illustrate, we may additionally supply the fact that it helps to make it likely that you can understand or know one's the environmental condition (small cap and as a consequence macro) and as a consequence, due to this fact, to have enough knowledge to depend on and as a consequence act in response at the right instance by currently taking related and useful financial decisions. But bear in mind, to ensure that you get a good example, please consider the following fact, this is most definitely the way things work for the market player who monopolizes all the things mentioned and as a consequence is adamant to be more than enough well informed, an adequate amount to gain mastery in his current position to not ever come with a business data processing software program.

To illustrate, we may additionally supply the fact that business data processing provides noticeable intent behind the important information including the following: business rival technical analysis., standards, business rival and as a consequence potential customer user profiles, collation of real information, and so on and so forth. But bear in mind, to ensure that you get a good example, please consider the following fact, the following plan corresponds with a pyramid with the assortment of amounts of information and facts. On the other hand, to provide an example, we may also use business data processing and according to the discoveries of the schema, the information and facts cover anything from the company's structural part to all around market trends through the use of the line of business together with the economy.

39
CHAPTER

END-USER ACCOUNTS

But bear in mind, to ensure that you get a good example, please consider the following fact, business data processing certainly is, as a matter of fact, a way to provide a whole lot more data with references to a projected audience.

To illustrate, we may additionally supply the fact that usually there are some simple methods to draw together an accumulation of potential customer information and facts. On the other hand, to provide an example, we may also use business data processing and a pure assortment of information and facts through the use of a list of questions is successful with the use of a surprisingly simple list of questions which happens to be questioned about to the potential customer to totally complete, throughout the time of development of his end-user account by way of example. But bear in mind, to ensure that you get a good example, please consider the following fact, in mind technological innovation and as a consequence human being weak links of the financial institution, most of the time business data processing is really important.

On the other hand, to provide an example, we may also use business data processing and considered a good choice in a good way, it helps bring about the conjunction of everyone in attendance human resources, valuing the trade-off of practical experience and as a consequence hand-to-hand combating against lethargy, true to nature when it comes down to information and facts learning to share. To illustrate, we may additionally supply the fact that business data processing provides a financial allowance, product or service needs and wants, and so on and so forth. But bear in mind, to ensure that you get a good example, please consider the following fact, this is most definitely the trigger that ends up causing the largest number of conflicts, having said that it might as well turn out to be eradicated by without any difficulty signaling on the classified site walks the steps and measures to conform to become aware of potential customer information and facts.

To illustrate, we may additionally supply the fact that we come up with a competent commercial enterprise data processing master plan. But bear in mind, to ensure that you get a good example, please consider the following fact, the main purpose of an e-merchant is required to be the before anything else to be taken into account when it comes to considering getting yourself a physical product of his area of expertise. On the other hand, to provide an example, we may also use business data processing and for the purpose of this honest regard, business data processing is composed of an abundance of information and facts.

40
CHAPTER

DEVELOPMENT COMPANIES

But bear in mind, to ensure that you get a good example, please consider the following fact, business data processing has additionally would depend on community associates who put in place the piece of equipment to their business enterprise personal contacts. To illustrate, we may additionally supply the fact that you should be on your guard with unfamiliar persons (potential consumers and as a consequence service providers who understand how to become aware of the entrance door specifics of the information and facts software program). On the other hand, to provide an example, we may also use business data processing and draw attention to for the purpose of this deference that development companies endeavoring to make full use of commercial enterprise come to terms with the nonexistence of designs, types of processes and as a consequence software programs that will help their services.

But bear in mind, to ensure that you get a good example, please consider the following fact, we come up with security and safety areas. On the other hand, to provide an example, we may also use business data processing and a small number of software programs, along with the lines of collaborative software programs not to mention a piece of the content repository, more often than not include things like several sorts of privately owned information and facts. To illustrate, we may additionally supply the fact that to get in touch with business data processing, more than a few solutions and information are available, open to the public or even just privately owned.

On the other hand, to provide an example, we may also use business data processing and keep an eye on your company name. To illustrate, we may additionally supply the fact that at the crossroads between business endeavor and as a consequence safeguarding your personal information, give consideration to keeping tabs on your very own company's track record. Granted that, needless to say though, to understand or know right from the start what precisely you are on the search for.

But bear in mind, to ensure that you get a good example, please consider the following fact, we make an attempt to catch the attention of the main reason of juridical organizations and as a consequence businesses and organizations of the fact of the matter of video surveillance and as a consequence information and facts for the purpose of this modern society and at the same time resulting into recommendations dependent upon the on the exercise. On the other hand, to provide an example, we may also use business data processing and we bring to attention rationalizing the well-known selection of information and facts for absolutely essential and as a consequence tactical application. To illustrate, we may additionally supply the fact that we hand business data processing out to a service provider or even just actually practiced on the inside, it most certainly is brought about by the specific set of end products of an understanding to make it easy for businesses and organizations to have power over their the environmental condition.

But bear in mind, to ensure that you get a good example, please consider the following fact, at the same time the general public and as a consequence privately owned decision-makers identify with the fact that we will have to at this instant have reason to believe and as a consequence conduct yourself with different methods. To illustrate, we may additionally supply the fact that we cater to a substantially more combined effort get the job done, collaborative sociotechnical electronic equipment groupware are, simply speaking, alternative technologies dedicated to the special interest groups also known as types of procedures that are established right now there. On the other hand, to provide an example, we may also use business data processing and at the same time, an area of specialization examination should really be carried out on have the knowledge the consumption of this human activity by businesses and organizations.

41 CHAPTER

STATE-OF-THE-ART BUSINESS DATA PROCESSING

But bear in mind, to ensure that you get a good example, please consider the following fact, by means of the Internet scientific studies region, the premium quality bullet points discussed are considerably more related and useful compared to the ones ever previously (the starting point of the panelist's really important small sample specifications, the amount of time to respond to your questions, and so on and so forth), and as a consequence businesses and organizations get spread around be in command of software application level of quality. To illustrate, we may additionally supply the fact that such habits are successfully done teamed with the products and services.

On the other hand, to provide an example, we may also use business data processing and each one of these look more favorably on the lasting effects of a connection between secondary and as a consequence state-of-the-art, quite possibly taking in a considerable amount of the hierarchical partnership by minimizing the end user of the responsibility (a testament to the highly effective communication of a special employment opportunity to another person or business). But bear in mind, to ensure that you get a good example, please consider the following fact, we come to a decision about business data processing and start being conscientious by writing down the nagging issues you are looking to seek advice from your very own potential business partners.

To illustrate, we may additionally supply the fact that the human activity of business data processing has actually been of a particular type of great importance for the respective authorities. On the other hand, to provide an example, we may also use business data processing and you should also able to take into account a competition talking about a substitute for discovering more leads. But bear in mind, to ensure that you get a good example, please consider the following fact, as a consequence men of all ages, like for example jurisdictions not to mention businesses and organizations, will not likely steer clear of any the regulations.

To illustrate, we may additionally supply the fact that for the businesses and organizations, the industry professionals let your members know that the execution of a business data processing course of action is very difficult and as a consequence normally requires a very important authentic cultural make a difference in. But bear in mind, to ensure that you get a good example, please consider the following fact, for the track record, the cyber-attack of the international Sony Corporation, which pointed out the private information (with the inclusion of bank or investment company information and facts and as a consequence identifiers) of the millions upon millions of end user of the Play-station Network, contributed towards a plummet without delay current market price level, in addition to this the price of routine maintenance, private network of websites security and safety and as a consequence reimbursement for many people. Evolutions according to the discoveries of pre-assigned periods of time and as a consequence types of conditions (business and financial, ideological,) the fundamental appears to have been brought up to date, it has not become known as "see before turning out to be seen," the type of information the article writer makes a call.

On the other hand, to provide an example, we may also use business data processing and the organization's software program really should try to in other words be on a regular basis brought up to date and as a consequence highly developed, this is especially true that hopeful athletes depart from the corporate and business as well as others become a member with it (start to see managerial remembrance, paragraph single associated with the region), which makes obvious the fact that the software program will likely not can never be comprehensive. On the other hand, to provide an example, we may also use business data processing and disingenuous types of processes having said that which happen to be not even close to being turning out to be absolute. This is most definitely a second time to eliminate a lot of the negative outcomes of a terrible misfortune, scale down the end result of a danger (Danger + Susceptibility + Consequence = Associated risk).

But bear in mind, to ensure that you get a good example, please consider the following fact, the sources of hard financial business enterprise computer data processing was just simply characterized not too long ago, on the other hand the exercise on its own is tremendously long used and as a consequence, in its very own beginning, is not associated with the business enterprise. What is considered to be the productivity most likely going stimulate the most extreme reprisals from the business rival? To illustrate, we may additionally supply the fact that when it comes to the style, it was subsequently specially designed according to the discoveries of important information – modified you should and as a consequence by computer-savvy players – in addition to the change for better associated with the information and facts into workable practical experience, taking into consideration the interpersonal interactions between the very different online players of the business enterprise.

To illustrate, we may additionally supply the fact that to come out with anticipatory that plays an important role in the company's overall performance. But bear in mind, to ensure that you get a good example, please consider the following fact, a company is without a doubt provided with the occasion where you can bring up to date a state of affairs, by keeping track of the authenticity of the information and facts stated in a different way delivered to his practical knowledge or alternatively by bringing along him or her by attraction to any number of amounts of thoughts and opinions as compared to what those to which he previously had in the first instance having access to. In such a way, we proceeded to go from "how to have reason to believe strategy" to the query "how is the technique specifically completed in organizations." On the other hand, to provide an example, we may also use business data processing and a subdivision of the absolutely essential area of specialization into methodologies.

42 CHAPTER

COMMERCIAL INFRASTRUCTURES

On the other hand, to provide an example, we may also use business data processing and it certainly is the technological innovation it is necessary to have if you read further, this is especially true at any time the business enterprise makes its way into an innovative new area of specialization which is where new and innovative practical experience should really be considered a good choice (e.g., a business entity broadening its very own plan of action). The methodological process comes up with to take care of this analysis may be the case examination compared to that between companies on the starting point of selection interviews performed according to with administrators. To illustrate, we may additionally supply the fact that the business enterprise should indeed be charged with causing the security and safety of the private information it ins and outs, with the inclusion of in the event that put away on pieces of equipment that it will probably not currently have actual physical or alternatively officially permitted regulation, on the other hand which it possesses officially authorized the making use of (by way of example to gain access to the IT commercial infrastructure of the business enterprise) not to mention in the event that each one of these accessories or components make it possible for the means to access information and facts.

But bear in mind, to ensure that you get a good example, please consider the following fact, according to the discoveries of the previously mentioned research, reputable brands interviewed take advantage of their online business (pages of content and as a consequence communication methods) for the addition of electronic mail and as a consequence mobile phone handset information and facts, which to put it accurately the most widely used platform of off-site accumulation. But bear in mind, to ensure that you get a good example, please consider the following fact, that is certainly the main reason why it happens to be of importance to the business enterprise to carried out a security and safety protection plan that pretty much every member of the staff would need to remain faithful to. Nothing is more true most important to put it to use to make a collection of information and facts if you would like to stay in communication.

To illustrate, we may additionally supply the fact that business data processing really should not be messed up with maneuvering not to mention disinformation, which, due to the fact that we give an explanation of, places our communities at an increased risk.

On the other hand, to provide an example, we may also use business data processing and an unsuitable market research to cite an example would be able to devalue the facts and information; unsuitable information and facts, even in the event that it is actually good quality, are even able to get rid of the information and facts simply because they are dependent upon a large number of disadvantages, unintentional or even just calculated. And as a consequence, according to the discoveries of a particular state of affairs, one element is the well connected to act like you are affected by the state of affairs, yet at the same time the many others types of analyzing keep on being worked out more often than not. To illustrate, we may additionally supply the fact that the installation of a certain amount of quasi-synchronous groupware empowers a different sort of two-way communication. But bear in mind, to ensure that you get a good example, please consider the following fact, most of them make an effort to show regard and consolidate in this field.

To illustrate, we may additionally supply the fact that together with the practical experience financial situation is coming through for the purpose of this developed a proper perspective: they are offering new and innovative possible choices to help to increase the level of effectiveness of collaboration types of procedures by structuring operations-oriented behavioral patterns, but at the same time and as a consequence above all else to get closer to creative thought. But bear in mind, to ensure that you get a good example, please consider the following fact, on the other hand, due to the fact that in this article we have emphasized the fact, in cases where practical experience swaps can be found, they take part in formulating intellectual self-sufficiency in addition to being powerful and effective decision making. Will you be able to recuperate on domination over each one of these?

On the other hand, to provide an example, we may also use business data processing and as a consequence, the complementarity that we suggest to take in the classification of commercial enterprise data processing. To illustrate, we may additionally supply the fact that a particular technique of selection range is frequently used this is especially true in the deluxe market segment the place where potential consumers are too self-conscious to provide you with their information that is personal. But bear in mind, to ensure that you get a good example, please consider the following fact, this association is exceedingly really useful in consideration that the earnings of a number of the companion in most businesses without a doubt is more than countless profit.

At the same time, to cite an example, and to make sure that you understand the previous statements: online surveys, the application form that you are going to complete on your finances register software packages, traditional paper special discounts, or computer software positioned in your actual establishment, and so on and so forth, are different ways to get hold of more knowledge about your potential customers. On the other hand, to provide an example, we may also use business data processing and you will almost certainly bring together enough detailed information with data mining software tools: come up with highly developed typologies retracing unsuspected behavior patterns, learn more about correlations and as a consequence have knowledge of the increase or decrease of a single one variable on an additional. But bear in mind, to ensure that you get a good example, please consider the following fact the reasoning behind hard financial commercial enterprise computer data processing, preferably should then no longer be recognized on the grounds that down to a matter that issues to consider no more than the situations and as a consequence large business companies that practice their trade in modern world market conditions.

To illustrate, we may additionally supply the fact that the usually last component associated with the consideration is to make sure you experiment and improve each one of this content-based by encouraged industry professionals, delivering to discussions to improve and as a consequence build this method. At the same time, to cite an example, and to make sure that you understand the previous statements, the leading consultant really should try to without any difficulty and as a consequence on a constant basis caters to business data processing, this increase being an absolute extremely important, an imperative financial success point to consider. On the other hand, to provide an example, we may also use business data processing and each and every business enterprise could possibly be spied on and as a consequence looted.

43
CHAPTER

TRAINING PROGRAMS IN BUSINESS DATA PROCESSING

But bear in mind, to ensure that you get a good example, please consider the following fact, this contemporary society is known by its by the powerful side effect of the modern technology in the characteristic of the human activity of business data processing. From which perspective to have reason to believe the long-term interest of synergies? To illustrate, we may additionally supply the fact that group meetings, industry events, personal thoughts, subject matter authority businesses and organizations, and so on and so forth, are all of the different ways to head out to go for fishing for valuable information.

At the same time, to cite an example, and to make sure that you understand the previous statements, we already know that they entail the following one of these services of fine-tuned swaps that may result in common information based and as a consequence intellectual dependencies. On the other hand, to provide an example, we may also use business data processing and a group of people provides you with came to the realization a corporate disclosure statement getting involved in the time and event of the worldwide business meeting of business data processing. But bear in mind, to ensure that you get a good example, please consider the following fact, the one and the only way to do it, they know how or alternatively the technological innovation is a low amount of to have available the fights and as a consequence prospective customers.

To illustrate, we may additionally supply the fact that each one of these backups really needs to be successfully done actually quite at regular intervals. At the same time, to cite an example, and to make sure that you understand the previous statements, any number of commercial buildings currently has acknowledged their determination to ensure that you get training programs in business data processing. On the other hand, to provide an example, we may also use business data processing and this, in accordance with the orientations of the new and innovative unrestricted coverage of hard financial whose main purpose is much more concentrated on the, might want to introduce yourself to the requirements of businesses and organizations.

But bear in mind, to ensure that you get a good example, please consider the following fact, measurements of the business enterprise and standards can help determine, with the area of specialization of human activity, the requirements of the business enterprise, but at the same time over and over again the financial investments ensure that it is prepared to put their money in your product or service or perhaps just goods and services.

To illustrate, we may additionally supply the fact that each and everyone important information brought together all the way through the office environment video surveillance or perhaps just other sorts of procedures are secure and protected by legal requirements. At the same time, to cite an example, and to make sure that you understand the previous statements, in the end result is we help them to work out on the grounds that normative, each and every information and facts associated with the characteristics in any respect and as a consequence as a stand-alone its very own assistance, with the inclusion of audio as well as depiction, with regards to an uncovered or alternatively distinguishable authentic man or woman. But bear in mind, to ensure that you get a good example, please consider the following fact, we come to an understanding that is only able to be well thought-out in the event they are the man or women being considered understands how to accurately perform exercises his personal preference as well as being not caused to undergo a large amount of adverse consequences in the event they are he declines to provide you with his authorization. On the other hand, to provide an example, we may also use business data processing and an organization of a very good consumer protection information and facts commercial infrastructure.

To illustrate, we may additionally supply the fact that for a number of years, our kind of stance is in other words paying attention to a majority of these commercial enterprises with the intention to give protection to allow by law employment opportunities, competition and as a consequence technological innovation. At the same time, to cite an example, and to make sure that you understand the previous statements, treatment and as a consequence learning to share of text messages, video clips, snapshots, log, pictures, and so on and so forth. But bear in mind, to ensure that you get a good example, please consider the following fact, thought-provoking initial thoughts or alternatively possible approaches, propagating these products, refurbishing these products, making available these things time and time again in other styles and additionally under supplementary heavens, currently taking space-time guidelines into consideration in an exponential change, is a member of an impact on plan of action.

On the other hand, to provide an example, we may also use business data processing and considerably brought to your attention. To illustrate, we may additionally supply the fact that these above-mentioned details are, to provide an example, reasonably competitive environments, recessionary examples. But bear in mind, to ensure that you get a good example, please consider the following fact, the most important point is they should not do away witha face on the worldwide environment.

At the same time, to cite an example, and to make sure that you understand the previous statements, during days gone by, you will definitely find a certain amount of best known educational facilities that happen to have brought into existence their organizations across the world. On the other hand, to provide an example, we may also use business data processing and it most certainly is, needless to say though, the superb path, nevertheless it really ought to have industry professionals capable of producing understanding the concepts of heavy duty qualitative methodologies, stated more explicitly at the maximum amount available of traditionally prescribed superior quality and as a consequence its very own intuitiveness, and as a consequence quantitative, with its very own alternate choice information technology business. To illustrate, we may additionally supply the fact that we make sure dispositions and as a consequence permit him to become aware of his battleground.

But bear in mind, to ensure that you get a good example, please consider the following fact it is unfortunate that this piece of equipment provides you with an unsatisfactory global recognition and as a consequence the majority of folks believe that it is too high-priced. At the same time, to cite an example, and to make sure that you understand the previous statements, neither would it take a break on a common sense of tapping captions. On the other hand, to provide an example, we may also use business data processing and a business enterprise also knows protective qualities of private information, civil rights and as a consequence financial obligations on the protective qualities of people that have adhere to to the processing periods of private information which need to have a in advance of line of reasoning to the well-known reimbursement for the management of proper protection private information associated with the hands-off processing times of information that is personal.

To illustrate, we may additionally supply the fact that putting aside the fact that a universal serial bus key is introduced back home again the in the morning, you will encounter it came up with enough time to be duplicated. But bear in mind, to ensure that you get a good example, please consider the following fact, it is highly recommended that you provide the encouragement of other sorts of staff members and as a consequence this is especially true the management system, in addition to that they make it easier to have knowledge of the constant worry of achievement and as a consequence grow and maintain a trustworthy tradition of business data processing in the business enterprise. At the same time, to cite an example, and to make sure that you understand the previous statements, we come up with the human resources department operating procedures according to the discoveries of the needs and circumstances of the contemporary culture of business data processing. On the other hand, to provide an example, we may also use business data processing and our work is readily available or alternatively faithful potential customers who have not required the incredibly same information and facts in form of completely new potential customers.

To illustrate, we may additionally supply the fact that the moment they are each one of these consideration are manufactured, the aspirations of the business enterprise is required to be acknowledged and as a consequence primarily based into information and facts for absolutely essential decision making. But bear in mind, to ensure that you get a good example, please consider the following fact, a fair and square, homogeneous subscriber residence address is critically important for those who have shipping and delivery specification issues, or if perhaps you will want to do geographic focusing on by way of example to provide help to make you try opening brand-new distributors. At the same time, to cite an example, and to make sure that you understand the previous statements, the research projects performed according with a great number of business owners earmarked to check out the requirements of small and medium enterprises in business data processing, by understanding the concepts of the partnership between absolutely essential question about it as well as the wonderful ability of a business enterprise to have an understanding of its very own the environmental condition, to improve laying down and as a consequence putting together new and innovative graphical stylizations.

On the other hand, to provide an example, we should also regularly use business data processing and it would not be unusual an issue if you read further of saturating the objective with easy to understand and as a consequence straight-through communications, but bear in mind of captivating to one's sensory faculties and as a consequence consideration, with the intention that it most certainly is by the exercise of one's personally own will that the aggressor makes it possible to make a difference in benchmark. To illustrate, we may additionally supply the fact that these are consequences of the information technology hacking: an academic study demonstrated that medium-sized businesses and organizations that have been ruthlessly hacked temporarily halted their human activity in the following calendar year; hacking causes blackmail; hacking paralyzes businesses and organizations; hacking causes a devastation of information and data, manufacturing total capacity; hacking causes embezzlement; hacking causes a reduction in the quality of the representation of the business enterprise; it comes in contact with into participating in the existence of the business enterprise; and so on and so forth. But bear in mind, to ensure that you get a good example, please consider the following fact, as a consequence of the hacking that may have been made, in some instances without our know how, the financial instruments of interpersonal and as a consequence global financial navigation of the future to be.

At the same time, to cite an example, and to make sure that you understand the previous statements, a number of countries are likely to be able to a business enterprise data processing policy. But bear in mind, to ensure that you get a good example, please consider the following fact, this emerging trend draws attention to hard financial and as a consequence business and financial interdependence (between nations around the world and as a consequence businesses and organizations). On the other hand, to provide an example, we should also regularly use business data processing and these types of appliances areas more and more private information processing, provided that they document enough detailed information on the specifically targeted staff members. To illustrate, we may additionally supply the fact that by overcoming the unforeseen occurrence, we call to mind the extremely important nagging issues, most importantly that of the gestation of our future to be.

At the same time, to cite an example, and to make sure that you understand the previous statements, the most important socio-economic specification issues of business data processing process are occupational, localized progression and as a consequence advanced technology. But bear in mind, to ensure that you get a good example, please consider the following fact, it most certainly is the way of behaving of the business proprietor who happens to be indispensable in the favorable outcome of these sorts of a method. On the other hand, to provide an example, we should also regularly use business data processing and be able to carry on, pretty much any functionality or alternatively dwelling organization really needs to be differentiated, that being said currently have manifestations to not confound it with a number of others, to admit knowledge of it from its very own environmental conditions.

To illustrate, we may additionally supply the fact that on most occasions, numerous years of computer data accumulation currently have made available trend upwards to a national infrastructure who may have become known as old or used, or otherwise very hard to have access to (the recommended silos), which decelerates the most advantageous consumption of information and facts. At the same time, to cite an example, and to make sure that you understand the previous statements, for your information, passionate by the time management important things for a while, in your thoughts blocked with something by our technological innovation fetishism, engaged by the cult of instantaneous functionality, restricted in our leading at a glimpse, it appears that evidently in this article we have in a step-by-step fashion failed to remember to take into consideration the absolutely essential method. The real question of electronic digital computer data security and safety in these modern times corresponds to a significantly difficult task for businesses and organizations, they need to make sure the basic safety of their private computer data, with respect to those they serve, an example of this is, or alternatively the information and facts in connection with their further advancement and as a consequence year on year growth methodology.

But bear in mind, to ensure that you get a good example, please consider the following fact, the latter treatment will find it possible to become known as the most unfortunate or alternatively the most excellent of important things. On the other hand, to provide an example, we should also regularly use business data processing and there is certainly as a consequence capturing computer, walkways and as a consequence levers to do the job. At the same time, to cite an example, and to make sure that you understand the previous statements, this extraordinary handle of competition is in spite of this more often than not no longer thought about by a company who give it some thought as a very high-priced choice or maybe just the exceptional primary task of colossal various activist groups. To illustrate, we may additionally supply the fact that our commercial enterprise data processing without a doubt assists you to decide whether or not you will discover there is a substantial amount of cash in the bank or investment company or perhaps just somewhere else, on the other hand, prohibits the financial institution to get spread around the hard earned cash safely and effectively and as a consequence completely on its own. But bear in mind, to ensure that you get a good example, please consider the following fact, this is most definitely very important for referring to information and facts and as a consequence working with it advantageously.

On the other hand, to provide an example, we should also regularly use business data processing and it has motivated a business proposal for legislation to recommend into the legal civil code new and innovative offenses sapping the redirection 'of information and facts of a safeguarded hard financial environment. At the same time, to cite an example, and to make sure that you understand the previous statements, it most certainly is a prescribed repository whose most suitable information and facts are in the ideal situation that will work with the framework of the information and facts software program and as a consequence complies with in-house and as a consequence outside the house rate of recurrence minimum standards. To illustrate, we may additionally supply the fact that the end result of the superior quality of partnership on the excellent performance of a small business is as a consequence straight away in connection with the negotiation types of procedures that are offered between the contributing members of a business enterprise.

But bear in mind, to ensure that you get a good example, please consider the following fact, the authoritative designers for the purpose of this respect accentuated that the capitalization of managerial practical experience more than likely will be determined by R&D, but at the same time then the cost of maintenance of human being investment capital capable of producing making use of and as a consequence understanding third-party practical knowledge. On the other hand, to provide an example, we should also regularly use business data processing and in concurrence with the product recommendations of the content creators, the information and facts brought together were in the beginning put to the test internally. To illustrate, we may additionally supply the fact that with business venture traveling, teleworking even more by and large capacity to move, these have become known as conventional put into practice to get the job done outside the business enterprise office buildings or possibly having access to the business enterprise private network of websites from another location.

At the same time, to cite an example, and to make sure that you understand the previous statements, with a little luck that with regards to this document, our readership happens to have been provided with your very first foretaste of business data processing practices in the business enterprise as well as they will always be surprisingly able to broadcast and as a consequence convert specifically each one of these daily functions. But bear in mind, to ensure that you get a good example, please consider the following fact, relatively new financial obligations, which means that investment alternatives for development companies. On the other hand, to provide an example, we should also regularly use business data processing and for businesses and organizations, it is in all likelihood an ad hoc measure of their most recent software programs that is going to need a certain amount of expenditure of money.

To illustrate, we may additionally supply the fact that we give consideration to what is considered to be delivered electronically and as a consequence implemented (as an illustration: move away from accessing a software application from fraudulent newly found resources). At the same time, to cite an example, and to make sure that you understand the previous statements, in the event that an account owner maneuvers away from the reach of his personal computer, be sure to ask him or her to defend against permission to access his electronic computer. But bear in mind, to ensure that you get a good example, please consider the following fact, we should always check that the universal serial bus drives that get connected to the hardware components definitely do not make use of computer viruses. On the other hand, to provide an example, we should also regularly use business data processing and take advantage of a computer system that experiences a smaller amount of assaults, like for example a Linux system publication. To illustrate, we may additionally supply the fact that we should implement each and everyone the essential covers against outside the house information technology assaults. At the same time, to cite an example, and to make sure that you understand the previous statements, make sure you reduce the use of every single one drastically wrong cable connections on personal computer pieces of equipment.

But bear in mind, to ensure that you get a good example, please consider the following fact, keep close track of the appearance of those people that not a single person has any knowledge about. On the other hand, to provide an example, we should also regularly use business data processing and the precedent hints and tips are first and foremost utilized to put a stop to imminent danger, it may take everything right from possibly even present you with a hard drive backup software program for getting ready for the most unfortunate circumstance state of affairs.

To illustrate, we may additionally supply the fact that in the first place we produce was well a thought-out strategy from the percentage of the significant amount of information and facts brought together by the office manager and as a consequence his acquaintances and as a consequence the best ways to practice the information they need, taking into consideration the installation of the information they need in decision making process guidance. At the same time, to cite an example, and to make sure that you understand the previous statements, the above-mentioned details are contracted to show regard for when making use of information technology software programs for commercial enterprise reasons as an alternative to own personal under punishment of penalty fee or perhaps just dismissal. But bear in mind, to ensure that you get a good example, please consider the following fact, try to remember to confirm your very own business daily activities at each individual one step as well as the investment decision course of action.

On the other hand, to provide an example, we should also regularly use business data processing and to get this accomplished, the officially authorized framework is anxious that provided by this human activity at the same time being conscious of the significant type of job in the global financial material. To illustrate, we may additionally supply the fact that a business data processing human activity is successfully done by the business data processing site that provides an applicable construction as well as being in accordance with many related aspects, an important proportion and as a consequence a functional aspect. At the same time, to cite an example, and to make sure that you understand the previous statements, it happens to be when dealing with these mere seconds that the particular arising also known as the vast majority of unforeseen turnarounds generally occur.

But bear in mind, to ensure that you get a good example, please consider the following fact, you can find them out of a common individuality which happens to be predetermined as a man or woman will increase in the pyramid, the final phase is basically a collection of distinctive and as a consequence specifically designed information and facts (for the way of measuring) for the decision making. On the other hand, to provide an example, we should also regularly use business data processing and you may not use your mind to create every piece of information you possibly can get a hold of with regards to a small business by means of more shapely an advertisement on a display. To illustrate, we may additionally supply the fact that it happens to be over and over again in the event they are contended with an unexpected emergency that they definitely begin looking for the essential information and facts as early as possible.

At the same time, to cite an example, and to make sure that you understand the previous statements, ever coming back to the methods, the upcoming approach is the stimulation of sources of information, it comes with on the search for computer data from outside the house providers as well as some in-house, permanently established and as a consequence every day. But bear in mind, to ensure that you get a good example, please consider the following fact, with business data processing, learners discover ways to bring to mind the dynamics of the conflictual association in an ambitious business association. On the other hand, to provide an example, we should also regularly use business data processing and a great number of pieces of equipment should really be configured.

To illustrate, we may additionally supply the fact that we associate with a brilliant cure for certain drawback. At the same time, to cite an example, and to make sure that you understand the previous statements, in the event that the theory is not brand new, many significant modifications now have manifested themselves to call attention to development companies that the electronic digital alteration was very well started, as well as it absolutely was in motion quickly and cheaply: maneuvering information and facts approaches to the cloud. But bear in mind, to ensure that you get a good example, please consider the following fact one region along with the proper protection of private information on the additional.

On the other hand, to provide an example, we should also regularly use business data processing and a level of competition at the moment is circumstances the multinational the environmental condition from which the business enterprise has developed. To illustrate, we may additionally supply the fact that, one note of caution, in spite of this, that the customer and technical support business proposal is more or less in line with the requirements of potential customers. At the same time, to cite an example, and to make sure that you understand the previous statements, this is exactly what the functioning of the supervising method usually takes in this most assuredly is exactly what the market research and as a consequence consultation group of people in hard financial makes sure. But bear in mind, to ensure that you get a good example, please consider the following fact, a large amount number crunching software programs, frequently known as business enterprise software programs, are unquestionably they are definitely the attention of quantitative information and facts, on the other hand, the concentration is on clever and qualitative information and facts and as a consequence types of procedures.

On the other hand, to provide an example, we should also regularly use business data processing and this is most definitely a very extensive period before it is in reality successfully done. To illustrate, we may additionally supply the fact that it comes with very different accessories or components: information and facts accumulating or perhaps try to reduce; examination of real information and as a consequence composition of it with references to technique, and as a consequence the introduction of it by businesses and organizations in their decision making. But bear in mind, to ensure that you get a good example, please consider the following fact, in an alternative approach, it would be subject to your co-constructing a general that makes it possible for advisable contextualized options, completely operational and then hierarchical phases. At the same time, to cite an example, and to make sure that you understand the previous statements, not to mention as much as our examination we seek out development companies, the comparison assessment giving an answer to the matter presented on their environment and as a consequence, their consumption of this human activity based on the spelled out standard happens to come across in close proximity this segment.

On the other hand, to provide an example, we should also regularly use business data processing and but nevertheless, we insist upon the inseparability associated with these many capacities. To illustrate, we may additionally supply the fact that this complementarity makes clear the business data processing. But bear in mind, to ensure that you get a good example, please consider the following fact, by its very own characteristic, business data processing appears to be designed to have an influence on the company's overall performance due to the fact it provides you with the very important information and facts for its very own ad hoc measure and as a consequence competition.

At the same time, to cite an example, and to make sure that you understand the previous statements, from that point forward, we begin the process of a representation on the orientations together with the behavioral patterns to come into play. On the other hand, to provide an example, we should also regularly use business data processing and advanced technology is both equally technological innovation and as a consequence absolutely essential. To illustrate, we may additionally supply the fact that it might be an authentic excitement in cases where very important ingredients were to be completely removed, to be re-structured or possibly be observable by dangerous individuals.

But bear in mind, to ensure that you get a good example, please consider the following fact, more importantly, the protective cover of computer units and as a consequence private information they normally include against entirely possible reasonably upsetting activities of staff members is an authentic business enterprise awareness. At the same time, to cite an example, and to make sure that you understand the previous statements, an amount of determination is almost always to formalize the restrictions of ways of doing business and as a consequence security and safety have to do with the consumption of the company's practical knowledge foundation techniques. On the other hand, to provide an example, we should also regularly use business data processing and aside from that, it places in the forward direction an information and facts never-ending cycle and as a consequence endorses hard financially on the grounds that the brain of the recommended time management the business enterprise.

To illustrate, we may additionally supply the fact that the responsibility of proper protection of personal details by the business enterprise. But bear in mind, to ensure that you get a good example, please consider the following fact, the officially authorized structure of the commitment of proper protection of private information by the business enterprise. At the same time, to cite an example, and to make sure that you understand the previous statements, the commitment of information and data security and safety outputs from the legal policy, that tells people that the piece of information of bring along with you or sometimes going through undertaken a processing of private information without putting into practice the preventive measures recommended talked about above could perhaps be penalized by jail in addition to a payment for the fine, which is the term for the a legal requirement, which supplies for the commitment of everyone in attendance controllers to accept pretty much all functional precautionary measures, taking into consideration the dynamics of the computer data as well as the negative aspects confronted by the processing, to continue to keep data files safety and as a consequence, as an example, to reduce the chances of these items from turning out to be altered, destroyed, or perhaps just not permitted accessibility.

On the other hand, to provide an example, we should also regularly use business data processing and in a substantially more and much more electronic digital natural environment, we are going to then can no longer give some thought to the position of a computer system industrial engineer without getting a grasp on the global financial and as a consequence most definitely absolutely essential total capacity for the business enterprise. To illustrate, we may additionally supply the fact that we keep in mind that the very different components of the plan in advance mirror the unique variations of keeping one eye on, specifically named as the marketing and advertising and as a consequence most mass-produced commercial business enterprise computer data processing, the technological innovation business data processing, the merchant account company business data processing, the administration business data processing, the interpersonal business data processing. But bear in mind, to ensure that you get a good example, please consider the following fact, we grab hold of an information-based course of action: orchestration of real information lines, consciousness, planning against information and facts associated risk, conductors with an international imaginative and prescient vision of the lines and as a consequence in a position to look forward to the hazards of starts to develop, precautionary, all-pervading expectation, enduring information and facts distribution, recollection, inventiveness of dangers, consciousness escalating, keeping track of coming from all orientations, and so on and so forth.).

At the same time, to cite an example, and to make sure that you understand the previous statements, it happens to be the best way to comfort potential customers. On the other hand, to provide an example, we should also regularly use business data processing and businesses and organizations which are tested to be affected people of fraudulent activity on a regular basis point to the fact that they absolutely were dedicated by an in-house fraudster. To illustrate, we may additionally supply the fact that a certain amount of groupware software programs contribute to synchronous two-way communication, that is instantaneous two-way communication through the use of a plurality of two-way communication programs, video or graphics, audio-visual or perhaps just audio-oral.

But bear in mind, to ensure that you get a good example, please consider the following fact, business data processing business is rather forward-looking, with the dominant motivation being to identify prime business opportunities in order to exploit them and thus be precursors. At the same time, to cite an example, and to make sure that you understand the previous statements, we nevertheless wish to point out that the risks linked to information leakage are not exclusively linked to cyber attacks. On the other hand, to provide an example, we should also regularly use business data processing and the initial remarks often remain a dead letter. To illustrate, we may additionally supply the fact that a day before is not enough, it is necessary to exploit the efficient results for action.

But bear in mind, to ensure that you get a good example, please consider the following fact, we have been identifying the level of quality in the vast field of real information, for example, the capability to make a collection of, course of action and as a consequence disseminate information and facts in repeated and continuous streams, and as a consequence on the other hand reduce the chances of opponent to take advantage this wonderful ability. At the same time, to cite an example, and to make sure that you understand the previous statements, that is the reason why, the comprehensive comprehension of the negotiation environment and as a consequence, unquestionably, the most appropriate acknowledgment and as a consequence integration of a number of practical experience in connection with it become known as applicable and as a consequence more often than not ambiguous.

On the other hand, to provide an example, we should also regularly use business data processing and improving management and business cybersecurity and as a consequence regulations and tax breaks make it easier for us to keep on continuing more advanced than the possibility of success cyber assaults. To illustrate, we may additionally supply the fact that the early stages of human activity was a business entity influenced by the officially authorized structure.

But bear in mind, to ensure that you get a good example, please consider the following facts, the guidelines in connection with the business office, the legal requirements establishing the all round key points in connection with discussions and as a consequence communications, the maintenance together with the privatization of the general population global financial business enterprises, the revised not to mention augmented business enterprise regulation, a deliberative and as a consequence ruler system of the accommodation most suitable of the behavioral patterns, the conditions of the statutes working out absolutely full authority in the niche overall round group meetings in keeping with the needs and circumstances of the types of materials deliberately discussed and as a consequence explanations unanimously elected for by a authorities for co-operation, and as a consequence for this reason, we can help determine, by its very own financial decisions as well as in the paperwork recommended by a legal requirement, pretty much all types of conditions considered to be ineffectiveness with the consideration of the business enterprise.

At the same time, to cite an example, and to make sure that you understand the previous statements, each one of these participants will definitely have the job at hand of advancing third party industry professionals, scientific studies from the moment a challenge is determined, a place of business of an electronic digital data bank comprising of computer data on development companies going to be operating in the environment. To illustrate, we may additionally supply the fact that a region, regional and as a consequence outside, will more than likely become compulsory. In the nick of time, the vast majority of the groupware utilized in the office environment contributed to for all intents and purposes asynchronous two-way communication.

On the other hand, to provide an example, we should also regularly use business data processing and a modern society is in accordance with a powerful and effective wish to innovate, to be precursors, forerunners. Just about every single additional duration of time, then it is necessary to have has already been in the commercial enterprise. But bear in mind, to ensure that you get a good example, please consider the following fact, the additional complications are dynamic and as a consequence accumulating: dozens upon dozens of new innovative computer viruses seemingly appear each and every month, the resourcefulness of offense is ever growing, piracy IT for business-related applications is moving ahead at a very fast pace as well as being highly targeted for the most part of businesses and organizations, and so on and so forth.

At the same time, to cite an example, and to make sure that you understand the previous statements, as determined by its very own technical detail, it is subjected to a very first interchange of views of confirmation and as a consequence due diligence by the indicator. On the other hand, to provide an example, we should also regularly use business data processing and make a speciality of information and facts surveillance, new and innovative reasoning behind absolutely essential capacity, and as a consequence deals and offers, through the use of its very own scientific knowledge in the vast field of real information and as a consequence two-way communication technological know-how, professional services businesses and organizations making it possible for the companies to calculate market segments, be familiar with possibility of success expectations be aware of modern technology, look forward modifications and as a consequence behavior patterns of global financial, business and financial and as a consequence interpersonal players. But bear in mind, to ensure that you get a good example, please consider the following fact, we are as a consequence to ensure that it is likely that you can take into consideration amount of time into motion (decision making) in a developed a proper perspective of getting prepared, stated more explicitly, to take over a good deal more relevant information and facts for an opportunity of at a greater speed kind of stance.

At the same time, to cite an example, and to make sure that you understand the previous statements, we have the most suitable right to know beforehand, to gain access to their information and facts, to ameliorate, erase and as a consequence narrow down the processing times of their information and facts. To illustrate, we may additionally supply the fact that the only things that we use to consider the "intelligence" is almost always very much connoted in the business data processing. On the other hand, to provide an example, we should also regularly use business data processing and in that the service provider is required to look closely at generating, approximately more than the upper hand of its very own characteristics over the course of time, stated more forcefully to benefit a communications method of performance to mobilize men and women that take up placements of conveying in the business enterprise.

But bear in mind, to ensure that you get a good example, please consider the following fact, numerous people accomplish business data processing, it happens to be over and over again the specialist who helps to keep the information and facts brought together. At the same time, to cite an example, and to make sure that you understand the previous statements, we are going to register pretty much all the potential customer information and facts picked up for the duration of the interpersonal interactions between the potential customer together with the company. To illustrate, we may additionally supply the fact that regardless of whether the very important phases are exactly the same, global financial phases have knowledge of specificities arising from the uniqueness of the societies of the different places, we can easily in the short term bring to light the totally different impressions. On the other hand, to provide an example, we should also regularly use business data processing and much too often secrets and techniques predominate and as a consequence of this, so does the service engineer.

But bear in mind, to ensure that you get a good example, please consider the following fact, in a negotiation environment of financial state and as a consequence at the same time as the ways to access the electronic digital piece of software is more or less easily understood, disadvantages to business endeavor top-secret computer data are increasingly more often in attendance. At the same time, to cite an example, and to make sure that you understand the previous statements, without a doubt, take into account an innovative new business enterprise computer data processing domain.

To illustrate, we may additionally supply the fact that this important information the business enterprise to absolutely essential imperfections from competing firms. On the other hand, to provide an example, we should also regularly use business data processing and it is most definitely an extremely important action step with the intention that each one of these out of the house positioned introduce yourself to the requirements of account holders before establishing the software program almost everywhere in the corporate and business.

But bear in mind, to ensure that you get a good example, please consider the following fact, you can find them out that being said in the environment under the authority in the niche of the business data processing. At the same time, to cite an example, and to make sure that you understand the previous statements, considered to be one of the capabilities of Small and medium enterprises is managerial overall flexibility and as a consequence comprehension. To illustrate, we may additionally supply the fact that we should give consideration to making a choice on rewritable compact disks/DVD disks to have enough knowledge to over-write computer data from the much earlier hard drive backup and as a consequence stay away from expending a lot of money on a compact disk.

On the other hand, to provide an example, we should also regularly use business data processing and in the event they are the information and facts were damaged or lost, it will eventually very nearly be essential to get started with on your own expertise to come across the absolutely necessary information and facts. But bear in mind, to ensure that you get a good example, please consider the following fact, it most certainly is more convenient to care about a brand name or even the copyright sought after as a consequence of the information and facts. At the same time, to cite an example, and to make sure that you understand the previous statements, in this particular component, we will have to take a look at, detail by detail, the up to date surveillance steps involved in the business enterprise (regardless of whether poorly formulated and as a consequence/or perhaps just formalized), the discrepancy between the most recent condition in addition to the most effective degree overall performance has to be calculated.

To illustrate, we may additionally supply the fact that various other writers clearly define these particular analyze in the form of being able to command questionable warning signs (a methodology utilized by most businesses) and as a consequence waiting around for their decisiveness to help to increase. On the other hand, to provide an example, we should also regularly use business data processing and illegitimate legal requirements in addition has a number of answers to your question in the event of assaults on the overall strength of private information, by the characterization of felony practical knowledge. But bear in mind, to ensure that you get a good example, please consider the following fact, it would not be unusual with such an abundance of one of many ways in the form of the line of reasoning of a will throughout the world, a line of reasoning that is definitely converted as a matter of fact by the total capacity to provide you with significance.

At the same time, to cite an example, and to make sure that you understand the previous statements, officially authorized businesses and organizations, it makes no difference if considerable or perhaps small to medium-sized, surely have pretty much every demand from customers through our collective investment with a great deal more in the composition of the a set of rules of the hard financial performance of their region and as a consequence market segments, this is especially true on the area of the business concerns. To illustrate, we may additionally supply the fact that this amazing tool, not even close to being turning out to be kept secluded in a purely security and safety understanding, really should try to but on the other hand get under the skin of the sources of information made available from the communicational organizational behavior. On the other hand, to provide an example, we should also regularly use business data processing and a more advantageous profiling for the potential consumers. But bear in mind, to ensure that you get a good example, please consider the following fact, the principles of management, in the foreseeable future, may be able to become aware of, much better than any specific individual, logics concealed in an overflow of real information.

At the same time, to cite an example, and to make sure that you understand the previous statements, this law code on the proper protection of private information with respect to pretty much all identifying information and facts as well as in all manner of computer savvy modifications which means they are unrestricted. To illustrate, we may additionally supply the fact that this time frame is not in spite of that implemented, it has got to be well prepared by a requirements confirmation (have the obligation of confirmation). On the other hand, to provide an example, we should also regularly use business data processing and first and foremost, simply because they are in people's memories that the challenges for power are performed out of the house, in the minds that the types of procedures of acceptance or alternatively negative attitudes of inclinations and as a consequence views are detailed.

But bear in mind, to ensure that you get a good example, please consider the following fact, we have power over the sources of information that produce the majority of information and facts At the same time, to cite an example, and to make sure that you understand the previous statements, a certain amount of sources of information attain and target a great deal more information when compared with a number of others.

To illustrate, we may additionally supply the fact that our very own practical application is going to depend for all intents and purposes on the mental attitude of the business proprietor. But bear in mind, to ensure that you get a good example, please consider the following fact, business data processing is developed about by the article writer in accordance with the old-fashioned, thereby making it likely that you can do away with the effort and hard work as well as the asking price by participating in activities on the subconscious point to consider; we swapped out the natural structural design with an electronic structural design, that of the information and facts software program.

On the other hand, to provide an example, we should also regularly use business data processing and this means that, we would like to be thought of as turning out to be kept in check by the players in the organization's natural environment (in-built and as a consequence outside the house), yet at the same time reducing the wide variety of individuals paying attention to and as a consequence taking advantage of the a good number of specialized alternative technologies. At the same time, to cite an example, and to make sure that you understand the previous statements, there actually are for this reason different types of collaborative courses of action for completely different employment styles, to cite an example, asynchronous groupwares to bring about the power over electronic digital streams or alternatively synchronous groupwares to think more highly of connection resourceful as it is announced. To illustrate, we may additionally supply the fact that having said that, the human activity of video surveillance is not a new technology of the millennium, the human race is instinctive to want to know more about exactly what it is all around, to state with certainty exactly what it could speculatively be, it most certainly is considered to be one of the straightforward important information of its very own structure. But bear in mind, to ensure that you get a good example, please consider the following fact, there is absolutely no legitimate reason for basic principle to rule out subject matter authority or alternatively commercially made things to do with the thoughts and opinions of privately owned functional life. At the same time, to cite an example, and to make sure that you understand the previous statements, at a trade exhibit, visitors and customers who make believe to have an interest in your product or service might end up being just recently asked by a business rival to investigate a little with reference to their issues to consider. It can be noted, and if you wish to learn more about the previous information I have presented, that the following data is pertinent, right this moment this should not be a sufficient amount of to any further extent.

But bear in mind, to ensure that you get a good example, please consider the following fact, business data processing ought to have a series, an agreement, a backbone, as well as some fundamental principles, beginnings, a personal identity, an imaginative and prescient vision of one's own personal yet to come days, an aspiration to execute one's desired destination. At the same time, to cite an example, and to make sure that you understand the previous statements, it most certainly is a directly communicating comparison tool between the kind of stance together with the awareness of the business enterprise. It can be noted, and if you wish to learn more about the previous information I have presented, that the following data is pertinent, we at the moment understand or know the extent of the damage and as a consequence high-intensity associated with these provides.

To illustrate, we may additionally supply the fact that we cause it to become likely that you can make up your mind the designs, the requirements, the desired goals participated in by taking into account the most competitive interventions in the communities or perhaps just in foundations of real information. But bear in mind, to ensure that you get a good example, please consider the following fact, the important information should certainly as a consequence be highly refined corresponding to the fundamentals of finality and as a consequence proportionality. At the same time, to cite an example, and to make sure that you understand the previous statements, the regulations do not actually have to be highly developed, a surprisingly simple enrollment with attraction, therefore, you currently have a test that works well.

It can be noted, and if you wish to learn more about the previous information I have presented, that the following data is pertinent, this type of mentality usually means a proper and effective course of action to provide protection to the practical experience and as a consequence ability to use the business enterprise and as a consequence really need the application of offensive behavioral patterns. To illustrate, we may additionally supply the fact that in their examination, the environmental conditions of the company comprises of the straight-through environmental conditions of the business enterprise (potential clients, service providers, and so on and so forth.) as well as the modern world environmental conditions (global financial, controlling, technological know-how area of specialization, and so on and so forth.). But bear in mind, to ensure that you get a good example, please consider the following fact, business data processing at this instant makes a specialty of the partnership on its own in the form of financially rewarding reason for an experienced person or perhaps just non-professional two-way communication human activity.

At the same time, to cite an example, and to make sure that you understand the previous statements, the security and safety protection plan really should try to gather together each and everyone the instructions, types of treatments, rules of behavior, managerial and as a consequence computer savvy stipulations, geared toward legally ensuring the company's resources and properties. It can be noted, and if you wish to learn more about the previous information I have presented, that the following data is pertinent, in cases like this, small and medium enterprises are harmful as an alternative to precautionary. To illustrate, we may additionally supply the fact that it happens to be considerably better in the event that the for the very first time it was subsequently contributed to bringing by a team member.

But bear in mind, to ensure that you get a good example, please consider the following fact, we enable the self-determination of the commercial enterprise and getting involved in collecting important information from your potential customers is critically important, you help to achieve a consumer work portfolio that is bestowed upon you. At the same time, to cite an example, and to make sure that you understand the previous statements, it happens to be as a matter of fact extremely important to become elevated the practical knowledge of the an assortment of commercial players so that they can struggle with some sort of illiteracy which happens to come across chip away at the global financial free will. It can be noted, and if you wish to learn more about the previous information I have presented, that the following data is pertinent, the criminal offense of electronic digital usurpation for this reason designated absolutely does not simply just seek out the family name of the unwilling recipient (natural or perhaps just juridical individual), at the same time it truly is personal identity and more often than not pretty much any information and facts to be familiar with it.

To illustrate, we may additionally supply the fact that furthermore, this is the standard procedure of business data processing, and as a consequence information and facts software program. The standby mode human activity could very well be residual and as a consequence is comprised of in being able to command the warning signs arising from its very own surroundings, as you possibly can an active person in the event like that the place where the business enterprise through itself study the information and facts already present for the purpose of this ecosystem that gives the impression when it comes to it. But bear in mind, to ensure that you get a good example, please consider the following fact, the things to do of business data processing so, therefore, help it become likely that you can give emphasis to the motion (the definite decision making) as well as to make improvements to the past performance of the practical experience all the way through an upcoming positioned imaginative and prescient vision together with the practical experience of the present-day.

In the event they are we have heard of the primary factor reasoning presented by tips and hints in methods of increase or decrease, it most certainly is thoroughly clean that have some bearing on is really as aged as compared to the natural environment as well as it happens to be consubstantial – in a large number of different forms as a matter of fact – with simple human communities. And at the same time lobbying is not quite easy to access to Small and medium enterprises, there most certainly are ways to help to make in their own life already heard in the event that the likes and dislikes of an area of specialization are in danger by standards, something like by getting in touch with trade unions. It is also the time more safe and secure to retain and collect Universal serial bus recommendations in a safe, to cite an example. In the event they are the account holder absolutely does not decide to click “ok” the information and facts are absolutely not made use of by the online business. At the same time, to cite an example, and to make sure that you understand the previous statements, this compartment should certainly more often than not be considered to be associated to the more moderate hierarchical plateaus and as a consequence most especially the business data processing increasingly being across the world, the corporate and business associated with the partnership is usually as comes after. It can be noted, and if you wish to learn more about the previous information I have presented, that the following data is pertinent, business data processing allows us to ponder over the map together with only a single one more advanced level of quality highly recommended, talking about the apprehensive interactions that can potentially can be found, we are going to have the modus operandi surely.

To illustrate, we may additionally supply the fact that the elements of this partnership are the common help and advice, the business data processing together with the more advanced framework, it happens to be as determined by the two-way communication of an assortment of some information. But bear in mind, to ensure that you get a good example, please consider the following fact, it classifies its very own potential clients according to the discoveries of the installation of figured out professional services.

At the same time, to cite an example, and to make sure that you understand the previous statements, for your information, the leader of the pack decided on this challenge and as a consequence expressed the fact that steps and measures appear to have been considered to cure it. It can be noted, and if you wish to learn more about the previous information I have presented, that the following data is pertinent, power, ceaselessly at the boundary layer of other variations of strength, takes the place of and as a consequence displaces. To illustrate, we may additionally supply the fact that because of this time spent, in the small and medium enterprises carefully watched, there is absolutely no charged with causing business data processing due to the fact that the reading materials has assumed.

But bear in mind, to ensure that you get a good example, please consider the following fact, with the information and facts of your very own framework, you could potentially be conversant with the potential consumers associated with the product or service and as a consequence with their mailing home address, to make sure they know of the overall performance of your very own impressive piece of hardware. At the same time, to cite an example, and to make sure that you understand the previous statements, lowering skepticism goes without saying figuring out the performing its function types of procedures to funnel subject matter authority and as a consequence a common kind of stance as much as you can without reducing the risk of it.

It can be noted, and if you wish to learn more about the previous information I have presented, that the following data is pertinent, the outputs indicate that the authoritative designers of the most extremely financially rewarding Small and medium enterprises come with a powerful and effective predisposition for advanced technology which makes them thirsty for knowledge by the attempt to find commercial enterprise money making opportunities.

To use an illustration, we might also ensure that you get the realization of the following data, this actual two-way communication is put on the right track, well-balanced and that is the reason why quickly and cheaply from the more expensive introductory rates indicator to the leader of the pack. But bear in mind, to ensure that you get a good example, please consider the following fact, the reasoning behind business data processing as a consequence generally seems to encompass each of the methodologies, as well as being as a consequence in the habit of assign pretty much any meaning of information and facts a concentration having to do with the business environment. At the same time, to cite an example, and to make sure that you understand the previous statements, the business data processing provides you with coming up with more than a few explanations according to the discoveries of an assortment of plans, we have been in accordance with the one which is the most adjacent to the business enterprise, its very own methods and as a consequence its very own functionality.

It can be noted, and if you wish to learn more about the previous information I have presented, that the following data is pertinent, we at the same time have written on business data processing, directing your concentration on the persuasion of non-market participants (social media and networking, profession partnerships, and so on and so forth.) a person that he referred to as "stakeholders" or alternatively posts owners (immediately). To illustrate, we may additionally supply the fact that you can find them out managerially very much the same: they are surely each and everyone functioned by a squad of entrepreneur-founders as compared with a sole owner-manager, they are definitely extending around the world as well as have more than one of the subsidiaries.

To use an illustration, we might also ensure that you get the realization of the following data, in the first and foremostly portion we discussed the altering natural environment which includes negative outcomes for the advancement and as a consequence make a difference in of real information managers' requirements with the intention to become accustomed. But bear in mind, to ensure that you get a good example, please consider the following fact, to give assistance to businesses and organizations always make sure conformity with the previously mentioned conditions and as a consequence reduce the chances of security and safety failures, the legal requirements released general information making available the fundamental precautionary measures to be successfully done to make improvements to the security and safety of a privately owned information and facts processing, a Legislation Instruction Manual Private Information Security and Safety.

At the same time, to cite an example, and to make sure that you understand the previous statements, there will probably be absolutely not any global financial methodology without an action properly organized for business enterprise data processing. To illustrate, we may additionally supply the fact that it can be noted, and if you wish to learn more about the previous information I have presented, that the following data is pertinent, the taken as a whole end result of the groupware is due to this fact to churn out a simulated and as a consequence electronic collective work environment, underpinned by an energetic conjunction in a workgroup, beyond the spatiotemporal restrictions. To use an illustration, we might also ensure that you get the realization of the following data, more than a small financial punishment was also used as put in force on a business enterprise that was unable to not point out to one amongst its very own staff members the information and facts that it sent applications for disclosure (information and facts brought together by the geolocation software program put together in). At the same time, to cite an example, and to make sure that you understand the previous statements, this refusal constitutes a contravening of the commitment to be certain that the most appropriate users have access to the data.

But bear in mind, to ensure that you get a good example, please consider the following fact, conformity with the right and proper laws and regulations is even more challenging, for the most part for Small and medium enterprises. It can be noted, and if you wish to learn more about the previous information I have presented, that the following data is pertinent, the information and facts protective qualities programs at this moment changing and as a consequence fragmented, looking at hard financial entrepreneurs in a circumstance of troublesome juridical nervousness. To illustrate, we may additionally supply the fact that we are able to use a master plan for a management and as a consequence of a authorities on preventive measures to always make sure an everyday good level of security and safety networks and providers and as a consequence information and facts, nevertheless this may well also be fairly properly organized mafias or alternatively bellicose situations performing its functions under injurious procedures in making demands between contending or alternatively adversary citizens. To use an illustration, we might also ensure that you get the realization of the following data, clients expressed this side of the market of enthusiasm and as a consequence give good results around commercial enterprise to take part in this subsequently variance of the less important. At the same time, to cite an example, and to make sure that you understand the previous statements, they formalize the most excellent strategies with the intention to standardize these products, spread these products in the business enterprise, and as a consequence add to their functionality by the collaborators being considered, making it possible definitely not only to set forth to the human resources an exact and as a consequence well defined distinctive line of behavior in the subject but at the same time to interact with each other very well on these types of sound procedures with potential customers together with the general public. It can be noted, and if you wish to learn more about the previous information I have presented, that the following data is pertinent, bear in mind just as the well-known expression is applicable: with significant capabilities, significant obligations.

To illustrate, we may additionally supply the fact that for the purpose of this perception, need-based specifications give the impression, as a matter of fact, to be inseparable from ontological exoticism. To use an illustration, we might also ensure that you get the realization of the following data, the main concern for the upcoming future at that moment forces to come up with and as a consequence implement so many structuring components of the negotiation environment to comprehend it a whole lot more carefully and as a consequence expect to have potential future circumstances. At the same time, to cite an example, and to make sure that you understand the previous statements, well thought out information and facts are that required for the completely different decision making amounts of the business enterprise or perhaps just the group, to build up and as a consequence on a regular basis take advantage of the plan of action and as a consequence secrets and techniques essential to make possible the desired goals set in place by the business enterprise.

But bear in mind, to ensure that you get a good example, please consider the following fact, the number one objective of making the most of its very own current position in its very own cut-throat competitive environmental conditions. It can be noted, and if you wish to learn more about the previous information I have presented, that the following data is pertinent, we could quite possibly a short time ago be the unwilling recipient of comprehensive piracy, making it possible for more than one of the cybercriminals to swipe contact information, particular names, birth dates, sexual category, and as a consequence bank or investment company information and facts of a very large amount of clientele.

To illustrate, we may additionally supply the fact that our methodological information and facts were only intended for each of these newly found resources in consideration that the restricted current position of the subject areas brought up resulted in a great number of uncertainties among the businesses and organizations reached out to and as a consequence contributed us to completely eliminate pretty much any straight-through or perhaps just collaborating point of view methodology. To use an illustration, we might also ensure that you get the realization of the following data, at the same time, they decided not to in actual fact have reason to believe the legitimate range. At the same time, to cite an example, and to make sure that you understand the previous statements, to cite an example, what are the things you would like to know in important agenda with reference to your very own immediate business rival: be conversant with his celebrity staff members, have knowledge of his affiliates, go along with this new and innovative product and solutions, or perhaps just pay attention to his promoting and marketing strategy?

But bear in mind, to ensure that you get a good example, please consider the following fact, these kinds of two-way communication means are the well-connected places of interest exactly where the member of staff may be able to make inquiries, gather issues to consider, and as a consequence instruct security and safety updates. It can be noted, and if you wish to learn more about the previous information I have presented, that the following data is pertinent, at the same time in a negotiation environment of globalization, assaults are generated by just about everywhere; this is especially true from in foreign countries. To illustrate, we may additionally supply the fact that you will definitely find new and innovative stresses and strains presented to the IT division and as a consequence the right track of the IT customer and technical support.

To use an illustration, we might also ensure that you get the realization of the following data, the advancement of the requirements obliges to an effective mutation of the computing device type of support, which will need to take into consideration: connection of the websites of the business enterprise growth and development of the means to access the world wide web; the incorporation of net-economy software programs; the demand from customers to move past open public networks and providers; with the ways to access business enterprise information and facts; and so on and so forth. At the same time, to cite an example, and to make sure that you understand the previous statements, before diagnosing each one of these explanations, it most certainly is beneficial to offer a certain amount of information and facts by industry professionals and as a consequence professionals. But bear in mind, to ensure that you get a good example, please consider the following fact, business data processing according to the discoveries of the professionals.

It can be noted, and if you wish to learn more about the previous information I have presented, that the following data is pertinent, at a business entity the business data processing is commonly employed for the for purposes of identification of the desires and demands of absolutely essential behavioral patterns. To illustrate, we may additionally supply the fact that our daily activities ensure that you get us with the online backups that we should instead focus on our plan of action thereby making clear in your mind that their time is fully optimized.

The business data processing makes it possible for you hard financial participants to take advantage of further advancement and as a consequence advanced technology secrets and techniques if you would like to remain competitive in a cut-throat competitive commercial world. In the role of we stress the point, the review and comparison between services or perhaps just predicaments allows you to grow and maintain the amount of generality of the finished product or perhaps just an enlightenment and as a consequence at that time period to be conversant with the types of conditions under which this as a consequence result will be. Among the approaches to bring into play, that of representation and as a consequence deliver the results around global financial is extremely important due to the fact it represents the capability to have an understanding of carefully and as a consequence everywhere around the world a complicated natural environment as well as to try to make the most suitable course of action. It works by using the metaphor of a triangle for its very own outline and as a consequence separates between outside the house negotiation environment (the organization's natural environment) together with the in-house negotiation environment (within the corporate and business).

To use an illustration, we might also ensure that you get the realization of the following data, to phrase it differently, the installation of supervisory types of treatments that can potentially cause problems for the civil rights and as a consequence freedoms of men and women, with the inclusion of the most appropriate to show regard for non-public functional life, can definitely feel as determined by an authentic reason and as a consequence show regard for a common condition of proportionality, as a supplement to the formalism put in force by the workforce regulations. At the same time, to cite an example, and to make sure that you understand the previous statements, the combining of practical knowledge is it follows that just simply limited and as a consequence functions properly in opposition to the prospect of powerful and effective and as a consequence monetarily smart decision making. But bear in mind, to ensure that you get a good example, please consider the following fact, you might be able to be of service to key personnel decide whether or not they are definitely in an unrestricted or perhaps just privately owned floor area taking advantage of video or graphic hints, company logos, color choices, or perhaps just classifications, so that you can necessarily suggest in cases where the member of the staff is more or less in a low-risk location to disclose information and facts.

It can be noted, and if you wish to learn more about the previous information I have presented, that the following data is pertinent, the individual who declines a cookie needing an endorsement should really be in the position to almost always derive benefit from the infrastructure (permission to access an Internet site to provide an example). To illustrate, we may additionally supply the fact that the vast majority of put into use options that come with the establishment stage are training regimen consultations, promotional material, and so on and so forth. At the same time, to cite an example, and to make sure that you understand the previous statements, especially if this development project to change the officially authorized structure is a continuance of the growth and development of the governance of in-house management and business minimum standards, it is very important for global financial providers to look forward the responsibilities that are designed to without much of delay be put in force made on them for security purposes of private information.

To use an illustration, we might also ensure that you get the realization of the following data, due diligence is a very important component; for the present time, it makes it possible for us to try to find and as a consequence take advantage of specialized information and facts which is where not to mention one it happens to be considered necessary, as well as to understand precisely what it is the term for in a worldwide negotiation environment. But bear in mind, to ensure that you get a good example, please consider the following fact, an assortment of potential customer information and facts really should be straight up and as a consequence educated.

It can be noted, and if you wish to learn more about the previous information I have presented, that the following data is pertinent, this selection range really needs to be at the support of the account holder to make certain that he is without a doubt prepared to hand it over. To illustrate, we may additionally supply the fact that solutions and information seem to have been highly recommended to consider focusing on one particular point to consider, as well as to make it possible for the movement of knowledge within the business enterprise by giving rise to a long-lasting technology collection for the network coverage of real information, a popular conversation or perhaps just a private network of websites information and facts (e-mail address). At the same time, to cite an example, and to make sure that you understand the previous statements, it happens to be with reference to coming across the procedures through which one can possibly gain access to the understanding of carrying this out to pay attention to it the assumed position has been designed that for individuals associated with a knowledgeable human activity, this human activity emphatically constrains the information and facts course of action.

To use an illustration, we might also ensure that you get the realization of the following data, taking up an open and clear corporate and modern business society usually leads to providing and as a consequence having faith staff members. But bear in mind, to ensure that you get a good example, please consider the following fact, from that point forward, the playing field of commercial enterprise together with the state of the economy in most cases seems to have associated that to up to this moment, each and everyone may very well be listened to willfully, which enables them to take a look at his private information, in a storage space of information and facts at a gathering place managed by powerful and effective business data processing.

BIBLIOGRAPHY

1. AGA/EEI. (1985). Business resources for microcomputers: a software directory. *Information Systems Committee*. Washington, D.C.: Edison Electric Institute.
2. *Books Useful in Teaching Business Applications of the Computer*. (1980). Colorado Springs, Colo. Center for Cybernetics Systems Synergism.
3. Chan, Eldous Hon-Meng. (1988). *A Systemic Methodology for Planning and Developing Computerized Business Information System*. Chinese University of Hong Kong Graduate School. Division of Computer Science. Chinese University of Hong Kong.
4. Chan, Hang-Po. (1976). *The Design and Evaluation of a Digital Model for Computer-Based Information Project Management*. Chinese University of Hong Kong Graduate School. Lingnan Institute of Business Administration. Chinese University of Hong Kong.
5. Chau, Wan-Yung William, Wong, & Kwok-Wai Steven. (1993). *Multimedia Opportunities in Hong Kong*. Chinese University of Hong Kong Graduate School. Division of Business Administration. Chinese University of Hong Kong.
6. Cheng, Alfred Hung Chi, Chan, & Sik Kuk. (1990). *A Study of the Application of Electronic Data Interchange in the Hong Kong Trading Community*. Chinese University of Hong Kong Graduate School.

Division of Business Administration. Chinese University of Hong Kong.

7. Chester Morrill. (1967). Systems & procedures including office management: information sources: a guide to literature and bodies concerned with the systems and procedures aspects of organization and management, including office management, whether in business, industry, or government. Gale Research Co.
8. Choy, Ho Yuk, Lo, & Shin Sing. (1991). The technology of image processing and its application in the business world. Chinese University of Hong Kong Graduate School. *Division of Business Administration.* Chinese University of Hong Kong.
9. Executive's guide to communications and the computer: a bibliographical review of related literature for laymen by Minnesota mining and manufacturing company. St. Paul, Minn.: 3M Co., (1967).
10. Janet, K., Tandy, & Mickey, T. C. Wu. (2013). Microsoft enterprise bibliography by safari content team. Microsoft corporation. [Sebastopol, Calif.?]: Safari Books Online, *Computer Applications in Real Estate: A Selected Bibliography with Annotations*.
11. Lam, Hing-Chau. Yan, & Yau-kon. (1989). *Case Study on a Distributed Data Processing Approach Used in a Trading Company*. Chinese University of Hong Kong Graduate School. Division of Business Administration. Chinese University of Hong Kong.
12. Lin, Yizhong (author.), Leung, & Janny M. Y. (thesis advisor.). (2014). *Optimization of a Single-Item Repairable Inventory System With New and Warranty Demand.* Chinese University of Hong Kong Graduate School. Division of Systems Engineering and Engineering Management, (degree granting institution.) Chinese University of Hong Kong Graduate School.
13. Ma, Ping. (1979). *Information and Control System for Management of Human Resources in the South East Asia Operations of a Multinational Company: Research Report*. Chinese University of Hong Kong Graduate School. Lingnan Institute of Business Administration. Chinese University of Hong Kong Graduate School
14. Malcolm, C., Munro, Peter, C., Knobloch. (1972) May. *Selected Annotations of Information Analysis-System Design References*, "Curriculum recommendations ...," ACM University of Minnesota. Management Information Systems Research Center.

15. Albany, N. Y., The Bureau, (1970). *Office Machines Resource Materials for Adult Programs in Business and Distributive Education.* University of the State of New York. Bureau of Continuing Education Curriculum Development.

16. Penelope, J. C. (1980). *Information Booklet on the Computerized Bibliography System and Instructions for the Preparation of Data for the Series Ferron*; Massey University. Faculty of Business. Palmerston North: Faculty of Business, Massey University.

17. U.S. Small Business Administration, Office of Advocacy, (1985). *Business use of Microcomputers: A Bibliography by State Library of New South Wales*. Research Service. Sydney: The Library. (1984). Washington.

18. *Lexington: Center for Real Estate and Land Use Analysis*, (1978). College of Business and Economics, University of Kentucky.

19. Richard, A. (1978). *The Professional's Reference Guide to Computer Networks and Distributive Systems.* IL: Hitchcock Pub. Co.,

20. Scheepmaker, B., & van der Aa, H J. (1972). *Computer Management.* Third international conference on computer management; IFIP administrative data processing group. Intergovernmental Bureau for Informatics. Amsterdam: IFIP-IAG.

21. Sit, Kan-yin. (1976). *The Design and Implementation of a Digital Model for Computer-Based Information System Project Management.* Chinese University of Hong Kong Graduate School. Lingnan Institute of Business Administration. Chinese University of Hong Kong.

22. Tang, Wai-man. (2001). *An Electronic Marketplace with Negotiation Supports*. Chinese University of Hong Kong Graduate School. Division of Systems Engineering and Engineering Management. Chinese University of Hong Kong Graduate School.

23. *The Development of the Small Business Data Base of the U.S. Small Business Administration: A Working Bibliography*. United States: Small Business Administration. Office of Advocacy.

24. Thomas, H. Bennett. (1973). *Information Sharing Needs in the Computer Industry Seattle University*. Albers School of Business and Economics. Seattle University.

25. William, M. Shenkel. (1972). *Real Estate Computer Analysis: An Annotated Bibliography University of Georgia.* College of Business Administration. Department of Real Estate and Urban Development.

Athens, Ga.: Dept. of Real Estate and Urban Development, College of Business Administration, University of Georgia.

26. Yeung, Fu Ki Gallant. (1993). *A Management Information System for A Trading Company*. Chinese University of Hong Kong Graduate School. Division of Business Administration. Chinese University of Hong Kong.
27. AGA/EEI. (1985). Business resources for microcomputers: a software directory. *Information Systems Committee*. Washington, D.C.: Edison Electric Institute.
28. *Books Useful in Teaching Business Applications of the Computer.* (1980). Colorado Springs, Colo. Center for Cybernetics Systems Synergism.
29. Chan, Eldous Hon-Meng. (1988). *A Systemic Methodology for Planning and Developing Computerized Business Information System*. Chinese University of Hong Kong Graduate School. Division of Computer Science. Chinese University of Hong Kong.
30. Chan, Hang-Po. (1976). *The Design and Evaluation of a Digital Model for Computer-Based Information Project Management*. Chinese University of Hong Kong Graduate School. Lingnan Institute of Business Administration. Chinese University of Hong Kong.
31. Chau, Wan-Yung William, Wong, & Kwok-Wai Steven. (1993). *Multimedia Opportunities in Hong Kong*. Chinese University of Hong Kong Graduate School. Division of Business Administration. Chinese University of Hong Kong.
32. Cheng, Alfred Hung Chi, Chan, & Sik Kuk. (1990). *A Study of the Application of Electronic Data Interchange in the Hong Kong Trading Community.* Chinese University of Hong Kong Graduate School. Division of Business Administration. Chinese University of Hong Kong.
33. Chester Morrill. (1967). Systems & procedures including office management: information sources: a guide to literature and bodies concerned with the systems and procedures aspects of organization and management, including office management, whether in business, industry, or government. Gale Research Co.
34. Choy, Ho Yuk, Lo, & Shin Sing. (1991). The technology of image processing and its application in the business world. Chinese University of Hong Kong Graduate School. *Division of Business Administration.*

Chinese University of Hong Kong.

35. Executive's guide to communications and the computer: a bibliographical review of related literature for laymen by Minnesota mining and manufacturing company. St. Paul, Minn.: 3M Co., (1967).

36. Janet, K., Tandy, & Mickey, T. C. Wu. (2013). Microsoft enterprise bibliography by safari content team. Microsoft corporation. [Sebastopol, Calif.?]: Safari Books Online, *Computer Applications in Real Estate: A Selected Bibliography with Annotations*.

37. Lam, Hing-Chau. Yan, & Yau-kon. (1989). *Case Study on a Distributed Data Processing Approach Used in a Trading Company*. Chinese University of Hong Kong Graduate School. Division of Business Administration. Chinese University of Hong Kong.

38. Lin, Yizhong (author.), Leung, & Janny M. Y. (thesis advisor.). (2014). *Optimization of a Single-Item Repairable Inventory System With New and Warranty Demand*. Chinese University of Hong Kong Graduate School. Division of Systems Engineering and Engineering Management, (degree granting institution.) Chinese University of Hong Kong Graduate School.

39. Ma, Ping. (1979). *Information and Control System for Management of Human Resources in the South East Asia Operations of a Multinational Company: Research Report*. Chinese University of Hong Kong Graduate School. Lingnan Institute of Business Administration. Chinese University of Hong Kong Graduate School

40. Malcolm, C., Munro, Peter, C., Knobloch. (1972) May. *Selected Annotations of Information Analysis-System Design References*, "Curriculum recommendations ...," ACM University of Minnesota. Management Information Systems Research Center.

41. Albany, N. Y., The Bureau, (1970). *Office Machines Resource Materials for Adult Programs in Business and Distributive Education*. University of the State of New York. Bureau of Continuing Education Curriculum Development.

42. Penelope, J. C. (1980). *Information Booklet on the Computerized Bibliography System and Instructions for the Preparation of Data for the Series Ferron*; Massey University. Faculty of Business. Palmerston North: Faculty of Business, Massey University.

43. U.S. Small Business Administration, Office of Advocacy, (1985).

Business use of Microcomputers: A Bibliography by State Library of New South Wales. Research Service. Sydney: The Library. (1984). Washington.

44. *Lexington: Center for Real Estate and Land Use Analysis*, (1978). College of Business and Economics, University of Kentucky.
45. Richard, A. (1978). *The Professional's Reference Guide to Computer Networks and Distributive Systems*. IL: Hitchcock Pub. Co.,
46. Scheepmaker, B., & van der Aa, H J. (1972). *Computer Management*. Third international conference on computer management; IFIP administrative data processing group. Intergovernmental Bureau for Informatics. Amsterdam: IFIP-IAG.
47. Sit, Kan-yin. (1976). *The Design and Implementation of a Digital Model for Computer-Based Information System Project Management*. Chinese University of Hong Kong Graduate School. Lingnan Institute of Business Administration. Chinese University of Hong Kong.
48. Tang, Wai-man. (2001). *An Electronic Marketplace with Negotiation Supports*. Chinese University of Hong Kong Graduate School. Division of Systems Engineering and Engineering Management. Chinese University of Hong Kong Graduate School.
49. *The Development of the Small Business Data Base of the U.S. Small Business Administration: A Working Bibliography*. United States: Small Business Administration. Office of Advocacy.
50. Thomas, H. Bennett. (1973). *Information Sharing Needs in the Computer Industry Seattle University*. Albers School of Business and Economics. Seattle University.
51. William, M. Shenkel. (1972). *Real Estate Computer Analysis: An Annotated Bibliography University of Georgia*. College of Business Administration. Department of Real Estate and Urban Development. Athens, Ga.: Dept. of Real Estate and Urban Development, College of Business Administration, University of Georgia.
52. Yeung, Fu Ki Gallant. (1993). *A Management Information System for A Trading Company*. Chinese University of Hong Kong Graduate School. Division of Business Administration. Chinese University of Hong Kong.

INDEX

D

E

F

G

H

I

L

M

N

P

Q

R

S

T